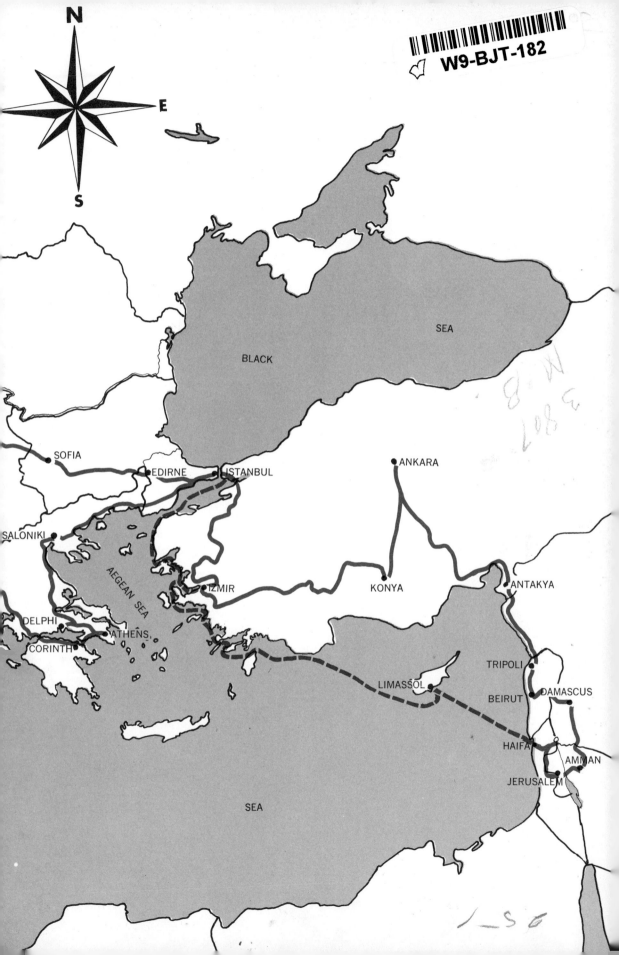

N

E

S

W9-BJT-182

BLACK SEA

SEA

SOFIA

EDIRNE   ISTANBUL

ANKARA

SALONIKI

AEGEAN SEA

IZMIR

KONYA

ANTAKYA

DELPHI

ATHENS

CORINTH

TRIPOLI

LIMASSOL

BEIRUT   DAMASCUS

HAIFA

AMMAN

JERUSALEM

SEA

Safari for Seven

Safari for Seven

Thea B. Van Halsema

BAKER BOOK HOUSE   •   GRAND RAPIDS, MICHIGAN

Card Number 67-31150
Library of Congress Catalog

For David, Nancy, Clark, Emily, Dick Jr.
to help them remember

and for the Revener
to thank him for planning it all

Preface

A safari, says Webster, is a journey or an expedition. In that sense this is the story of a safari. It is also a travel record, including details of route, mileage, money, and lodging for which people have asked in planning their own travels to Europe and the Bible lands.

This part of the world has changed some since 1962. A week of war in June, 1967, gave the Israelis the holy places west of the Jordan; the Mandelbaum Gate was dismantled. East Berlin shows remarkable building progress and tourists move more freely into that city and into East Germany. Hungary has relaxed some of its curbs on visitors. Prices, especially in European countries, have gone up.

But this book does not pretend and was not written to be a travel guide or a report on people and places. It is simply the record of an unusual family expedition, written to fasten the experience more securely in our memories and to share it with others, some of whom may contemplate a family safari of their own.

Speaking of family, I also want to record the debt I owe my husband for photos, title, and all kinds of help, and my mother for painstaking proofreading and indexing.

T.V.H.
October, 1967

Photographs on pages 111-130 are reproduced from 35 mm. Kodachrome slides by Dick L. Van Halsema and from other materials provided by him.

Contents

North 1

South 38

East 74

West 195

Photographs 111

Index 242

North

SHAGGY-NOSED TUGS edged the ship away from the Hudson River pier. The deck moved beneath our feet, shouts and waving grew frenzied, and our dream burst into reality. We were on the way to Europe and the Middle East for four months with five children, on a preacher's salary. Who says only rich people can travel?

But of course you must begin with a dream, the Rev would say. A good dream, a dream for which you sacrifice, a dream you want your children to share because in its fulfilment their lives will be enriched and challenged.

After an initial trip to Europe, we began to dream of taking the children there. We wanted them to live some weeks in the land of their grandfathers. We wanted them to see something of Europe, of its people especially, so that their horizon would be enlarged beyond the comfortable Michigan city where the norm is to grow up and grow old in the same well-padded rut.

So we tacked a big map of Europe on the family bulletin board and began to gather information. This takes months, maybe a year, depending on how far one is going. How far could *we* go? One midnight over mugs of tea and a table full of travel folders, we boldly expanded the dream to include the Middle East, especially the areas of Biblical history. To fly that leg of the trip was too expensive. Rome-Cairo-Beirut-Rome costs as much as New York-Rome round trip, multiplied by seven of us. But we could drive it — and see more. The Rev recalled from *Frontiers* magazine the account of two Italians who had driven from Trieste to Beirut. So it could be done.

Alongside the map of Europe we hung the *National Geographic*'s map of Bible lands. Our information search expanded until there was a bulging folder for every country we hoped to visit. We read newspapers, magazines, and books with a new purpose. Revolution in Damascus, escapes in Berlin, excavations at Sardis, gunfire on the Sea of Galilee — these were table conversation. With appropriate concern we noted that Venice was sinking into its canals at the rate of half an inch a year and that the lean on the tower of Pisa was increasing precariously. Clearly we could not procrastinate. Over many midnight mugs the Rev computed kilometers into miles, divided miles into days, and experimented with itineraries.

We held a family council. If the denominational board will give us unsalaried leave of absence and if we go the cheapest way possible — camping, roadside eating, native hotels — and if each child pays his own round trip ocean fare, we can go.

"Hurray," shouted Dicker, nearly four. "We're goin' t'broad. I got five dollars from my birthday and three pennies from a coke bottle I found."

"That, my boy," said his father, "will take you just past the Statue of — "

"Liverty," finished Dicker triumphantly.

The ocean voyage was booked for the last off-season sailing in April: two cabins in the least expensive of the tourist class on an excellent ship, the *Rotterdam,* pride of the Holland-America Line. Four of the children were eligible for half-fare rate. Each of the five had nearly two hundred dollars in the bank.

We ordered a Volkswagen microbus, red to photograph well, windows all around, paid for at home, to be picked up upon arrival in the Netherlands. The small Volkswagen purchased on our previous trip we sold, and made plans to sell our Ford station wagon after it had carried us plus luggage to the ship. Having shocked the Dutch relatives with news of our adventure, we asked them to find us housing for seven weeks. Nothing fancy, we said, knowing that Dutch rents are high and housing scarce. Maybe a summer place unused so early in the season.

Thanks to the Rev's active reserve status, the Navy clinic gave us full treatment in inoculations. "If you're drivin' through Turkey, sir," said the yeoman, "you better have all we give our boys goin' there for duty." "All" was eight or nine shots per person, plus a vaccination, and a polio booster jabbed in for bonus. We felt quite immune after those sessions, and quite sore.

On my passport photo the five children clustered angelically around me. The Rev appeared alone on his. This left him mobile in case he had to answer an emergency from somewhere in the backwoods of someplace. I hated to think where this left me. At the AAA he got his international driver's license. So did I, a month later and at my own suggestion. While this document empowered me to operate a vehicle anywhere from Singapore to Dublin, in the course of fifteen thousand miles I drove the redbus once, for thirty miles, on a German *Autobahn*. It is reassuring to believe that this was not so much mistrust of my navigating skill as preference for my services in other departments, such as making cheese sandwiches on my lap when we were behind schedule, persuading Dicker that he wasn't thirsty, clocking the time until the next rotation of seating, and assessing emergencies (must we stop right now or can you wait a little longer?).

With pins and red yarn we plotted our course on the map. We would disembark in Rotterdam with all our luggage, leaving London for the return trip. During two months in the Netherlands we would make a side trip to Germany, south as far as Heidelberg for some research and then east to Berlin before returning to Holland. Mid-June we would begin our long trip, leaving cool weather clothes behind, go directly to Italy and save Austria and Switzerland for the return when these countries would be warmer. From the heel of Italy an overnight ferry to Greece, overland through Greece to Istanbul, two weeks in Asian Turkey, and then south via Beirut-Damascus-Amman to Jerusalem-Jordan and after that through the Mandelbaum Gate into Israel.

The knottiest problem was to get out of Israel with a car. Once one crosses from Arab Jordan into Israel, he is *persona non grata* in any Arab country. Not allowed to return the way he came, he must leave Israel by air or ship for some non-Arab country. After long correspondence with Istanbul and Haifa and much juggling of our schedule, we booked passage on a Turkish ship sailing from Haifa to Istanbul via Cyprus and Izmir. We booked first-class accommodations because the only other class was kept in ship's hold for the three-day trip. From Istanbul on the return route we hoped to travel through Bulgaria, northern Yugoslavia, Hungary, to Vienna. In Berchtesgaden the Rev would participate in a U.S. Army retreat and after that we would return to Holland by way of Switzerland, France, and Belgium.

We charted the trip so that each weekend would be spent in a large city where we wanted to stay for several days. In these cities we made reservations. During the weekdays we planned to camp. The round trip Amsterdam-Jerusalem (excluding ship from Haifa to Istanbul) would be about nine thousand miles. We tried to estimate a couple hundred miles a day on full travel days, less on sightseeing days, and we left the weekends to rest from the road. For this part of our stay abroad we allowed about ten weeks.

The Rev avoids travel agencies whenever possible, partly because travel agencies cater to people who travel more elegantly than we, partly because agencies too must write for information about out-of-the-way places, and mostly because it is more exciting and satisfying to make plans directly. We did use agencies to book our Atlantic crossing, to reserve cabins on the Italy-Greece overnight ferry, and to request entry into Bulgaria and Hungary which Budapest informed us could be done only through certain recognized agencies in the United States. Ironically, on the Italy-Greece ferry we found rows of empty airline-style bunks to be had for half the price of the cabins which were the only thing available through the travel agency. The Bulgarian transit visa was incomplete and caused us trouble at the border. And our Hungarian visitors' visa was denied, perhaps because we would not specify dates and cities for our visit, though we did advance $140 to cover hotel costs. So we got our own transit visa later at the Hungarian consulate in The Hague.

By direct mail we made YMCA reservations in Rome and Jerusalem. In Istanbul the YMCA director arranged lodging in a small native hotel. Missionary friends gave us a listing of Christian hostels in Europe which ranged from houses to hotel-like places. In Beirut it was the University Christian Center to which we wrote, in Ankara a lonesome airman whose name we found on the magazine mailing list of our church's youth magazine. We wrote a colonel friend in the U.S. Army in Verona, Italy.

Piece by piece we put it all together. From Esso Touring Service in Rockefeller Center came excellent maps of each European country, from Seattle the *Camping Europa* guidebook listing in detail hundreds of campsites all the way through Greece and Yugoslavia. From the U.S. Printing Office in Washington we ordered language books, put out for the military during World War II and slanted to the problems of capture and occupation. David practiced phrases like *Vannak errefelé csapatok? Látott gépfegyvereket?* which is Hungarian for, Are there any troops around here? Have you seen any machine guns? and wondered whether he could create an international incident.

Several months before we sailed I began carrying around a clipboard with lists on it. Whenever I thought of something, it was written down. There was a list for each child, divided into warm clothes for the weeks in Holland and summer clothes for travel to Jerusalem. The list for camping was small — only silverware, seven plastic bowls, a collapsible army shovel, Halazone pills to purify water, and sleeping bags which we stuffed into two army duffel bags. In Holland we planned to buy a small tent and camping stove.

On a separate list were the household needs for the flat reserved for us in a seaside town by a Dutch cousin. The landlord sent a German inventory of the flat, German because the Dutch seacoast is taken over largely by German people during the summer months. I was not sure what six *Vorrapstöpfe* were in the *Küche,* but it did appear that we would have a *Kühlschrank,* a *Heisswasserapparat,* and a *Doppelgaskocher* which were essential. There were thirty *Gläser,* six each for *Trink, Wein, Sherry, Likör, und Bier,* but only four chairs at the *Esstisch.* There were enough blankets, even *Satinsteppdecken,* but only four single beds. The landlord graciously, and for a considerable sum, had agreed to pack the seven of us into a flat for four. Probably one of us could sleep in the *Wohnzimmer* on the *Dreisitzbank* and the other two of us would repose in sleeping bags anywhere on the *Fussteppich.* After the luxury of the ship this would be good preparation for the rigors of camping. Besides, weren't the dunes a stone's throw away and the sea itself a five-minute walk through Zandvoort town?

From such ecstasies of anticipation I returned inevitably to the lists. List nine was things to be purchased, not many. List ten told what had to be arranged before we could leave — cancel music lessons and newspaper, arrange for mail and lawn care, secure permission for four children to be excused six weeks early from school with books and assignments (their mother will tutor them in the flat for four).

The Rev kept his own lists: photography equipment, financial jugglings, information needed, reservations, correspondence with Dutch church leaders whom he would see while we were in Holland.

Meanwhile we were fending off a variety of reactions from friends and relatives. Most often it was, "But your children are too young. Wait until they can remember more."

"I went when I was ten," the Rev would answer, "and I remember all kinds of things. Who knows what will happen if we wait? The colorful Dutch family members are getting older, and they may be gone."

One mother of teen-agers came to our rescue. "Travel now before your children are working, going steady, and planning their own lives," she said. "These are the years when they are still yours and you can do things together."

There were also the wide-eyed folk who implied that we must have money trees growing in our back yard, or some more hidden source of wealth. You can try all you like to explain to such people that a family of moderate income *can* travel if they want to badly enough and if they sacrifice or even rearrange their set of values. Overlook the green sofa grown lumpy and threadbare from fifteen years of jumping children and parsonage visitors. Don't go out for dinner. Make the car and winter coats last a few years longer. Or, as I said to one cousin, "Sell your boat and water skis and you can go, too."

We grew weary of explaining after a time, and the Rev would say with a disarming grin, "Well, my wife writes books, my children have money in the bank, so I am the only one who has to earn his way." This was a great over-simplification, but a tolerable explanation for curious people whose minds are not given to dreaming.

E IGHT DAYS IN A floating palace works miracles to remove the exhaustion of packing and to restore one's energy for adventures to come. Dicker's fascination with the ship's playroom lasted the whole trip and earlier nightmares about losing him overboard were superfluous. The other four children explored the ship, joined tournaments, entered contests, played games, watched movies, wrote cards, swam in the pool, and made new friends. At first the Rev was busy arranging Good Friday and Easter services with the chief steward and two other pastors on board. I curled up in my deck chair, snug in a blanket, accepted bouillon at ten and tea at three, read six novels from the ship's library, and slept. It was marvelous. When necessary I replied to the elderly Swiss social worker next to me who talked incessantly in a high breathy voice.

"Yes, the clouds are moving from west to east, that is, from left to right, from left to right," she would say as if instructing a child. Or, when a telegram was announced, she remarked, "Isn't the wireless a wonderful invention, a wonderful invention?" The second day she jolted me out of *Decision at Delphi* with, "Hello, hello, and what is your trouble?" But her face was lifted to communicate with a sea gull hovering over the deck.

The motion sickness pills from brother Gerry's Pfizer company were doubly effective. They had a drowsying effect upon our energy-packed children. They also carried us through a day and a half when the sea churned, the *mal de mer* bags appeared in their racks, and the stewards made an endless round of cabins, carrying pails of water to mop up accidents. Some poor dear got caught without a bag halfway up the red carpeted steps to the main lounge, but we never missed a meal. Perhaps we should have, because we soon learned that one's digestive system can accept only a fraction when the typical luncheon menu offers choice of hors d'oeuvres, soups, eggs, fish, meats, vegetables, cold buffet, salads, cheeses, breads, desserts, fruits, and beverages!

On Easter Sunday the Rev preached, the dance-band pianist played the joyous hymns as slowly as possible, and after the service the three ministers with their wives were invited to have coffee with the captain. Here the retired minister from Syracuse, who had declined to preach, described his personal acquaintance with Helen Keller and J. Edgar Hoover while his wife simultaneously explained how she had solved the race problem in Washington, D.C. Even the captain's canary fell silent.

For the eighty-nine children on board there was a children's party the day after Easter. Dicker, looking desperate, sang "Jingle Bells" off pitch because every playroom child had to do something and because this was the way to get a sailor doll. The Rev was prevailed upon by his five to enter the *zaklopen* race for fathers, and hopping with both legs in a burlap sack, he managed to outjump a philosophy professor by two lengths. Dave and Nan collected balloons to release from the ship's stern.

On the seventh day gulls reappeared, wheeling and crying. A few fishing boats lay in sight. Luggage for Southampton waited in the halls. In the darkness lighthouse warnings flashed along the English coast and by morning we were in the channel fog.

After Southampton, through more fog, past unseen ships calling out, we broke into warm sunlight at LeHavre. But the fog waited at the edge of the harbor to enshroud us again, blowing streaks across the retreating sun and forcing us inside, shivering.

Breakfast at six the final morning. Luggage in mountains on the decks. Dark water running by as we pass through the Waterweg that leads to Rotterdam harbor. We are late in docking and after the ship is tied up, we wait two hours to disembark. The spell in the floating palace is broken, the lounges deserted. A grey humor sifts down through the ship. But on the pier we have spotted Oom Johan, bald head shining, cigar clamped firmly in his front teeth. And Tante Da, carrying tulips. Soon Tante Kundien is there, too, with her minister husband, Oom Henk. From the deck we wave and call as excitedly as if we are arriving home.

On the pier some of our luggage lies under "V," some under "H," and one duffel bag turns up from "R" in the first-class area. Twenty pieces, checked off on a list in my notebook, stamped by the customs official for whom we need to open nothing (wait until American customs when we return to New York!). Porter and cart in tow, we hurry down the ramp to kiss the *ooms* and *tantes*. Somehow we and they and the luggage and tulips are telescoped into Oom Johan's Opel and Oom Henk's Morris and off we go, whizzing through the Maas Tunnel, out of the city, past bulb fields where stretches of pink and purple hyacinths and squares of red tulips are framed by canals, and garlands of yellow daffodils wait at roadside stands to adorn the hoods of sightseeing cars.

In a little inn we sit around a low round table covered with a carpet-like cloth, drinking coffee and hot chocolate and talking in a torrent of Dutch and English. The children are the center of attention. I murmur to Nan to look happy even though she is tired, to Dave to be gracious even though he is starving. Clark thrives on people and needs no prodding, only some restraint. Em is off on one of her dangling sentences, and Dicker obviously needs to use the W.C. (the Vay-Say, the Dutch say, and the letters are imported from the English, who speak of the "water closet").

Suddenly I am struck by the big difference between this trip and the previous one. The difference is five children. Out of the panic of that moment evolved, almost spontaneously, the technique with which five unpredictables were controlled in public for four months. Since we rarely encountered people who spoke English natively, I found that by speaking softly and swiftly in full hearing of others and with a smile on my face, I could issue commands when necessary and be understood only by the children. These commands ranged from, Be sure to thank *tante* when we leave, to, Be quiet while your father answers questions (this at border crossings), or, still with a smile and usually to Dicker, Sit down and be quiet or I will spank you very hard tonight. Perhaps it was not so much the form of discipline as the challenge of novel situations, but neither before nor since have we achieved the good behavior of those memorable months abroad. We must make another trip, I guess.

8

WHEN THE LAST of the relatives had departed with love and kisses, we surveyed Flat 77, our home for seven weeks. It was on the upper floor of a new U-shaped complex of summer flats built on a hill. Each flat had a picture window on the outside of the U and ours looked down over the red roofs of Zandvoort to the North Sea. On the inside of the U were the entrances, opening onto a covered cement walkway. From the courtyard below the *melkboer,* the *groenteboer,* and the *broodman* sounded their horns insistently each morning and the women of the flat streamed down to buy their daily supply of milk, vegetables, and bread.

The flat was attractive. And small. Charming for two, snug for four, crushing for seven. One tiny closet, no dressers or drawers, six hangers for seven people. The kitchen, galley-type, scarcely wide enough for two people to pass sideways, was between the living-eating area and the W.C., so there would be much sidewaysing to be done. In the W.C., clammy cold and without towel bars, the sound of the flushing resembled a diesel train passing at arm's length and the toilet paper felt like rough wallpaper even though it was pink and marked *prima qualiteit.*

But why complain? The living-eating room was nice, the view lovely, and three bouquets of fresh tulips lent their charm. One bouquet stood on the round table in front of the picture window. This is the mark of a well-kept house or flat — fresh flowers visible from outside in the center of a clean picture window. Drapes on picture windows are usually not drawn at night. In this fishbowl existence, with houses wall to wall, the Dutch preserve their privacy with a formal courtesy in their speech to one another. Their words, rather than their drapes, serve as guardian of their privacy.

The twenty pieces of luggage were waiting on the walkway to be stuffed into the flat. Hopeless. But here the rules of family travel apply. The first rule is, Be organized. The second, Be flexible. And the third, or maybe it should be first, Never lose your sense of humor. The latter two dictated a walk into town and to the beach before attacking the luggage and making beds.

Rule one suggested that we organize the march into town. There is little decency in roaming like a motley pack. People will be looking out of their picture windows while they drink tea. Besides, we will be walking in many strange places these months, so we may as well begin properly. The girls first, then Dave and Clark, and then we, hopefully with Dicker. And quietly.

Zandvoort is a quaint peaceful town until late May when it becomes a bedlam of resorters and beach lovers who clog the streets, shops, and shore.

Fortunately we were there before most of the vacationers. From Zandvoort tower, the town landmark, one can see for miles, to the belching smokestacks of IJmuiden on the coast, inland to the spires of beautiful Haarlem, and all around to the *dorpjes,* the little villages snug among the dunes. In the back streets of Zandvoort the smith and cobbler work. On the brick street in front of the post office the herring cart offers its specialty with raw onion. Nearby is the *patats frites* stand. We took the individual sacks of french fries — no mayonnaise, thank you — and nibbled on our way.

Several big hotels preside over the beach. On the sand huddled dozens of hooded wicker chairs in which bathers of warmer days wriggle in and out of bikinis or sit sheltered from the wind. It was cold on the beach. A desolate wind swept the dusk across the grey sea. The harbor light at IJmuiden began to flash. People scurried through the streets to reach the cozy lights of home.

In early evening the landlord arrived at the flat with his wife. She brought tulips. He received our check for five hundred *gulden* rent. Expansively he demonstrated the expresso coffee maker and the *olie kachel,* the portable kerosene stove. There was a small electric heater, too. "You will need it," he said apologetically. "This is the coldest, rainiest spring anyone can remember." It would be.

To the girls we gave the seven-by-seven-foot twin bedroom. Clark and Dave took the bunks in the five-by-seven room because we wanted to use the living room evenings after the children were asleep. Suitcases slid under beds were a substitute for dressers, though there was scarcely room to pull them out and lift the lids. Dicker had the *Dreisitzbank* in the living room after starting the night in the boys' bunks. In one end of the living room was an extra cot, the bottom half made rigid by our footlocker hidden beneath. This was my bed. The Rev spread a sleeping bag over an undulating mattress made with four chair pillows of varying sizes. Nightly he arranged the whole assemblage at an angle to allow W.C. access without falling over him.

Such makeshift living did not augur well for receiving uninvited guests. That was the fiasco of the first Saturday night. We had managed to get each child through a swift rinse in the chilly W.C. by spacing showers far enough apart to allow the little *Heisswaterapparat* over the kitchen sink to build up lukewarm water five times. Sunday clothes were ironed and draped over chairs for want of hangers. I was converting the sofa into Dicker's bed when the doorbell rang. The Rev spoke cordially to some stranger and invited him in. Chagrined, I yanked the sheets and blankets from the sofa. As I flung them over my shoulder they hit the ceiling chandelier. The guest emerged from the kitchen, the chandelier crashed in pieces at his feet, and I managed a feeble greeting with a blanket over my head. It was not the ideal way to receive a lawyer who owns a sixteen-room house in fashionable

Aerdenhout and whose cousin in Chicago had written him that we were arriving. Rule three applied here.

Sometimes the living room became a clothes dryer. Handwashing could be hung on the cement walkway when and if the sun shone, or it dried on chair backs around the *olie kachel*. For general laundry we tracked down a laundromat in nearby Haarlem. It was on the Wittevrouwenstraat, the White Ladies Street. The first time there, we spent twenty minutes convincing the proprietor to leave the white and colored clothes in separate loads. He insisted that in his machines maroon towels should be washed with white cottons because all cotton belonged together. It was useless to explain in perfectly good Dutch that I had been washing in such a machine of my own for twelve years. At such times the Dutch have an exasperating trait. They are utterly gracious and polite in their condescension, but whether you speak of foreign policy or of maroon towels in white loads, they always know better. In the case of the towels I finally said, not too graciously, that I would take the responsibility and pay the cost if he washed the white and colored things separately. The next time, certainly to irk me, the man returned unwashed my white cotton gloves and the children's white shoe-strings. For these he said his water was too hot!

This laundromat had no dryer, so we strung lines from the drapery rods of the picture window to the iron poles of the bookcase, hung the wash, and reduced the living room to damp tunnels. By moving the *olie kachel* along beneath the clothes we encouraged the drying process. Please, no doorbell now. Nancy wrote in her diary on one of those laundry days, "We couldn't see each other across the room and we had to crawl to get anywhere and we stayed up late because the sheets weren't dry. We heard a good story about Rocky the seal from BBC in London and we ate some good cheese on raisin buns."

Supermarkets have not reached the villages of Holland. Neither have free paper bags. There are separate stores for milk, meat, bread, even soap. The second day in Zandvoort we shopped to fill our empty cupboards, leaving the children at the beach with new shovels and an orange ball. In the Albert Heijn store, which came closest to being an all-purpose store, we loaded staples into a shopping cart, only to discover at the checkout that each housewife brings her own container, whether string bag, baby carriage, or bicycle pouch. Rather than return what we had paid for and needed, we tried to load our pockets and my big purse. Oatmeal, sugar, and one hanger (they had no more) refused to be stuffed. We had not yet made purchases at the meat, milk, and bread stores. Reluctantly the children left the beach to serve as carriers. Their pockets were already loaded with shells they wanted to keep.

Expedition completed, we straggled seven blocks and up the hill to the flat. This was no matter of walking in orderly fashion. It was a question of reaching the flat at all. Balance the loads: shells, sugar, shovels, soups (we should have bought less), rolls, flour, cocoa, rice (the Dutch buy for only a day at a time), rusk, oatmeal, bread, milk (don't drop the bottle, Clark), cheese, butter, coffee, tea (get the orange ball — it rolled off), hanger, jam, meat, salt (just up the steps now). *Gekke Amerikanen,* crazy Americans, the people watching from their picture windows must have thought. Why buy all that food at once and with nothing to carry it in?

The fourth day the red microbus was ready in Amersfoort, fifty miles away, and the Rev left by train to get it. It was almost dark when he blew the horn beneath the window and we all rushed down to go for a trial run. Sitting high above the bicycles and cars, we drove to Haarlem to locate the nearest cousin, a probation officer. It took three hours of going in circles and making polite inquiries to find his flat on a new block-long street. Truthfully, we never did find it, and in answer to our third telephone call, cousin Geert came on foot to where we waited beside an unused ferris wheel in a vacant lot. "After all, it's my business to find people who have gone astray," he said as we sat down to drink coffee together near to midnight.

The next day we continued exploring nearby. Spaarndam and the bronze statue of the boy with his hand in the leaking dike. Tiny Spaarnwoude's Romanesque church and graveyard called Akker Gods, God's Acre. We drove to the sluices of the North Sea Canal at IJmuiden, past Saturday soccer games and flower wagons and colorful calliopes making merry music in the streets. There were nearly a hundred bicycles and only one other car with us on the ferry across an important canal. At another canal we watched the bridge tender collect his fee on the end of a long pole held out to barges passing through.

Between excursions the days in the flat assumed a predictable pattern. The Rev and the redbus left early for meetings, conferences, and observation in various cities. I reached out from my warm cot to turn on the electric heater and when it generated a small circle of warmth, I got up to light the *olie kachel.* The children wakened mid-morning if we had been out late the night before. Sometimes, to keep warm, they had breakfast and books in bed. Every morning they studied, made diary entries, and learned five Dutch words their father left for them.

All this was not as serene and well-organized as it sounds. Between dealing out arithmetic and language assignments, keeping Dicker out of trouble, marking papers, settling arguments, draping handwash, and wondering when the rain would stop, I had some doubts about the value of paying money so that I could baby-sit, school-teach, and hand-wash abroad. Gloomy thoughts persisted as I swept half the dunes out of the flat door and bemoaned a missing arm of Emily's grey cardigan which had dried too close to the *olie kachel.* I was not very patient about refusing to admit more treasures to the flat, and so they piled up outside the door — a cracked *klomp,* hunks of cork, a tin cigar box, bottle caps, sticks of sea-smoothed wood, and the overflow of shells after the plant ledge under the picture window was full. There was also a green bottle Dave and Nan found on an eight-mile hike along the beach to IJmuiden, in which there was a note saying, *Het was lekker* — it was delicious. Kees, the caretaker, cast a baleful look at the treasure pile every time he came to call us to the central telephone in his locked shed.

Afternoons were for the dunes, often with lunches to be eaten in some sheltered spot. Cheese sandwiches mostly, with some fruit. The Rev bought a sixteen-kilo cheese, thirty-five pounds in our weight, shaped like a solid wagon wheel. It cost about six dollars. Like good Dutchmen we ate cheese with tea for breakfast because eggs were too expensive. All the way into Greece we hacked away on the cheese. The last of it, deteriorating and bad-smelling in the heat, was abandoned at the campsite in Salonika.

In slacks and sweatshirts, or hooded jackets for a drizzle, the children roamed the dunes for hours. They discovered pools and flowers and cozy nooks for telling stories. There was a tall dune to jump from, a flat place for drawing sand pictures, a natural amphitheater for giving plays, and a secret hiding place where no one could find them. There were grasses for weaving and trails for walking and sometimes a wanderer to talk with or a dog to befriend. Often we all went hiking after "sinner" which was our name for dinner-supper served at 4:30 after late brunch in the morning. Sometimes we played kick ball or follow the leader, and sometimes we sat atop a dune to watch the sunset settle into the sea. If we waited longer, the herring boats appeared like phantoms out of nowhere, gliding across the dark water, each guided by a light on its bow.

HﾠOW CAN ONE summarize two months in Holland? They linger in our minds as a string of vivid experiences, unconnected, focused on certain days, certain places, and of course, certain people.

There are the days of April 30 and May 4, when within a week the Dutch commemorate with joy the birthday of Queen Juliana and with deep sadness the death of many countrymen under the Nazi occupation of 1941-45. No other week of the year matches this one for intensity of national feeling.

The queen's birthday in 1962 was a special occasion because Juliana and Bernhard also celebrated their twenty-fifth wedding anniversary. Royalty flew into Schiphol airfield from everywhere. Radio and newspapers described the arrivals of the Shah and Farah Diba, Queen Elizabeth and Philip, King Baudouin and Fabiola, and members of other royal houses.

Loyally we sprinkled orange *hagel* on our breakfast bread before we left for Amsterdam. Flags with orange streamers flew everywhere. Pine trees were decorated with orange balloons. Children with masks, horns, and hats watched parades in the smaller towns. Bicycle traffic was at peak.

In the Amsterdam apartment of cousins Gerard and Tineke there were small Dutch flags for the children and apricot tarts with coffee. Dessert at noon featured orange-flavored yogurt with orange slices in it. *Oranje boven* — the House of Orange above all!

In the afternoon, cameras in hand, we joined the crowds along the route of the queen's carriage. Few tourists are in Holland so early in the season, and we smiled at the comments about the *Amerikanen* as we passed. Is it the boys' crewcuts that identify us so readily?

In the first carriage rode the top-hatted *burgemeester,* the mayor of Amsterdam. Then came the royal carriage. There was a sprinkle of polite applause. People on the continent do not shout and wave as we undignified Americans do. Prince Bernhard looked jovial and relaxed. The queen looked weary and much powdered under her white tulle hat. (But never venture such comments aloud because the Dutch are protective of the royal house, at least to foreigners.) The next carriage brought the four princesses, each wearing a different colored tulle hat. The horses passed at a swift trot and the carriages disappeared into the Rai, a large exposition hall where the royal family received greetings from assembled dignitaries. We walked along canals lined with daffodils to catch a glimpse of the golden barge on which the queen's party would float to its next appearance.

In stark contrast, the people of Holland make their *stille tocht,* their silent march, on May 4, the eve of Liberation Day. From a central meeting place in every village and city they walk to the graves of war dead, to the crossroads graves of a few as well as to cemeteries for thousands. Nearest us was the military cemetery in the dunes outside Overveen. Here lie 368 heroes of the Dutch underground, two of them *onbekend,* unknown.

More than five hundred people gathered at the tower in Overveen. Many carried flowers. At seven, just before dusk, they began their march paced by a drummer, moving out of the town onto the main highway along the coast. For forty-five minutes they walked, children, men, a crippled woman, a *dominee* straight and imposing in his preaching garb. No one spoke. There was only the loud rustle of a thousand feet and the steady roll of the drum. Down the empty highway, over the crest of a hill, and, more slowly now, up the curving walk that rises through the dunes to the cemetery itself. The marchers poured through the gate like water seeping into a maze until they filled the brick walks of the cemetery. While the bell tolled they laid their flowers on the graves. Boy Scouts were there with more flowers so that every grave had its offering. After the bell a bugler on the wall blew a long blast. Silence followed, absolute except for the cry of a gull wheeling late in the dark sky. No speeches, no bands, only a silent gazing and weeping and remembering. And then a final blast from the trumpet on the wall. Until the funeral of President Kennedy, we had never seen anything as moving and impressive.

There was nothing national about the paintings and pewter day. It was important only to us. The rain falling in Zandvoort had not yet reached Amsterdam when we parked the redbus in the courtyard of the red brick Rijksmuseum, best-known art museum in the Netherlands. Armed with a diagram of the galleries, we moved from room to room, picking favorites. Nancy liked the serene face of Van Heemskerk's *Anna Codde*. Clark was properly impressed with the mass of figures in Rembrandt's *Nightwatch*, which is to the Rijksmuseum what the *Mona Lisa* is to the Louvre. The Rev liked Rembrandt's sorrowful *Jeremiah*.

But the painting that belonged to all of us was Nicolaes Maes's *Biddende Vrouw*. The old peasant woman prays over her dark bread, fish, and soup while the cat claws hopefully at the tablecloth. Throughout my childhood a large sepia-colored print of this painting hung in my parents' dining room and now the children live with it above our table. Emily found the painting. She and Clark made us close our eyes while they led us to it. We were entranced with the colors, the reds especially, and the light on the old woman's face. The guard, curious that seven people should stand so long at one painting, came to joke with the children about the cat that had been trying for a hundred years to reach the fish.

For five *gulden,* a dollar and a quarter, one can purchase eight-by-ten-inch reproductions of paintings, glazed and mounted on masonite for hanging. It was hard to be frugal. Nan took her *Anna Codde,* Clark his *Night Watch,* we the *Jeremiah* and the Maes *View of Haarlem,* our favorite city, as well as five *Biddende Vrouw*'s to share with friends. We should have taken more.

When we left the Rijksmuseum, the coastal rain had reached Amsterdam. But the Rev kept his promise. He took the children on a cruise through the canals while I shopped for pewter. *Tin,* the Dutch call it. We had decided to make a few significant purchases on our trip. Pewter, a painting, and perhaps a brass tray from Istanbul or Damascus. Things to enjoy as a family in our home.

The Kalverstraat is pewter headquarters in Amsterdam. It opens off the Dam, pronounced "dum," originally the raised plain in the Amstel River on which the city was built when much of Holland was still marsh and swamp. The dam in the Amstel — Amsterdam. Today the Dam is a four-block open rectangle in the center of the city. Facing it stand the imposing grey palace where the queen rarely stays, the Bijenkorf (Bee Hive) department store, and the Krasnapolsky Hotel. In the center of the Dam is a white monument erected after World War II.

Under a crimson umbrella I squished from one elegant shop to another, out of the rain into warm circles of lamplight where pewter is laid out on velvet squares. At the end I returned to Hoyng, probably the finest shop, to purchase a coffee and tea service in heavy Zeister pewter which is not exported. I bought it complete with creamer, sugar, and the typical Dutch *lepeltje vaas,* a container for little spoons, of which we have a collection. The whole set, five pieces and a teakwood-and-pewter tray, cost no more than one lighter-weight Dutch pewter coffeepot purchased in the States. The saleswoman made out an invoice for U.S. customs.

There was time left for a walk along the Dam and leisurely coffee in an expresso place before the redbus and its lively occupants would return. *Koffie met slagroom,* with whipped cream and a sprinkle of nutmeg, a coffee for festive occasions. It suited my mood. Perched on a stool at the counter built against the window, I looked out through the rain-streaked glass to watch the bicycles and umbrellas of the five o'clock rush for home, to scan the faces, to think in peace, and to feel a surge of gratitude for a husband who would shepherd five children through a rainy afternoon so that his wife could buy pewter.

Dicker said as the redbus inched its way out of the city, "Know where we went, mom? We went on a boat down all canals to the ocean, and then we came right back to you."

This was better than pewter and *slagroom* coffee. Back to the flat. Happily.

W E REMEMBER HOLLAND also for certain things and places.

Flowers, for one thing. A colorful garden, however miniature, for every house, and windows full of plants protected from too much sun by newspapers draped over them. Wagons, stands, and open markets of cut flowers in every town and city. Long-stemmed carnations, a dozen for eighty American cents. We liked the light pink ones best and were always happy when an invitation gave us reason to buy some for our hostess.

Dutch flowers have their most beautiful setting in the Keukenhof, near Lisse on the road from Haarlem to Leiden. Keukenhof means "kitchen courtyard," though it is sixty acres of landscaped gardens with ponds, trees, and paths around which bulb growers display their best tulips and spring flowers. In May when the flowers are at their peak the Keukenhof attracts people from everywhere.

There is an annual *bloemencorso,* a flower parade with floats made of flower petals, pretty girls, bands, prizes, and crowds along the parade route through several villages. In Sassenheim Dave and Nan stood on the iron railing of a canal bridge with their arms wrapped around the neck of some big-hearted stranger who invited them to see without falling into the canal. Clark burrowed through to the front of the crowd and got lost. And of course it rained, so the pretty girls were wrapped in plastic sheets and their coiffures dripped, but the floats kept coming for nearly two hours.

The Dutch have another use for the hyacinth blooms stripped to improve the bulbs. They make flower mosaics along the roads through the bulb fields. Some are ten feet square, designed flat on the ground or on raised frames. From the individual petals are fashioned intricate advertisements for margarine, Indus watches, jewelry, or they form the face of a clock or the figure of a white duck against a pink and purple background. Somehow the petal pictures remain intact for days.

There are endless names of places that trigger clear pictures in our minds. Rotterdam means the Euromast and the Erasmus statue and the new zoo in this gleaming city which has risen in the past two decades from bombed-out rubble. The Hague means stately parliament buildings reflected in the water of the Vijver, and the Binnenhof with the twin-towered Knight's Hall built in the 1200's, roofed like a Viking ship upside down, and hung with precious rugs and tapestries. Here the queen arrives each September in a golden coach to deliver her message to the States General. The province flags hang on the walls and the names of the oldest cities are etched in the stained glass windows.

Andrew Carnegie's Peace Palace is in The Hague, too, but it is not as exciting as the miniature city of Madurodam, gift of a Dutch couple from Curacao whose only son died in Dachau concentration camp after fighting for Holland in the Second World War. In Madurodam everything is one twenty-fifth of normal and nothing is missing. Ski lift, harbor, airport, canals and locks, trains, oil pumps, castles, zoo, Euromast, Binnenhof, carnival, calliope, and dozens of typical streets and stores. We spent a whole day there while the Rev had conferences in The Hague.

Say Delft and there rise to view the two venerable churches in whose crypts lie the bodies of greats and royalty. Admirals Tromp and Piet Hein are buried in the Oude Kerk, while all the deceased House of Orange members lie in the Nieuwe Kerk, which is not very new, dating from the 1400's, and has the misfortune to be without a W.C. I know because Dicker needed one, but the attendant at the entrance to the nave said there was none. Such details, reducing the sublime to the strategic, the Rev is not pleased to have included in this record though he concedes that travel is vitally affected thereby.

To return to the sublime, William the Silent, assassinated savior of his country, reclines in sculptured marble in the Delft Nieuwe Kerk, two marble tasseled pillows under his head and his favorite dog at his feet. More recently Queen Wilhelmina was buried here in an all-white funeral, according to her wish that it be symbolic of the resurrection. On a sunny day after a climb of 370 steps, the view from the Nieuwe Kerk tower is worthwhile, though one may climb higher, 454 steps, in the Dom Kerk in Utrecht.

Leiden means poems carved into the stone façade of the city hall, com-memorating Dutch bravery during the Spanish siege in the Eighty Years' War. Alkmaar on a Friday morning is the *kaas markt*, where men in bright brimmed hats of red, yellow, and green weigh and carry piles of cheeses on sleds of colors to match their hats. Only a display for the tourist, says the lawyer cousin living there! But Hoorn is real, a quaint little village on the old Zuider Zee, with gabled roofs and leaning houses decorated with painted poems. From Hoorn ships sailed to exotic ports, and Jan Pieterzoon Coen is remembered with a big statue as the man who captured Indonesia for the Dutch.

Loosdrecht is lake country. Fleets of white sailboats skim across blue water. Here we watched men smoke eels, and we drank tea in a thatched cottage with a half door. Do not expect such friendliness in Staphorst. This Drenthe village is openly hostile to visitors. Its people protest any photo-graphing of their green and blue doors and shutters, and they vanish magi-cally when one raises a camera to record the *klompen* and costume which they wear as a matter of conviction. The children of Staphorst may be obliging, but some adult will call out to berate the visitor and order the children inside.

Bolsward makes us think of the Martinikerk with its huge key and the intricate pulpit carved from a single block of wood. "Some rich American wanted to buy it," snorted the custodian dressed importantly in black as he conducted a tour of the church with an oratory to match the Sunday sermon. In tiny Piaam, the mailman stopped to point out that all the gravestones around the old church face east, toward the rising sun, for the resurrection day. And at Zoutkamp old sailors leaned on their sticks and shared salty comments as they watched the younger generation sail the herring fleet to sea for the first time in the spring.

Just outside Zwolle we found the stone to Thomas à Kempis on the site where he lived in a monastery of Brethren of the Common Life. In the Zwolle railroad station restaurant we found that coffee cost as much as a roast beef sandwich. Coffee is expensive in Holland. It is not included in the price of a dinner and no second cups are offered.

Above all cities, Haarlem is our favorite. We hear the organ pealing in the magnificent church of Saint Bavo. Intriguing shops lean against its ageless foundation and Frans Hals, famous citizen, is buried in the choir. The Bavokerk stands on the square, in the middle of which is a statue of Laurens Koster, inventor of printing. People sit in yellow wicker chairs on Brinkman's terrace to eat croquettes in the sunshine while they enjoy the medieval beauty of the meat hall, the *stadhuis* (city hall), and the church. Tucked into the streets that radiate from the central square are wonders like the Frans Hals museum, its inner-court gardens candlelit and music-filled for the anniversary year. Or one can enter another world through gates which shut out city noise and open into immaculate *hofjes,* peaceful clusters of one- and two-room homes for the elderly. Walk the streets of Haarlem at night while bells of many sizes call out the hours to each other and every turn in a cobblestone street brings shadowy surprises.

Sometimes we make a game of recalling little places. Among these, too, we have favorites like the Kraantje Lek, the "Leaky Faucet," a restaurant near the coast at Overveen with a big sand dune behind it for children to climb while parents enjoy dessert of crisp waffles with *slagroom* and confectioners sugar. That, in turn, reminds us of Brederode Castle in nearby Santpoort, an ivy-covered ruin with a drawbridge over a flowing moat, a knights' hall, and open stone staircases on which a single misstep can plunge one into the gaping dungeon below. And don't forget the Lage Vuursche restaurant, serving pancakes the size of wagon wheels on oversized Delft plates. The night before Oom Johan took us there the queen had used the restaurant to entertain her Soesdijk Palace staff in honor of her anniversary. A stroll after eating brings one past the gate of Drakensteyn, octagonal palace of Crown Princess Beatrix.

The Dutch, of course. would expect one to remember the colossal delta-works project in the southwest of the country where the delta of the Scheldt River is being contained and rechanneled to prevent flooding, to create a fresh-water recreation area, and to provide highway access to an area of islands isolated for centuries. This is the area of the disastrous flood of 1953. And in the north the work goes on behind the Afsluitdijk to reclaim land from the Zuider Zee. Some polders are so new that the salt is not yet out of the soil and the red brick farmhouses are brand new as are the *burgemeesters* appointed by the queen to rule the new villages being organized.

Sunday memories of Holland are of worship. An unconventional service in a youth center in the middle of Rotterdam after we had gone three times through the Maas Tunnel to find the place. Or Okke Jager preaching in the Good Shepherd Church of Haarlem about the angel Gabriel contending with the devil for the body of Moses, surely an unusual sermon text. Or the small village church of Ameide between whose narrow walls deacons must be dexterous to maneuver the long poles with velvet collection bags on the end of them.

In most churches members have their accustomed places and in some churches visitors may not seat themselves until the green light flashes to say that any remaining space is available. For us, unless a family member had us in tow, it was usually safer to wait until the service was about to begin, or we could be certain that some of the seven of us would occupy a place sacred to a regular worshiper. There are no ushers in Dutch churches but the *koster,* the custodian, is much in evidence checking and directing everything until the service begins. The people in the churches are not friendly, not at all, and the Rev liked to provide members with a shattering experience by greeting them warmly as we walked out of the sanctuary.

But the sermons and bells and organs make up for this. Sometimes we heard a cousin or an uncle preach. And oh, the pipe organs, small or great, coaxed and challenged by men at the console who know how to send a melody echoing among the pillars, who can improvise expertly a *voorspel, tussenspel,* and *naspel* (prelude, interlude, and postlude) for every psalm sung, who play with an authority and virtuosity of which no woman is capable, says the Rev. The women are in the pews, passing out peppermints from silver *doosjes* and if they are elderly, they share Boldoot cologne on a handkerchief to freshen one's face halfway through the sermon. After church there is coffee and talk, with no hurry for Sunday dinner. The children have handleless cups like small soup bowls and lots of warm milk in their coffee. But then, no Dutchman drinks his coffee black.

M OST OF ALL, Holland means to us *familie*. The family province is Groningen in the north. At Kloosterburen is the old dairy farm called Groot Halsem and in the whitewashed basement of the farmhouse we saw the beam with the deep-carved inscription, *Jakob Halsem Katrina Sin Huisfrow Anno Domni* 1599 *Den* 13 *Dessember.*

"Before the pilgrims," said Dave, wonderingly.

Old bachelor Hendrik Halsema told us, to the tune of his squeaking rocker, that it had been twenty-five years since a family member had visited the farm. Then it was a Halsema who was a civil engineer in Bagguio, the Philippine Islands.

"I met his son Jim there," said the Rev, as amazed as the rest of us over this coincidence. "In the spring of 1945 while I was in the U.S. Infantry freeing Luzon from the Japanese, I carried the family silver to him in Manila." Small world, converging in Kloosterburen. Behind his steel-rimmed spectacles, Hendrik Halsema considered this in silence and shook his head.

Men were putting new thatch on the barn roof. That makes the barn good for another hundred years, perhaps. In Europe the old things last. They are repaired and restored and treated tenderly. And so one walks each day in history and the past is precious in churches and town halls, in walls and barns and cottages. Unless bombs destroy, as they did in Rotterdam, the heart of a European city is old and meaningful. Streamlined modern buildings stand respectfully at a distance, aware of what they owe the generations before them, just as children in Europe seem to show more respect for older people than American children do.

Oom Bee — short for Berend and pronounced "Bay" — oldest living member of the family, was convinced that he could trace the Van Halsemas back to Charlemagne, though he had a few rude shocks in the process and his enthusiasm waned. For one thing, there was the woman who was jailed twice in the city of Groningen for cavorting with other women's husbands. And then the whole family turned out to have been Roman Catholic until the early 1700's, which was disappointing to a man whose father, son, brother, and six nephews were all *Gereformeerde dominees* — Reformed ministers — like himself.

It was the silversmith's wife, a Huguenot, who protestantized the family. She attracted the eye of her husband when he was on his way to Rome during study for the priesthood. In his marriage he was ambivalent about his promise to become a wholehearted Protestant, but his wife had the final word. She buried him in the floor of the Reformed Church in Wirdum. From that time on the Protestant branch of the family has been called Van Halsema, implying a departure from, while the Roman Catholic branch retains the Halsema name.

The priest-turned-silversmith became a prosperous businessman. In 1765 he purchased a distinguished country home called Rusthoven near Wirdum. It was for sale when we were there and someone steeped in the history of that area has purchased it now. The son of the silversmith was a jurist named Diderik Frederik Johan.

"Why didn't you give me a name like that?" asked Clark, stirred by ancestral glory.

The jurist wrote two books about history and practice of law which are still used, and he compiled the first dictionary of the Groniger dialect. He also kept a chronicle which was continued by a minister son and covered the eighty years from 1769 to 1854. Oom Bee unearthed it and the *Groniger Chroniek van de beide Van Halsemas* was published in 1957.

The silversmith and the jurist lie side by side in the choir of the Wirdum church. On their large flat stones and on the family pew enclosure is carved the family coat of arms depicting a knight with a raised sword. We had painted copies of it made and a signet ring in honor of the Rev's fortieth birthday.

More recent ties link us to the old cemetery and church in the village of Nijeveen in Drenthe. Opa, father's father, was *dominee* here for thirty-three years. He lies buried in the churchyard beside Oma, sharing double graves with two unmarried daughters.

In front of the Nijeveen church runs the shady road to Meppel, the nearest town of size, six miles away. Oma walked that road one day to pawn a large silver spoon because she needed money to feed her family of eleven children. Opa did not know she pawned it. No one knew until Opa visited father in Passaic, New Jersey, in 1930, which was thirty-five years later and after Oma's death. The son of the pawnshop owner had emigrated to America to a city near Passaic. When he heard that Opa was visiting father, he invited him to his home and showed him the spoon. "My father never sold it," he said, "because he always hoped the *dominee's* wife would be able to buy it back." So father redeemed the spoon and Opa took it home with him and Oom Bee told us the story with many flourishes of the big spoon which he had inherited as Opa's oldest son.

We stopped in Nijeveen on an afternoon when a burial was being completed in the newer cemetery. Bartel Kuyer, ninety-year-old former custodian, who boasted that he had helped to rear all the parsonage children, called to the people walking home from the grave.

"Here is Emo's son from America and all his children," he said, gathering a crowd around the redbus.

Everyone came eagerly to shake the Rev's hand, to peer in at the children, and to reminisce about father's frequent visits to Nijeveen. As if intensified by the mood of the funeral, the past rose up to be remembered. The redbus and its brightly-clothed children were encircled by the black-clad figures, eager to recall the brightness of their own younger days.

At last the circle drifted apart and Bartel Kuyer showed the children the church, leaving his *klompen* at the door when he entered. Today's *dominee* brought from the back room of the parsonage the chair on which Opa sat to teach catechism in that room, and the silver ash tray Opa left for continued use at smoke-filled consistory meetings.

We looked up at the attic window under the tile roof where father slept when he was a boy. Here Oom Frans asked him one night before they fell asleep, "Emo, what would you rather have, the kingdom of heaven or Koendert Haveman's new dog cart?" Father knew what he was supposed to say but, being a normal boy, he greatly admired the *hondekar* and so there was a long silence in the attic before he answered in a small voice, "'t koninkrijk Gods."

Oom Bee had many souvenirs of Nijeveen in the neat row house to which he retired in Hilversum. One of the souvenirs was a snake, preserved sixty years in a jar of formaldehyde. The first time we came with the children to the house on Gysbrecht van Amstelstraat (a good example of the impossible Dutch street names, chosen for important citizens, if not for the royal family whose names adorn streets, barges, boats, and bridges), Clark could scarcely weather the introductions before he asked to see the snake, the *slang,* he added, to hurry the process.

Oom Bee, who never walked if he could run or sat if he could stand, rushed upstairs to get the snake from the shelf above the washstand in his study. Triumphantly he set it down in the middle of the tea table. While Tante Yt poured tea into cups set in a circle on the table, the snake rocked in its formaldehyde and Oom Bee paced the room and dramatized the story.

"Zis snake, it is sixty years *oud,*" he began with preaching voice and gestures. It was an adder, brought in a carton by a helpful farmer to the Nijeveen parsonage so that Oom Bee could take it to his zoology class in Meppel high school. After supper the boys had opened the carton, and the adder got loose in the kitchen. Cornered, it struck and bit Oom Bee in the forearm. Opa and the boys killed the snake while the girls shrieked and fled. Soon Oom Bee's arm began to swell. During that long night father and Oom Bee walked the six miles to Meppel so that the doctor could lance the arm. Father had to hold the pan to catch the blood. This he himself told us, adding that he almost fainted.

"And zis is ze snake, and I have been keeping him all zeze years. Now, drink your tea before it becomes *koud*." It wasn't easy, though Tante Yt's cookies are the best anywhere.

They are even better than the cookies in the Gunnink *bakerij* in Kampen where Opa, a seminary student, met Oma in her father's bakery when he came to buy church peppermints there. It is still a good bakery, run by Oma's family. We liked best the *Kamper steur* butter cookies, shaped like a fish with the head dipped in chocolate, a gift given us in one of those pretty enameled tin boxes which the Dutch use for special cookies or tea bags.

On June 1, the date of Opa's birthday, we spent the evening with a few special cousins in Haarlem's Goede Uur. The Goede Uur, the "Good Hour," is a little place three steps down from street level in a nondescript neighborhood under the shadow of the Annakerk. It has cloudy leaded windows, uneven floor, rough-hewn stools and tables worn to a satin finish, big dark rafters, old bottles, and copper pieces. Lit by candles and lanterns, it serves cheeses on wooden squares with crusty bread, coffee, wines, and one kind of undecorated cake. By daylight no one would notice the place. It holds only twenty people. Silence is enforced during an hour of classical music, and one may pull himself up a ladder with the help of a rope rail to appraise the contemporary art hanging in the loft. We have not found anywhere a place to match this one.

Here, by the light of a fat dripping candle, we shared stories about Opa when we discovered that we were together on his birthday. The full flavor of the Dutch is untranslatable.

Did your father ever tell you the story of the retired *dominee* who came to visit Opa during the last years of his life? No? (Gerard of Oom Frans is talking — there are five Gerards in the family, all named for Opa.) Well, the *dominee* was in good health and, well-meaning, he spent part of each weekly visit exhorting feeble Opa to be prepared for death. As the old *dominee* took up his hat to leave one day, Opa said, "Brother van der Vegt, where are you going from here?"

"To the post office and then to the cigar shop."

"Be careful crossing the street," Opa admonished him, "or you may be in heaven before me."

Or the story of the *pruik,* the wig. You never heard it? In 1902 Tante Hendrika was born, the one who lived with Oma's rich sister who had no children. She was born at noon on Sunday in the parsonage so Opa did not preach in the morning. But everything went well and he decided to preach as usual in the afternoon. He noted with approval that the eyes of all the congregation were fixed on him intently as he began his sermon. It was surprising, however, that the attention remained so rapt that no one nodded or fell asleep as Opa traveled on to his second and third points. Opa himself was flattered that his sermon merited unusual interest. At the end of the service he retired to the consistory room to receive the handshakes of his elders. Each looked at him carefully. One lingered to say, "But, *dominee,* was it a very difficult birth?"

"Why do you say that?" inquired Opa.

"Because, *dominee,* before you had hair and now you have none."

Whereupon Opa ran his hand over his shiny head and realized that in his haste he had left his *pruik* at home on the bedroom dresser. He never wore it again.

Oom Bee was to our children what Opa had been to the Rev when he was ten and lived for a summer in Opa's house in Haren. We spent as much time as we could with Oom Bee and Tante Yt, took them with us in the redbus, and stored up the songs and stories Oom Bee taught us. The songs ran a gamut as wide as the life of the dear man teaching them to us. They ranged from one about the wonder of two bears buttering rolls to the family psalm which traditionally has been sung on Sunday noons for almost two hundred years.

"Hi-hi-hi! Ha-ha-ha!" Oom Bee would sing in the chorus to the bear song, with every filling and tonsil in full view, beating with his fists in rhythm on the table until the silver and glasses danced. Then, in a stage whisper, he would say to the children, "You know what my neighbors through ze wall will say? 'Zere goes zat crazy *dominee* again.'" Laughter rumbled loud and long from his chest and the tonsils hove again into view.

With the help of a magnifying glass (*"Ja,* my eyes are getting bad, just like Opa's did, you know"), Oom Bee wrote the words of a children's song which we learned and sang for morning devotions all the way to Jerusalem. The first verse of it was

> *Klokje klinkt, vogel zingt,*
> *Iedereen op zijner wijs;*
> *Kind, ook gij zingt daarbij*
> *Tot des Heeren lof en prijs!*

In literal translation that verse means

> A clock ticks, a bird sings,
> Everyone in his own way;

Child, you, too, sing along
Bringing praises to the Lord.

We sang the family psalm verse with the help of the Rev playing the reed organ in Oom Bee's dining room. And we still sing in solid unison every Sunday noon,

Zijn naam moet eeuwig eer ontvangen,
men loov' Hem vroeg en spa!
De wereld hoor' en volg' mijn zangen
met amen, amen, na!

a metrical setting for Psalm 72:19, "Blessed be his glorious name forever; may his glory fill the whole earth! Amen and Amen!"

One of the uncles told us, chuckling, "You know, we Van Halsemas are what is called *familie-ziek*."

Something of this wonderful sickness we hope to pass on to our children.

THE FIRST WEEK IN JUNE we made a week's shakedown trip into Germany to test our new camping equipment before making the trek to Jerusalem. We had research to do in Heidelberg and the old Palatinate area around it, and we wanted to see the two Berlins. Besides, German weather required warm clothes which could be left behind to lighten the luggage for the Middle East.

Haarlem's Sporthuiscentrum showed all the latest camping equipment. We chose a lightweight tent with waterproof floor, double top, and zippered closing, so uncomplicated that Dave could put it up unaided, so compact that the tent, aluminum poles, stakes, and ropes fit into a cloth bag two feet long and ten inches across. Europeans, who travel the continent with motorbikes and little cars, have developed ingenious camping materials. In American money the price is reasonable. The tent cost twenty-nine dollars. We bought a Camping-gaz stove, two burners screwed onto a pressure tank base. The tank was good for a hundred cooking hours and could be exchanged for a full one at the cost of a few *gulden*. Inch-thick, foam-rubber pads to avoid blowing up and patching air mattresses, a low collapsible table, a nest of pans, and one folding chair completed the purchases. For the German week each child took his zipper bag, no more, and wore a jacket.

Through the green rolling country around Arnhem we drove in high spirits, singing, across the German border onto the *Autobahn* where Germans think they only have the right to pass, particularly in Mercedes, and where every good driver wears leather gloves, even under a blistering sun. The older children began reading literature from the Germany folder, Clark and Em tried to decipher road signs, and Dicker said plaintively, "You know German, mom? Read me some."

At Hennef we left the *Autobahn,* cashed a traveler's check at a *Sparkasse,* and practiced some elementary German phrases on a boy in *Lederhosen.* Leaving the spires of Köln behind, we began to climb the steep green hills to the village of Herborn. This was part of the plan to stop at places important in the lives of three men — a prince, a preacher, and a professor — who together produced the Heidelberg Catechism, one of the finest Reformation creeds there is. The Dutch, Hungarian, and American Reformed churches have long used it as a guide to Sunday preaching. Written in 1563, translated into many languages, the catechism had an exciting origin and the prince's defense of it before Emperor Maximilian is comparable to Luther's stand at Worms. To write the story for the four-hundredth anniversary of the catechism, one had to explore the old towns and places of its history.

So here was Herborn, with castle and church looking down on crooked streets along the river Dill. A bazaar was being held under bright umbrellas and the people stopped to stare when the Rev dented a hubcap trying unsuccessfully to wedge the redbus up a narrow street to the church. The preacher Olevianus spent the last years of his turbulent life in Herborn. The castle with three turrets, an inn today, belonged to Count John of Nassau and he gave it for a Reformed university of which Olevianus was named head. The university was founded on the same day, July 10, 1584, that Count John's famous brother, William the Silent, was assassinated in Delft. In the choir of the church was the black marble wall marker of the preacher's grave. An organ student watched curiously while I wrote the Latin inscription in a notebook.

As we made our descent toward a camping place on the Rhine, home-going farmers passed, outlined with their oxen and wooden carts against the sunset. A man with a briefcase swung off a bus and began walking briskly down a pasture trail.

For two *marks* we set up camp at Campplatz Rhein-Mosel at the confluence of these two rivers and across the water from a floodlit castle which seemed at night to be suspended by unseen ropes from heaven. It was late and chilly, so we took the campground attendant's advice and went to the boat club across the road to eat. No one was there except a black-haired man who offered to make us soup with wurst. It would be ready *schnell schnell,* he said, ushering us to tables in a second-floor room lined with trophies. Shortly the man left the adjoining kitchen, locked the door, descended the stairs, and did not reappear for twenty minutes. Three times this happened. Up the stairs, unlock the door, stir the soup (presumably), lock the door, descend the stairs, stay away another twenty minutes. In answer to our rusty German, the man would say reassuringly, cigarette dangling, *"Jawohl, schnell schnell."* The third time, in desperation, the Rev inquired whether coffee was available while we waited.

"Schnell schnell schnell," replied the man, unlocking and re-entering the kitchen. The coffee was served with the soup. By then the children had memorized the trophy engravings and we were all making silly guesses about what treasure the man kept behind his locked kitchen door.

The soup was good, big bowls of it with crusty dark bread. Em was trying to say, *"Nein, danke,"* but she did not get it out fast enough to decline a second bowl. We drank our coffee and exited past the locked door.

Nan, Clark, and Em slept snugly in the redbus, one on each seat, sleeping bags rolled out, zipper bags on the floor beside them. Dave and Dicker bedded down on foam rubber in the tent and the two of us were invited for better-than-boat-club coffee with the Brintons in the tent next to ours. He was a University of California research chemist studying in Stuttgart.

At dawn the river traffic began. After washing themselves in an outdoor stone basin with nine spouts, the children perched on rocks at the river's edge and counted 105 boats and barges before breakfast.

Simmern was our next destination, birthplace of Elector Frederick III of the Palatinate. In the Mosel River Valley people were coming to work in the terraced vineyards, whose neat green rows ran vertically on the hillsides. Little ferries shuttled people, wagons, and bicycles back and forth across the river. Most of the workers were women, ageless in high shoes, kerchiefs, and wrinkled skin, pushing plows, wielding wooden hoes, bending, turning, lifting. Someone should write a German companion poem to Markham's "Man with a Hoe." In the Middle East women work because they are women. In Germany they work because wars have taken their men.

Simmern sat on its hill like most old cities, topped by the Stephan's Kirche. In a dim side chapel of the church are buried members of the family of Frederick III, including his parents and grandparents who were devoted followers of the emperor and of the Roman church, and his fourteen-year-old daughter. Bound to a pillar in the chapel is the nine-foot lance that Frederick carried into battle for the emperor against the Turks. Marble statues of the royal family contemplated us as we stood with the church warden deciphering from a German booklet something about the *Grab-malen* around us. The *Schloss* is unpretentious, as castles go, and has been converted into a museum and school.

The church warden in the Stephan's Kirche told us how near we were to an American air base. Thanks to him and to the Rev's active reserve status, we ate hamburgs and milk shakes for lunch at Hahn Air Force Base. The children were elated to see things American and Nancy made a sign which she held in the redbus window to offset our Dutch license plates. "We are Americans, too," it read.

Silence, blissful silence, descended on the redbus with the help of five new comic books as we returned to the Mosel Valley. Farmers were forking steaming manure while over their heads a succession of jets screamed in take-off. The Rev and I enjoyed the vine-clad hills and the winding river in peace. We are not in favor of comic books, but there are times!

Trier next, because Olevianus grew up there. An ancient Latin inscription in the marketplace declares, "Treves stood thirteen hundred years before Rome. May it continue to exist and enjoy eternal peace." This proud city on the Mosel makes several boasts. It had a first-century amphitheater for twenty-five thousand, eight hundred feet of imperial baths dating from Constantine, and its churches claim to possess the holy coat of Christ and the bones of the apostle Matthew. From Trier the Romans ruled their western empire which stretched from Britain to Spain.

To this cornerstone of the Holy Roman Empire Olevianus returned after studying. Most of the city was converted to Protestantism under his preaching. But the archbishop returned from a visit and laid siege to Trier, put down the Reformation there, and threw Olevianus and others into prison. Frederick III in Heidelberg sent an emissary with a trunk full of money and an appointment for Olevianus to the College of Wisdom. And so the preacher was ransomed with three thousand *florins* and brought to the Protestant university in Heidelberg in 1559.

We walked in the gardens at the Porta Nigra, the black gate that was the northern of four massive entrances into the city. Seventy-two feet thick and a hundred high, the sandstone fortress has blackened over the centuries. A procession of children passed, carrying flags in pilgrimage to a shrine. They were a reminder of the annual Olevian procession decreed by the archbishop to celebrate Trier's deliverance from the Protestant heresy preached by Olevianus.

From Trier we made an arc south and east through Saarbrucken and Kaiserslautern toward Heidelberg. This is drab congested industrial area and the *Autobahn* past Kaiserslautern is a relief. Dicker wanted to know when we would get to Jerusalem.

"First we have to go back to Zandvoort, dear boy."

"Why?"

"To get the army shovel, for one thing," I answered, trying to simplify the explanation.

"Dumb that we forgot to take it along now," he replied, and through the week he made frequent reference to the futility of going in a circle for the sake of a shovel. "After we get it," he would say, "we'll go in a straight line, for longer, to Jerusalem."

Ursinus, the professor of the catechism trio, spent his last years in Neustadt. *Camping Europa* listed a camping place five miles south of Neustadt in Saint Martin. To reach Campplatz Wappenschmiede we bumped up tortuous streets. Blurred by twilight, the faces, clothes, buildings, and flickering candles in wayside shrines could have come straight from the Middle Ages. The campground was above Saint Martin. In summer it might have been pleasant to sit at the orange tables on the terrace overlooking the vineyards. But now it was damp, cold, nearly dark, and overhanging vines and trees cast gloomy shadows on the uneven camping area big enough for ten or twelve tents. We were the only campers.

By the crisscrossing beams of two flashlights we made soup supper on the efficient new camping stove. The Rev set up the tent improperly so that the aluminum pole running along its spine broke at a bent point because it was forced beneath both layers instead of between them. What was left of the pole we propped upright in the middle of the tent to hold up the sagging canvas. Four of us wriggled cautiously inside and the tent collapsed no farther.

We entered Neustadt as people were leaving it on foot, wooden hoes over their shoulders, en route to the vineyards. It was a remnant of the medieval pattern when people lived in walled cities for protection and went out at daylight to work their fields around the town. The church on the square was red sandstone turned black like the Porta Nigra, and five unusually vicious gargoyles glared down from each side of the choir. In the stormy 1600's a wall was built inside the church to accommodate both Protestants and followers of Rome. The Protestants got the nave, the Roman Catholics the choir. Unfortunately for poor Ursinus, devoted Protestant professor, he had been buried in the choir while the whole church was temporarily Protestant. Today his grave is undiscoverable. Under the front portico between the defaced grave coves there is a plaque placed by the German Reformed Church of America on the 350th anniversary of the catechism. The effect is dismal.

Nan and I went to a bookshop on the square where we had to wait while a woman introduced her dog to the cat of the bookshop proprietress. When this had been accomplished with much cautious sniffing by the animals and even less appropriate noises from their owners, we asked for a book about old Neustadt. The lady sent us to the city hall, where I was escorted from office to office and each incumbent referred me to the next. At the end of the row someone gave me the address of the city hall and suggested I write for information!

The Rev had been more successful. At a sale he bought midget pillows to make sleeping more comfortable. They were covered in bright print remnants and cost thirty-eight and forty-eight cents apiece. A kind citizen showed us the road that led to Speyer, called the city of dead emperors because the bodies of twenty-two Hapsburg emperors lie in the cathedral crypt.

Heidelberg has had its charm and character affected by the overwhelming presence of the American military which has its European nerve center there. Still, does any castle stand more imposingly over its city than the one from which Frederick III ruled the Palatinate for seventeen years? Look at the panorama from the Philosophenweg, the hillside path across the Neckar River. Against the green mountainside stand the buildings of the castle. At its feet lies the city, from which the baroque spire of the Heiliggeistkirche rises highest over the aged roofs and chimneys. Below this the river flows to meet the Rhine, and it is spanned by the stone arches of the Alte Bruecke which Goethe called the most beautiful bridge in the world.

Germany's first university was established in Heidelberg by a Ruppert in 1396. Here Olevianus preached and Ursinus taught and Frederick III ruled from his castle. Together, in 1563, they produced the catechism which bears the name of the city.

Even in ruins the castle is outstanding. Cross the drawbridge over a sixty-foot moat and enter the inner court by passing beneath a wall of iron spikes that was raised and lowered for additional defense. The gate tower is 170 feet high with a lookout post in the top and a dungeon in the bottom. Admire the ruins of the hall of mirrors, and the graceful statues from Greek myth and Bible history on the red stone façade of Otto Henry's building. The castle was built by several electors. The grandson of Frederick III added a wing on whose façade he placed the catechism elector in company with Charlemagne and fourteen other royal ancestors. Casemier, son of Frederick III, contributed the largest wine vat in Europe, a feature which most tourists consider the distinctive thing about Heidelberg Castle.

At the university we had an interview with a church history professor who was preparing special lectures for the anniversary of the catechism. He suggested helpful books in the German language and showed us original copies of the catechism, though these were not as old as the one in Utrecht's university library from which we had photostatted several pages.

The shops around the Heiliggeistkirche sold spoons, ash trays, and jacket patches with the Heidelberg coat of arms on them. The Rev searched until he found an old print of the city from the sixteenth century when the catechism was written. "Not cheap," he said to me, "but ideal for the cover of your book."

O N TO BERLIN, the divided city. We stopped a day in Kitzingen to visit a chaplain friend. The desk clerk in the Bayerischehof Hotel there refused the Rev accommodations until he mentioned *fünf Kinder*. So, because of the children, we slept in two big rooms with plump coverlets and hot water. Better than the clammy vineyard at Saint Martin it was, and necessary because of the broken tent pole. But not as memorable.

It was interesting to note the improvement in German feeling toward Americans as compared with our previous visit. Now the German people speak of having fought the Russians, who today seem to be our common enemy. Bitter memories like the single bomb that killed six hundred children sheltered in a Kitzingen cellar are dimmed and replaced by new realities — the Berlin wall and the endless barricade that divides Germany East and West, captive and free.

The *Autobahn* uncoiled like a sleek ribbon past Erfurt and Göttingen to Braunschweig, the last city of size before Helmstedt and the East German border. Military vehicles formed an endless procession. In Braunschweig a kind man drove ahead to show us the way to the hospice after his wife had telephoned to see that space was available for us there. Refusing payment for his kindness, the man called to the children, *"Schlafe wohl."*

This was a large hospice decorated in institutional beige with Spartan furnishings. But breakfast was ample, offering hard-boiled eggs with the usual hard rolls, butter, jam, and individual pots of coffee or hot chocolate. Dicker sat a while in the W.C. down the hall from our rooms practicing Dutch loudly. Frustrated by German, he probably felt the need to bolster his ego with scraps of another foreign tongue. As we left the hospice, women passed us in the street, carrying big pans of unbaked strudel to the bakery.

We bought gas early and avoided the line of forty cars waiting at the last *Tankstelle* before East Germany. A helpful cousin had given the name of a Dutch minister in West Berlin who promised by phone to request lodging for us at one of the hospices. Lodging was scarce in West Berlin, especially in summer.

Cars pass easily through the Allied checkpoint at the East German border but the East German checks take longer. German cars were directed to one line, foreign cars to another shorter one. All occupants of German cars submitted to search inside the building. Foreign drivers went in to be interviewed through slots in a partition. The four East German checks included one by a Russian traffic controller. Armed *Vopos* in cars, on motorcycles, and on foot were all around. For twenty-five *marks* and a written declaration of money, cameras, binoculars, and such, the electric gates were raised to let us through.

Ahead of us on the highway through East Germany was a car from which a woman tossed out little packages of candy and cigarettes to men working along the road. People working in the fields responded readily to the children's waving. Beyond Magdeburg the big bridge over the Elbe River still was not repaired and the *Autobahn* narrowed to two lanes. No one exits from the highway and almost no one uses the gas stations along the way. Stolid-faced Russian soldiers in brown uniforms stood beside the East Germans in their greens as we cleared the check to leave East Germany. Through a double red-and-white barricade we entered the Allied corridor to West Berlin. Heavy barbed wire fences the corridor all the way and behind the fence the ground is cleared and mined.

Encircled by the desolation and bleakness of East Germany, West Berlin builds and thrives. Its teeming streets and towering glass-and-steel buildings rival New York. There is a kind of frenetic gaiety about the people as if, having survived the blockade of 1948 and the wall of 1961 and being cut off from the free world by a hundred hostile miles, they must eat, build, and be merry, for who knows what tomorrow will bring?

Down the Kurfürstendamm we rode in heavy traffic past fine hotels and shops to the beloved war ruin of Kaiser Wilhelm's church, a blackened tower left standing beside a starkly modern new church at the curve in the broad street. Shady 17 June Street brought us to the Brandenburg Gate and on the way we stopped to admire the golden victory statue of the Franco-Prussian War, the only war Germany won. Near the Brandenburg the streets were suddenly empty. Barricades keep tourists a block away from the gate. At its base runs the wall, and behind it is Unter den Linden, famous street of imperial Berlin. A victory goddess in a four-horse chariot sits atop the gate. She was carried away for a time by Napoleon and also had to be recast after the bombings of World War II. There was an army jeep near the wall and a few soldiers standing around.

"What's the wall in the middle of the street for?" asked Em.

"To keep people on the other side from getting out."

"How come? What'd they do wrong?"

The redbus had a servicing at the Volkswagen garage while we ate *Wienerschnitzel* in a paneled alcove of Bierstübe Hardtke. *Wienerschnitzel mit Kartoffelen.* Afterward we went window shopping. A cotton beach hat cost twenty-eight *marks,* a polka dot pajama and unlined robe of polished cotton could be had for eighty-nine *marks,* or twenty-two dollars! Clothing was chic and expensive.

The Dutch *dominee* whom we had telephoned about hospice space gave us directions to Pension Europa at Mommsenstrasse 6. It turned out to be the fourth floor of an older building and the proprietor came down the lift to greet us. There was utter dismay on his face when he saw the seven of us. He and his wife had expected only two people, two adults, he explained in swift German, rubbing his hands apologetically. Only one room was empty and the other *Pension* guests were elderly and permanent residents. He went to get his wife who looked compassionately at the children and said, *"Och, ja,* but where can we send them?" Even Dicker for the moment was sitting in respectful silence.

If we were willing to sleep in one room and if the children would be very quiet, they would take us. *"Frau Findeisen, wir sind Ihnen sehr sehr dankbar,"* said the Rev. We promised not to return until evening when it was time for the children to sleep.

It was expensive — four dollars a person — to take a bus tour of East Berlin. "Go in your own car," the Dutch *dominee* had urged. The U.S. Army captain at Checkpoint Charlie said the same. But he added, after writing down our names and license number, "Tell us when you plan to come back so that if you don't, we can start looking for you."

On this reassuring note we passed the four-language sign announcing the end of the American sector. The first barricade opened and closed behind us, hemming us in until we would be allowed through the second barricade which was at the narrow opening in the wall itself. All seven of us had to go into the processing building. Here West Germans with special passes are searched for anything they might be carrying into East Berlin. We sat forty-five minutes on wooden benches while our passports remained behind closed doors. Dicker made the East German, though not the Russian, guards laugh by peeking out of the doorway.

The second barrier was lifted and we drove into another world. In West Berlin at that five o'clock hour on Friday the streets were teeming, the sidewalk cafés full, and the city was gay with lights and laughter. East Berlin was a ghost town. The streets were almost deserted except for soldiers patrolling with guns. A few scraggly perennials, iris and delphinium, grew in a park where old people sat on benches, silent, arms and faces slack.

The KLM airlines office was a one-room storefront with a broken wooden step. Flower shops showed only pots of ivy in dirty windows. There was no color, no vitality anywhere except for the bright red propaganda signs and the WALTER ULBRICHT STADION letters over the gates of the empty stadium. Above a white reviewing stand on Marx-Engels Square, gold and red letters proclaimed, *Die Zukunft in ganz Deutschland gehört dem Frieden und dem Sozialismus:* The future of all Germany belongs to peace and socialism. Quite a future, judging by appearances! Ruined churches, rubble piles, bombed-out government buildings with grass sprouting in the cracks. We turned a corner and came near the wall which zigzags along. Instinctively the guards at the wall raised their guns into position so we waved and turned around.

Near the ruins of an Ev. Genade Kirche a young man was walking with his child. The Rev got out, ostensibly to photograph the church ruin.

"Gibt es heute schönes Wetter," he said to the man, first young person we had seen. The weather was a safe topic.

"Gott sei dank," answered the East German, using a common phrase.

"Gibt's ein Gott!" answered the Rev.

If there were not a God, answered the young father intensely, we could not exist on this side of the wall and we would be without hope in the world.

Silence.

"Wir beten für Ihnen," said the Rev softly. What else can one say?

The man explained that we were in a pocket of the wall and that we would need to turn around to get out. He and the Rev shook hands warmly. When the redbus was headed the other way, we all waved. But the man walked on without a flicker of response. In our mirror we saw the reason.

An armed guard walking his patrol route had appeared from behind a row of bushes which had blocked his view until then.

At the *Bahnhof* there were more people and a version of the news went round and round in lighted squares. The restored opera house boasted of its performances. But on Unter den Linden, five or six blocks from the Brandenburg Gate, one might not photograph. *"Nein, es ist verboten,"* answered the soldiers on the sidewalk when asked. So we took the picture through the windshield a block later, a twilight picture of a broad empty grey street lined with black trees, at whose far end is the six-pillared gate and beyond it, symbolically, a glow of light from the setting sun.

But no picture is engraved more clearly in our minds than the group of five people standing on the sidewalk at the edge of a canal bridge. Across the length of the bridge was an eight-foot wooden wall to keep out the view of West Berlin. But at the bank of the canal there was space, a few feet of it, before the buildings began. Here stood a group of five looking down the canal into West Berlin. An old man, leaning back on his cane with his hands cushioning the top of it. A teen-age boy on a bicycle shading his eyes against the falling sun. A middle-aged woman with an empty shopping bag. A young couple hand in hand. All motionless, suspended in silence like a photo in dimension, watching the free world.

We rode in matching silence, past the barred stone building where soldiers guard the tomb of unknown soldiers, back to the wooden benches in the processing building, back to the American captain who greeted us cheerfully and observed that we hadn't left anyone behind. But we had.

There is jagged glass imbedded in the cement along the top of the wall. Above this are rows of barbed wire. Guards, with binoculars and guns trained, sit in lookouts at regular intervals. Behind the wall twelve or fifteen feet of space has been cleared and in the buildings behind this the windows are boarded, the occupants relocated. At night searchlights crisscross the area. We drove as close as possible along the free side of the wall to the Bernauerstrasse to see a small monument with a cross and fresh flowers. It stands at the foot of the wall as a memorial to those who died leaping from the buildings above or who were shot to death trying to escape. A man came to talk. He and his family had jumped from a balcony in a now empty building, but his mother had remained behind the wall. Desperately he poured out his feelings about peace and President Kennedy and the wall. *"Und wenn Sie glauben —"* "And if you believe as I do," he said, grasping the Rev by both shoulders, "then I am your brother and my bed is your bed and my food yours."

The wall also sealed off the front door of a church on the Bernauerstrasse, leaving the church inaccessible and behind the wall. People have placed a small stone plaque against the wall there. "Pray without ceasing," it says.

Two by two we rode the lift with Mr. Findeisen to the top floor hospice.

On tiptoes we entered the room where two double beds and two cots were ready with starched linen. I stifled an exclamation until the door was closed. On the nearest white pillowcase sat a big black beetle. Then we saw that there were beetles on five of the pillows, and they were solid chocolate with foil covering and legs.

The elderly pensioners were still abed when we ate breakfast around a heavy carved table in the dining room. Mr. Findeisen did more than we to waken the slumberers as he told us about the landholdings he had left behind in East Germany. The key to the abandoned estate hung above photographs of children and grandchildren. Mrs. Findeisen kissed our children when we left and each one thanked her for the beetles. They had never seen such good children, they said. We had not often seen ours that good, either. Dicker rode in the first trip down the lift and waited until he was on the sidewalk to burst back into normalcy.

Checkpoint Charlie on the Friedrichstrasse was in full morning sun for photographing. A West German guard offered to take the Rev up on the observation platform. It was too hot to work inside his little booth, he said, and so he took the children, too, one at a time and each with a camera. As a result, we have many slides and pictures of that checkpoint — the red, black, and yellow East German flag, the tank traps to discourage wall crashers, telescopic pictures of individual Russian and East German soldiers. Dicker had no camera, but he saw a Russian using binoculars and he took ours from the camera bag on the sidewalk. For long minutes he and the Russian surveyed each other soberly through their glasses, a hundred yards apart. The American and West German soldiers laughed uproariously, and the white-helmeted MP watching from a high window overlooking the checkpoint thrust his thumbs up in approval.

Here, on a foggy night, a West Berliner brought his fiancé out of East Berlin by strapping her to the bottom of his car. While we watched, an old couple approached the barricade on foot. A young woman in slacks sat on her suitcase on the sidewalk, looking hopefully toward East Berlin. We bought jacket patches and a *lepeltje* with the West Berlin bear on them. And some fresh fruit, delicious but expensive, before we began to work our way back through the checkpoints to West Germany.

In the corridor Russian soldiers were inspecting a break in the double fence. At the passport control center before entering East Germany, one *Vopo* came to sit at the wheel of the redbus while another escorted the Rev into the office. But they were friendly. *"Viele Kinder,"* they said, laughing and poking each other. One was against having children. *"Zu teuer,"* he said, too expensive.

There were many *Vopos* around. Entering East Germany from the corridor, we inadvertently took the left fork in the highway which led to East

Berlin by circling around West Berlin. At once two *Vopos* on motorcycles roared out from the bushes at the side of the road to intercept us.

At Hanover we left the West German *Autobahn* to go toward Bremen. Life was relaxed again. In a country restaurant we admired a new litter of puppies and drank lemonade. The countryside was ablaze with red and purple rhododendron. Tree branches or green wreaths hung on buildings, car grills, house doors, and even on a steam shovel. For Pentecost, the sign of new life, explained the waitress in Westerstede where we ate pork cutlet and German potato salad. The local newspaper carried four pages of engagement notices in little boxes like advertisements, another Pentecost tradition.

A boxer was rolling with two small children in the back room of the restaurant. Our children felt like rolling, too. This was the meal when the Rev said, "Patience, honey, already your children begin to rise up and call you blessed."

"Better," I replied wearily, "that they called me that while lying down."

"Find the tin plates that mean barbershop," we cajoled them as we rode along.

At the Dutch border the official, also tired, brightened when he heard the Rev's Dutch greeting. "I thought," he said in Dutch, pointing to the BN license plate which means *Buiten Nederlander,* an out-of-the-Netherlander, "that I would have to speak that *rare Engels* again."

From Berlin to Groningen in the north of Holland had taken us about nine hours. Clark celebrated our arrival in the home of Oom Jan, the publisher, by plunging headlong down a back stairs which led from the second-floor living quarters to the printing shop below. In his well-meant effort to show Dave the way from a bedroom to the W.C., he forgot one turn and, stepping along confidently in the darkness, believed himself in the long hallway. We heard his cries in the living room where we were drinking tea, and followed them until we found him crumpled in his black abyss, shaking with fright.

It had been a long day from Checkpoint Charlie to the back staircase. I was talking a hopeless garble of German and Dutch. Please, someone, hang a green wreath on me!

HARLINGEN IS A North Sea town at the eastern end of the Afsluitdijk, and it is the birthplace of my father. He lived here in two rooms and an attic with nine brothers and sisters. He slept in a cupboard bed in the wall, fell into the *gracht,* the narrow canal in front of their home, and was reprimanded on a Sunday afternoon for taking a sugar *klontje* from the sugar bowl without permission. When we drove through Harlingen on our way back to Zandvoort after a pleasant Pentecost weekend, the children recognized the city hall and the harbor from paintings done by one of Father B's brothers. David has on his wall a painting of the sailing ship captained by my great-grandfather until it was sunk in a storm.

We stopped in Alkmaar for supper with one cousin, picked up there the family of another, which, added to two Groningen cousins returning to school in Amsterdam, made thirteen of us plus the week's luggage in the redbus. Singing and laughing, we arrived in Haarlem and pried out our passengers. One full day remained before we emptied the flat and began our trek to Jerusalem. The Rev and I stayed up until midnight unpacking from Germany and repacking the book suitcase and the footlocker with things we would not touch until Michigan.

On the last day in Zandvoort the Rev took laundry to the laundromat in Utrecht while he attended a final meeting. I sent the children to the beach via the Albert Heijn store where they returned a sackful of bottles for *statsie geld*. All kinds of bottles, from jam or other things, are marked with their return value and can be redeemed for a few cents.

Then I locked the flat door against visitors and pulled out from hiding all the suitcases and supplies we owned. Everything had to be evaluated in terms of leaving warm clothes behind, packing summer clothes into as few suitcases as possible, stripping beds, disposing of shells and other accumulated treasures, and cleaning the flat. Three o'clock the next morning we finished.

To avoid theft and bad weather we wanted to travel with everything inside the redbus. Each child had his small zipper bag, and in addition we took only three medium-sized suitcases for the seven of us for two months. The Rev had his briefcase, I a big travel purse. And the rest was gear — tent, sleeping bags, foam-rubber rolls, food supplies, medicine kit, five-gallon plastic water can, two-gallon plastic gas can, yellow plastic pail, camping stove, collapsible table, typewriter, two campstools, and one collapsible chair.

Everything else Tante Kundien had offered generously to keep for us in Utrecht until the voyage home. We worked a while to wedge all stay-behind and go-along possessions plus all of us into the redbus for the trip from Zandvoort to Utrecht. Even this small trip was punctuated with necessary stops.

First to the Zandvoort bank and post office, and to the hardware store to replace a knife we had broken in the flat. Next to Haarlem to replace the broken tent pole and have the salesman show us on a floor model how the pole must be inserted between and not under the two tent layers. Then to The Hague to deliver certain papers to the ANWB, the official Dutch tourist bureau, where we also asked information about which Swiss mountain passes were open. The ANWB had prepared the *carnet de passage,* a document necessary to get the redbus in and out of non-European and Communist countries.

The most important stop was at the Hungarian consulate in The Hague. We wanted very badly to visit the Hungarian family of a dear friend, a professor who had escaped from Communist prison in 1947 and had not seen his family since then. Contacts with the Hungarian Reformed Church also made us eager to visit there. But our Stateside request for regular visas had been denied despite the money we advanced. In 1962 Hungary was still very controlling about its tourists. No doubt the refusal was on file in IBUSZ in Budapest. But the Hungarian consulate in The Hague had promised by telephone that they would furnish immediately a transit visa, good for two days, usable anytime during the summer. It seemed too simple to be true. When we were admitted through the heavy doors of the consulate, an official was explaining to two motorcyclists why they had to pay so much money to enter Hungary on a regular visa. But we were back in the redbus in ten minutes with transit visas which cost sixteen and a half *gulden,* about four dollars. While we were exulting, we ran out of gas and coasted to a stop directly beside an Esso station gas pump!

After Utrecht we traveled southwest, through s'Hertogenbosch, past Eindhoven of Phillips' manufacturing fame. Cutting back a little east through Roermond to the German border, we came to Neuss below Düsseldorf where there was a *Campplatz* on the Rhine.

"Remember this date," said the Rev. "Wednesday, June 13, 1962, the beginning of our trip to Jerusalem."

"And this time we didn't forget the shovel!" Dicker.

South

"NOBODY GETS TO PRAY with their eyes open but dad," Dicker would announce anew each morning as we rolled along.

Every travel day began with morning devotions as soon as the redbus was on the road. One of the children read from the small Bible in his zipper bag, we sang Dutch songs Oom Bee had taught us and some English praise hymns, and then one of us prayed for the day ahead. When we reached Biblical areas, we read from chapters related to these places, aided by a Bible with concordance. It was always a good beginning to the day.

From Neuss to Zurich took a day. The *Autobahn* was full of construction delays and army vehicles until we passed the Heidelberg area. Everywhere families were haying in the fields. The children counted 564 hay wagons before they grew tired of counting. As we neared the Swiss border we took a shortcut around Basel through Rheinfelden, made a quick border crossing, and passed through Mumpf, where on an earlier trip we had eaten salmon in a restaurant overlooking the Rhine.

Just out of Brugg on the Reuss River that flows from Lucerne into the Aare, there is a delightful place called Restaurant Zoll. The river flowed past our terrace table, the sun laid a golden bridge across it, and plump red geraniums lined the low brick wall. It was a small peaceful place and the proprietor came to sit with us after he had directed the serving of the meal. Large plates of soup with bread were followed by salad and a main dish of *späezli*, as much as we could eat. All this, with orange drink, cost five dollars. The atmosphere alone was worth more.

With a stop at Baden's beautiful tower, we reached the lights of Zurich at dark. Everything was alight — cafés, boats, buildings, churches. The camping area was a stretch of manicured lawn on the river edge. It had a good store, airy washrooms in a cement building, and a stone promenade along the river where the lights of the city danced on the water and swans nested on the bank in the softer light of a full moon. It was the most elegant campground we found.

The higher we climbed out of Zurich, the more remarkable was the view of the Zurichzee below. We heard the first sound of cattle bells and passed barefoot children with schoolbooks strapped to their backs. Several children posed eagerly in a town south of Lucerne where we stopped to photograph the petition worked into the roofing tiles of a church. *SANCT. ANTONIUS, FÜR UNS BITT*, it said in six-foot letters.

Again we climbed, to Spiegelberg by Sattel overlooking the Laurezee. Snow-covered peaks above, and below a spired village on the blue-green lake and a small steamer churning a white wake as it left the dock. The road descended into Schwyz, a picture in color with murals on the town hall, geraniums against the dark wood of the hotel balcony, and fountains playing in the square.

"Mark this one for next time, for a week," we said when we saw the Sisikon campground on the southeast arm of Lake Lucerne. Altdorf had its 1307 statue of William Tell, Silenen a crew of stonecutters shouting to each other above the noise of a waterfall. Through the natural frame of a rock tunnel appeared another artist's landscape — blue sky, fluffy clouds, snow-capped peaks, and streams cascading into the green valley.

"In August when it's warmer we're coming back to Switzerland to drive through the length of it from east to west." This promise was the only way to justify driving past one breath-taking vista after another. Twenty-one switchbacks with a midway stop at Andermatt brought us up to the Saint Gotthard Pass. Snow stood twelve feet high on both sides of the road, the air was bitter cold, and the *hospicia* loomed large and grey in a fine mist. In the high altitude my pen emptied itself as I wrote. We turned on the heater for warmth. The children counted forty-three sharp switchbacks coming down and a steady rain began as we passed through heavy fortifications into Italian-speaking Switzerland. A one-legged man began his ascent up the road down which we had come. We watched his slow progress while we ate a lunch of rolls, sweet butter, fresh tomatoes, and Swiss chocolate in the redbus.

Heavy rain blurred the rose trees on the road to Lugano and obscured the castles on the hills above. It turned the blue lake grey and Mother B's glowing descriptions of their Lugano visit bore little resemblance to what we were seeing forty years later. The Italian border was a wet confusion, no place to park, no clear instructions. The Rev ran back two blocks' distance to buy gas coupons which are the economical way to buy gas in Italy.

In Milan we struggled through snarls of rush-hour traffic trying to get a look at the *duomo* where Ambrose preached and Augustine listened. Parking was impossible so we peered out between flicks of the windshield wiper and drove in circles until a boy on a motorcycle led us out of town onto the *autostrada* toward Verona. Dicker slept in my arms through supper in one of the glass-walled restaurants that arch across the *autostrada*. The Rev began computing 621 *lira* to the dollar. It was a heady feeling to be paying in hundreds and thousands.

HﾠOW SUNSHINE AND FRIENDS improve a travel route! In Verona we had both, a cloudless weekend and a total welcome in the terrazzo-floored apartment of an army colonel's family. The eleven of us spent Saturday in Venice.

"City of 120 islands, cut up by 150 canals, tied together by 370 bridges, the city where Browning died and Wagner and Lord Byron wrote their. . . ." Clark's folder reading stopped as we boarded the *vaporetto* to ride the Grand Canal past mansions and palaces to the Piazza San Marco. In the warm sunlight on the *piazza,* red-white-green Italian flags flew on tall poles, white-coated waiters stood at yellow wicker chairs and round tables, and a string ensemble played merry music. Imagine this in rain. Five-domed Saint Mark's, from which Pope John was elevated to the papacy, glittered with gold leaf, vibrant murals, lacy figures, and gold-winged angels. "Everything has arches," said Nan. "Lots more rounds than points," Em described it. Alerted, we found arches everywhere, on the Rialto Bridge and the Bridge of Sighs, the cathedral and the colonnade of the Doge's Palace, the openings in the red brick Campanile, which is the bell tower where two bronze Moors have been striking the hours since Columbus discovered America.

Pigeons perched on the children's arms to be fed. Friendly people stopped to run their hands over the blonde bristles of the boys' fresh GI crewcuts. A priest led his group of boys with long hair, short pants, and leather knapsacks. In the side streets glass blowers fashioned delicate animals before our eyes.

"Man, what a good day," agreed the younger set as they stowed away hot fudge sundaes after hamburgs, french fries, and malteds at the Vicenza U.S. Army base on the way back to Verona.

It was too early for Shakespeare performances in the city of Juliet's tomb, but there was swimming in Lago de Garde. On Sunday, which was both Flag Day and Father's Day, the Rev preached in the post chapel. Monday we left for Rome. We would see our friends again at the army retreat in Berchtesgaden. No words were adequate to thank them for making available to us American canned and packaged foods for camping meals.

Onward to the Eternal City! A breeze ruffled fields of red poppies and a mule clattered by with ears protruding through a fancy straw hat. Beyond the Po River bridge at Revere there had been a truck-car collision on the two-lane road. Umbrellas and blankets covered the bodies of three German tourists laid out beside the road, and a piece of print dress escaped the blanket. Morning prayers for safety took on new meaning.

The Autostrada del Sol provides smooth progress past Bologna and Florence with the help of many viaducts and tunnels. It was worth a toll of fifteen hundred *lira*. We tried to learn bits of Italian. Tunnel is *galleria*, exit *uscita, sempre diritto* the same as *recht uit* and *immer gerade aus*: straight ahead, keep going. *Alimentari*, a food store, reminded us of alimentary canal. Turn right is *gira a destra* and turn left, *gira a sinistra*. "Gyrate sinister, dad," said Dave, pointing out the interesting color of our word "sinister."

We left Michelangelo's Florence for adult study on another trip and opted for the leaning tower of Pisa. It stood on a street lined with souvenir stalls, whose hanging plates clinked together in the breeze. No one had told us that this landmark was *campanile* for the cathedral which stands solid but ignored in the rush to the leaning bell tower. Even the Russians have offered to help arrest the lean which is increasing alarmingly.

After the Arno River and the old fortified walls of Livorno, the children saw blue water. It was not the Mediterranean, as they thought, but the Tyrrhenian, a hard word to spell, Italy's own sea, bounded by Sardinia, Sicily, and the Italian peninsular boot. The geography was not important, only the sunbathers stretched on bright towels on flat rocks and the swimmers in sheltered coves.

"Can't we stop, dad? Puleeze! Here's good, right here!" This is why swimsuits must be kept handy in zipper bags.

Late sun shone on a golden landscape of wheat being cut by hand. White oxen with wire muzzles stood waiting in wooden yokes. A herd of goats came down the road and an old beggar was asking coins at a railroad crossing. The island of Elba rose from the sea. In Grosseto near dusk there was a funeral procession. Small boys walked with the priest ahead of the hearse, the priest chanting from the liturgy, and immediate family walking behind, the women heavily veiled. A large group followed, some carrying flowers, walking toward the sunset. The Dutch often place a small sheaf of grain on a coffin as a symbol of life's harvest. Here the two ideas seemed wedded, the somber procession and the wheat harvesters in golden fields. And the gay print dress under a blanket.

Rome was balmy and full of life at ten in the evening when we claimed our YMCA reservation on the Piazza Independenza. A suite of two rooms, hall, and bath cost fifty-five hundred *lira,* about nine dollars, for two nights. There was plenty of hot water for doing the first laundry of the trip.

In warmer climate laundry was usually a nightly affair. This allowed us to leave Sunday clothes and changes of outfit in the three suitcases from one weekend to the next. Between weekends we lived in the same clothes, washed and dried each night. Sometimes the liquid Lux had to work in cold spring water in the yellow plastic pail. I found the plastic hangers we had taken along much more effective for drying clothes than the clothesline and plastic clothespins. Shirts, blouses, dresses, even wash pants did better on the hangers. In this way we lived out of the zipper bags most of the time. Admittedly, by the end of the trip each of us had one outfit that he never wanted to see again. For the boys this was olive bermudas and light green Banlon shirts, for the girls seersucker pullovers with shorts for the road and a skirt for cities, and for me a black-brown-white cotton print, sleeveless, full-skirted, not a drip-dry fabric but quite agreeable to being treated that way. The Rev's long khaki pants were the hardest to launder, especially in the pail. Traveling this way, we accumulated no dirty laundry and we traveled light and clean.

Dave and Nan's Roman history class sprang into life when we began to explore the Eternal City. They explained to the rest of us the matter of Romulus and Remus and the wolf and the seven hills on the Tiber. And the Palatine hill on which Romulus built the city named for himself 750 years before Christ. Dicker liked the part about the wolf and showed unusual interest in the *lepeltje* we bought which was decorated with a scene of the boys taking nourishment from the animal.

The Rev had some facts to add. Did you know that the Roman Forum used to be a lake and then a swamp between two of the hills? It had a sacred way through the middle and it was never bigger than 670 feet. Sometimes they cleared it to make room for a whole new set of statues and temples. In the center was a bronze milestone from which the Romans measured the miles to the outposts of their empire. It was three and a half million square miles in the first two centuries after Christ. Listen to this: "amazingly rich with temples, basilicas, and columns, white with dazzling marbles and white-robed people, golden with gilt bronze statues, and here and there beautifully green with favored and sacred trees and flowers."

"You'd never know it to see it now." Clark.

"But the arches stood up pretty well, didn't they? One for Septimius Severus and here at this end the one for Titus. It says this one was built by the senate in 81 after Christ on the Via Sacra to celebrate Titus conquering Jerusalem. See if you find things from Solomon's temple in the carvings — the showbread table or golden trumpets or seven-branched candlesticks being carried by Jewish prisoners. The Jews really hated Titus. He made twelve thousand of them work on the Colosseum and lay the foundation stones for his arch. The arch over there next to the Colosseum is Constantine's. He was the first Christian emperor."

"He the one who saw the cross in the sunset or something?" David.

"Yes, and he's the one who built Constantinople which is Istanbul now. We'll see it."

"Today?" Dicker, tracing with a finger on the Titus arch.

We sat a while in a stone row of the Colosseum, wondering how it

had been when filled with fifty thousand shouting Romans watching bloody spectacles of human sacrifice. They must have been a callous people to find amusement and distraction in the agonies and gory deaths of fellow men. Imagine how many people died here by lions, fire, or crucifixion. The cross at one end is in honor of Christians who were killed here for what they believed. The arena floor is gone, revealing rooms and passageways beneath where animals and prisoners were kept. One emperor flooded this place enough to have a mock naval battle. The emperor had a special entrance and he sat on a throne under a canopy.

Past noon we rode out through Porta San Sebastiano, the southernmost gate, onto the Appian Way. The catacombs here were closed until three, so we rode on, past the round crenelated tomb of Cecilia Metella, along a high ridge on the famous old highway. Gnarled black cypress trees share the roadside with shrine ruins. We ate lunch under one of the trees, and no modern man or motor appeared to disturb our picture of Paul walking this way when he came to Rome the first time.

He came up from Puteoli, the harbor near Naples, and traveled more than 130 miles on the Via Appia. In Paul's day the highway was made of eight-sided blocks of lava, fitted together carefully. Nero was emperor then, about A.D. 61. Luke's description in Acts 28 provided our lunchtime devotions.

> And after one day a south wind sprang up, and on the second day we came to Puteoli. . . . And so we came to Rome. And the brethren there, when they heard of us, came as far as the Forum of Appius and Three Taverns to meet us. On seeing them Paul thanked God and took courage. And when we came into Rome, Paul was allowed to stay by himself, with the soldier that guarded him.

Peter, the rough fisherman, receives larger acclaim in Rome than the urbane educated apostle to the Gentiles. Saint Peter's church in the Vatican is the hub of Rome, and for many the hub of the world. It stands on the site where Peter supposedly met martyrdom in Caligula's Circus arena where Nero held most of his spectacular killings.

Constantine built the first basilica on the site and Michelangelo at the age of seventy designed the famous dome to rest upon the Greek-cross-design church of Bramante which took almost two hundred years to build. We walked slowly past the twin fountains and the obelisk in the immense square in front of the church. Two large wings of colonnade extend in half circles

43

to encompass the square, and endless marble statues line the top of the colonnades.

The interior of Saint Peter's was being readied for the first ecumenical council convened by Pope John. Rows of wooden bleachers faced each other in the nave. Straight ahead the light shone down in shafts through Michelangelo's dome onto the high altar. The Rev took one of his prize slides and only afterward — though no one believes this — did he see the signs forbidding photography.

Four relics are kept in the four colossal pillars which support the dome. They are exhibited only during Holy Week — the head of Saint Andrew, the veil of Veronica, the lance which pierced the Lord's side, and a portion of the true cross contributed by the indefatigable Helena, Constantine's mother who found relics and built churches all over the Mediterranean basin.

Other things were more convincing to us. The *Pieta* in its natural habitat in the first chapel on the right aisle was more impressive there than when seen against a backdrop of navy and stars at the New York World's Fair in 1964. It was hard to find the bronze statue of Peter which, my father often had told me as a child, had an outstretched toe worn shiny by the kisses of many worshipers. We found it, finally, behind some bleachers near the great altar.

Nancy and I explored the crypt with the tombs of popes after the Rev had seen enough of the relics and ornaments of Saint Peter's. He suspected that the big fisherman would have been dreadfully embarrassed at the elaborate homage paid him. In fact, the Rev was not greatly interested in any of the Vatican treasures. I think I heard a little sigh of relief when he discovered, after a comical exchange of Italian with the *carbonieri* on guard, that the Sistine Chapel was closed on Tuesdays.

"Remember, our real trip begins in Greece," he said restlessly, as if providing an excuse. "We can come back to Italy more easily on another trip."

"The shrine of the whole world," prompts a guidebook in describing the Pantheon. It would seem that the world has quite a stake in Rome. Saint Peter's and now this classical structure built for worship of the ancient gods. The traffic on the Piazza di Venezia does not encourage visiting the white marble Altar of the Nation, though it is awesome with a wide flight of steps which ascends halfway to heaven and a statue of the goddess Roma over the grave of an unknown soldier. Somehow we missed the Fountain of Trevi on our way back to the YMCA, so no coins insure our return.

"Let's have pizza for supper. It comes from here, doesn't it?"

The desk clerk recommended a place within walking distance. It was a place called Ricci with colorful sidewalk tables on the Via Genova. Nancy, always wary, ordered something that turned out to be dark bread topped with meat and gravy. The rest of us ordered pizza with coke and a bottle of

Chianti. When the masterpiece was delivered, there was a low groan. The pizzas were topped with fried egg, asparagus radiating like spokes in a wheel, ham, mushrooms, and in the center were small clams broiled in their shells. The Rev and I ate most of the top layers. The waiter offered an ash tray as souvenir and it stands on the television in the den, a reminder that the children think pizza tastes better American-style. It's like American chop suey and chow mein, which no Chinese regards as authentic.

Other families were strolling as we returned to the Y. Music floated in the warm air and a barefoot gypsy child darted in and out among the pillars of a building, begging. We bought fat strawberries from a fruit vendor. And Dicker barked like a dog all the way. It wasn't enough to be conspicuous with blonde hair and a brush cut. No, he had to bark and sniff, besides.

The next morning Americans whom we had met in post chapel at Verona rushed out to buy trinkets to take to Saint Peter's square where Pope John would bless the assembled crowd.

"But why do you want these things blessed?" we asked.

"As souvenirs for our friends back home," they said.

"Are your friends Roman Catholic?"

"Oh, no, but they'll think this is great."

After we had packed the redbus we set out in an opposite direction toward Saint Paul's Gate. Outside the gate is the pyramid of Cestius, a tribune for whom this unusual tomb was built in 12 B.C. Paul, if he was led to his beheading along the Via Ostiense through this gate, must have seen the pyramid.

Nearby, in the damp shade of the English Cemetery, lie the bodies of poets Shelley and Keats. Keats died first, in 1821 at the age of twenty-five, after an unsuccessful bid to regain his health in Rome. On his stone, where ivy droops over the oval-framed likeness of the poet, are these lines,

> This grave contains all that was mortal of a young English poet who on his deathbed in the bitterness of his heart at the malicious power of his enemies desired these words to be engraved on his tombstone, "Here lies one whose name was writ in water."

But Shelley did not feel this way about his idol. Glowingly he described Keats in his poem, "Adonis." The next year Shelley died, too, drowned in a storm at sea while returning from Pisa in his sailboat *Ariel*. When the body washed ashore, a volume of Keats's poetry was found in Shelley's pocket. Shelley is buried on the upper slope near the wall running behind the cemetery. With him lie the bodies of his friend Trelawney, his oldest child, and his biographer Symodis. His stone, below the Latin *Natus* and *Obit*, declares,

Nothing of him that doth change
But doth suffer a sea-change
Into something rich and strange.

Our final stop in Rome was at the church of San Paolo Fuori le Mura, Saint Paul Outside the Walls. Constantine built the first church on this site which is supposedly the burial place of Paul. It is Finegan who points out how appropriate it was to behead and bury the traveling missionary beside a well-used highway. In the church courtyard, surrounded by 150 pillars and a colorful mosaic façade, Paul stands in statue, carrying a sword and a Bible. Did he ever really carry a sword?

We were the only visitors at Paul's church. Apparently everyone else was at Saint Peter's. The old caretaker eyed us curiously.

"Not gonna see *il papa* today?" he inquired.

"No, I think not."

"He gonna bless," replied the old man.

"What's he gonna bless?" asked the Rev.

Wide-eyed at such ignorance, the caretaker threw up both hands in a broad gesture. "Ever-a-ting!" he said emphatically and shook his head as we drove away.

T O REACH NAPLES we chose the highway near to the sea. There was a turnoff to Anzio Beach of World War II, gay pottery was for sale in Latina, and Terracina stood between the blue sea and a mountain of olive trees topped by a shrine. The *carbonieri* everywhere wore spotless white. From Terracina to Gaeta there were wonderful sandy coves along the road. In Mondragone mozarella cheeses hung in the open. Many donkey and horse carts were coming in from the fields. Families sat atop burlap bags stuffed with field produce, and the family dog, tied, walked behind the wagon, often under the rear axle to keep out of the sun. We crossed the Volturno River — Uncle Tunis fought all through here, children — and passed Pozzuoli harbor — Paul landed here — and came down a long long hill into Naples.

We were looking for the Via Michelangelo Di Caravaggio and wondering how this would fit on a street sign if there were street signs, or how one makes himself understood when asking for this street. Someone told us eventually that it was up in the volcanic hills round the city. The redbus climbed and descended many hills before we found the U.S. NAVCOMMSTA buildings where men could tell us in English how to find the naval intelligence officer to whom we were bringing greetings. He lived in a new apartment building which, like other new buildings, had begun to fall apart before it was occupied.

From his balcony Vic showed us a refugee camp in the valley and, in the opposite direction, a concentration of Communist housing. Naples has the best harbor in Europe, according to Vic, but the people of this area are not very friendly to Americans. Too many Communists. Up north they are friendlier.

Carol, Vic's wife, was sure we wouldn't mind some American food. After the pizza of the Via Genova, we didn't mind at all! Jello with frozen strawberries for salad and a dessert of cake topped with crushed pineapple in whipping cream! And then we had devotions together and talked about home and churches and family and what it means to live away from all this. "Write us about Turkey," Vic and Carol said, "because we may be assigned there next. And call our parents when you get home."

In early evening we rode through the heart of Naples again, paying more attention this time. The city reminded us of Port-au-Prince, Haiti. It was noisy, crowded, dirty, sweltering in high humidity. Many buildings were half built. At the fishing docks people were gathered to watch boats come in with the day's catch. The streets were crawling with life. In the open market there was watermelon, by the half or piece, and oranges and lemons arranged on their waxy, dark-green leaves. Fish, clams, and mussels attracted flies. We made a wrong turn and were directed through a tiny street arched with washings and lined with people on steps or in doorways. Old men leaned intently over their card games and dominoes. I made some notes about the Garibaldi statue and the Castello dell' Ovo on a rocky island in the harbor.

The farther south we traveled in Italy, the noisier it became. There was no longer any need to curb our children's voices when they were out of the redbus. Everyone shouted. Arguing, singing, selling, conversing — all communication was in *fortissimo*. Perhaps there are fewer psychotics in such a population where people seem to repress nothing.

Above the town of Vesuvio there is a campground on the approaches to Mount Vesuvius. It is a colorful place set in an orange grove with a stone wall painted bright blue and bulbs painted bright green in the W.C., known to Italians as the *gabinetto*. The campground was clean, the proprietor spoke some English, and the cost was ninety-eight American cents. By nine we were all asleep, lying on top of instead of inside our sleeping bags. We rarely used sweaters or jackets again until the cool evenings in Jerusalem.

Thursday, June 21. We took note of the date after we discovered what a great feast day it was, and after this Feast of Corpus Christi almost proved our undoing. Guns were exploding and a man came up the road selling gladioli, in *fortissimo*. The children traded five Hahn Air Force Base comics for twenty gorier ones offered by children of an American army sergeant camped near us. When we re-entered Vesuvio, we could hardly get the redbus through the crowds on their way to church. Carrying flowers and wearing black, they pressed ahead on foot or in wooden-wheeled wagons with bell statues on the donkey harnesses. One boy stumbled on a broken piece of sidewalk where pine boughs were drying beside a pile of fresh un-wrapped bread.

Before the feast day created an emergency, we saw Pompeii and took the Amalfi Drive. Pompeii is a hot commercialized racket until one is safe within the walled-off ruins. Visitors are besieged on all sides by brash demanding hawkers and parkers. But once inside the Porta Marina, we bought a good guide book and map and charted our own way with no pressure from anyone. Dicker saw only the lizards hiding in every crevice and shady spot. He must have flushed out from hiding at least a hundred of them.

It is unbelievable that a city could be restored in such detail after being submerged beneath twenty-four feet of burning cinder. Intimacies of family life, details of daily living were all caught and preserved by the suddenness of the catastrophe. The museum at the gate showed plaster figures of volcano victims made by pouring liquid plaster into the natural molds left when bodies disintegrated in solid ash. A man clutching a bag of coins, a woman shielding her children, a man struggling to rise, another shielding his eyes. There was even the figure of a dog, chained and forgotten when his master fled.

We crossed the streets on high stepping stones placed to protect citizens from refuse and water and spaced to allow chariot wheels to pass. Forums, temples, shops, and arches were well identified in the guide book. Our favorite places were the House of the Faun, with a dining room for each of the four seasons, and the House of the Vettii, rich bachelors in whose garden a silver-eyed bronze boy held a duck from whose mouth water spouted into a little pool.

We paid a fortune for coke, retrieved our car for a price, and set out in the direction of Sorrento while Dave read aloud about Pompeii.

"Here in the garden was found another woman's skeleton with all her jewels. . . . on the stairs leading to the cellar lay the bodies of Diomedes himself and a slave; in his hand was a large silver key and beside him lay scattered quantities of coins and jewels. The slave held a lantern in his hand. Down in the cellar were found eighteen skeletons, two of which were little children." This was better than the twenty comics acquired at the camp-ground. Dave and Nan argued who would be the first to read *The Last Days of Pompeii* when they reached home.

THE SHIP FROM ITALY TO GREECE leaves Brindisi, on the heel of Italy, every evening at ten. We estimated the distance across the Italian instep from Salerno to Brindisi as less than 250 miles. So why not include a side trip to the Amalfi Drive?

After driving south to Castellammare, where Italian navy boats lay at anchor, we followed the northern coast of the peninsula to Meta. The beaches were full and bright orange rafts bobbed on the turquoise water. There was a tiny island with two palm trees on it. The southern coast of this little peninsula is the breathtaking one. Literally, that is. Here the road clings perilously to mountainsides that drop straight into the sea a hundred feet below. Beneath the clear water they keep on dropping. Most of the time the road is too narrow to accommodate passing cars comfortably, and nowhere are there guard rails or other protective devices. We were on the outer side of the road because we were driving east and sometimes instinctively we all leaned to one side to keep from falling off sheer cliffs into the pattern of blues made by rocky formations under the sea surface. At each hairpin turn the Rev blew the horn loud and long as good Italians do.

Towns cluster around small beaches from which the streets march up the mountainsides, branching horizontally to reach the rows of white-and-coral-roofed buildings which look like colored stepping stones. Positano was the loveliest, less commercialized than Amalfi. We shared a shady overlook with three townswomen sitting on a low wall above Positano. Bells chimed for the feast day. Below lay the town in shades of pastel, with olive tree greens and sky and water blues and a tawny beach punctuated with gay umbrellas as the turquoise of the sea was dotted with white sails.

When we arrived at Salerno, the Rev heaved a sigh of relief. He had negotiated every curve and brought us safely onto the highway toward Brindisi.

But his relief was momentary. The road from Salerno to Potenza, though free from peril of dropping off into the sea, is mountainous all the way. We averaged fifteen miles an hour. Volkswagen did not provide their 1962 microbus with the strong engine that later models have, so the ups and downs and turns required continual shifting of gears. Half of our progress from peak to peak was vertical, not horizontal. We met no other car for the whole of this distance, but there were many donkey carts and people on foot. Women carried water jugs or freshly done washing. Some were still washing in a river while others scrubbed on wooden boards at village fountains. Men stood in groups, talking. On the left before Potenza was the mountaintop village of Picerno, its flat roofs and cathedral spire etched against a pattern of clouds. How many gear shiftings would it take to get up there?

Potenza, provincial capital, is an old city with a fortification wall. We stopped for gas at a familiar Agip station with its sign of the six-legged black dragon blowing red fire out of his mouth. The attendant showed us a better route to Brindisi. Not the road which was once the old Appian Way through Matera and Taranto, but a more northerly route through Altamura and Ostuni. Only a black line on the map, but fewer mountains on the final stretch.

"You get Brindisi three *horas,*" the attendant guaranteed. This was good news.

"Is *non* road signs," he added, "so look look. Nineteen kilometers to —." Here he made a fork with his hands. "Go *sinistra*. Go kilometers —." On his fingers he showed thirty-five. "More *sinistra,* comes here Irsina. Is okay go on okay Altamura Ostuni Brindisi."

So we look-looked and counted nineteen kilometers and took the *sinistra* fork past three old women bent against a sudden hailstorm. Thirty-five kilometers farther — the man was remarkably accurate — we turned *sinistra* again and climbed steeply toward Irsina, past a little boy holding a donkey's tail to help him — the boy — up the hill. A man standing beside an old car waved for a ride up to the walled city. We dropped him off where he pointed and began the descent on the other side of the mountain. Irsina stands so high that five hills later we could still look back and see it. What a landmark it must have been for horsemen or pilgrims on foot plodding through this demanding terrain.

Decorated wagons were pouring into Gravina, probably for the feast day procession, though this explanation did not occur to us until later. An old woman in black led her donkey, on whose back a little brown dog stood erect. "Add a cat and rooster on top of them," said Dave, "and you've got the story of the 'Traveling Musicians of Bremen.'"

It was six-thirty when we came to Altamura and found the main streets closed off for the procession of Corpus Christi Day. Though large crowds lined the streets, almost as many people seemed to be marching in the procession that moved slowly, singing, through the town to the cathedral. First came the children, black-haired girls in white dresses, white veils, and blue sashes from shoulder to waist. Taller girls carried Italian flags with blue pennants attached. Then came the boys in suit coats and short pants, green or red sashes across their chests. More flags. The women were in black with mantillas and they sang most loudly of all.

Along the procession route balconies were draped with silk-tasseled hangings like bedspreads, pink, blue, orange. Finally the men came, preceding the bishop. Men in suits, monks in white cassocks or in black with white lace surplices, more flags, statues, crucifixes. Small boys in white surplices walked ahead of a canopy which was the climax of the procession. The boys swung censers of incense. Under the canopy carried by young men walked three distinguished servants of the church. The foremost carried a gold cross and as he passed, the onlookers bowed and crossed themselves.

The procession lasted almost an hour. We left the redbus in the middle of a street and stood with the people at the cathedral square. They were as much intrigued by us as by the procession. Several young people offered to talk English. One was a soldier who had been in England, another a girl whose only claim to English seemed to be the word "yes." For her own sake, we hoped someone would also teach her the word "no!"

Then the bells of the church drowned out the singing and the talk, the bishop passed, the crowds spilled into the street, and we inched the redbus through.

Seven-thirty. Two hours left until boarding time in Brindisi. Still no sign of the promised flat country, though the hills seemed to be settling a little.

We drove through two towns without stopping and then came Noci. Oh no, groaned the Rev as the unmistakable minor melodies of a procession reached our ears. As usual, the main street was the only access through the town. A policeman stood at the rear of the crowd blocking the way. The Rev got out to ask how we could go through.

"*Processio Christi*," replied the policeman with finality.

"Brindisi" — gesture of a ship riding the waters — "Corfu" — pointing desperately to his watch, replied the Rev with equal brevity and finality. After two such exchanges, the policeman led us through several alleyways to the end of the procession.

Any more processions and we'd miss the boat. In Alberobello we dodged around the end of one, and in Locorotondo the post-procession festivities had already begun. The ferris wheel was whirling and we honked our way through the gay noisy crowds. Then it was a train track. A woman holding a baby was working the gates in the darkness. There was no sign or sound of a train.

"*Brindisi, uno hora,*" called the Rev out of his window.

"*Si, si,*" replied the woman and went on rocking her baby.

We ate cookies to keep from chewing our nails. After fifteen minutes the train puffed by.

The last hour we rode in tense silence, seven pair of eyes glued to the road with intermittent glances at our watches. No one thought to say that he was hungry. The road began to level off, towns were cleaner and more modern, people better dressed as we neared the coast. At 9:50, ten minutes before departure time, we coasted onto the dock where a little black dog circled the redbus while the Rev produced proper papers to board ship and leave Italy.

Drooping over ham-cheese sandwiches and orange drink in the ship's dining room, we watched the lights of Brindisi drown in the blackness of the Adriatic Sea. At midnight, Greek time, we lay fresh-showered between clean sheets in first-class cabins, too weary to complain that there were rows of unused curtained bunks for half the price, though the travel agency at home had told us the ship was booked to capacity.

The first-class bliss lasted until seven in the morning when the girls appeared in their nightgowns, half asleep and clutching their zipper bags. Two substantial specimens of Greek manhood had entered their cabin to strip the beds of Dave and Clark who were already on deck. The girls fled. Never mind. Dress here. Lock the door.

When Dicker and the Rev went out to the W.C., the stewards knocked on our door, ready to strip the sheets from under us, too. I waved them back with a foamy toothbrush. No success. The Rev returned but New Testament Greek had not prepared him for this. He pointed angrily to his watch and motioned the men away. Grumbling, they assumed stations just outside the door, next to the boys' zipper bags which they had cleared out of the other cabin. Why the hurry? The ship was preparing to dock at the resort island of Corfu but our paid-for destination was the Greek coast an hour farther. For such treatment no tipping!

The United States aircraft carrier *Independence* lay in Corfu harbor belching white smoke. A helicopter whirred overhead. The boys waved madly and Smith or Jones or some other American navyman returned the greeting. It was almost like receiving word from home.

Little islands drifted by as we sat in the early sun on the top deck until we came to Igoumenitsa, not far south of the Albanian border. We could have stayed aboard down the Greek coast and through the Gulf of Patras but we wanted to see the back country of Greece. Few others did, and ours was the only vehicle with an IG sticker on the windshield.

The fewer the tourists passing through a place, the fussier the customs officials are. Townspeople watched the long procedure through a white metal fence. The children were busy with five copies of *Words in Pictures for the Tourist in Greece,* courtesy of the Hellenic-Mediterranean Lines.

"What's bread?"

"Psomi. We need it."

"We have just got off a *vapori,"* announced Clark, jerking his thumb in the direction of the ship.

"Let's hope we can stay in a few decent *xenodohions,"* tried Nan.

"Yeah, and eat in some good *estiatorions."*

"Whatta language!"

"That's nothing. Look at the signs. They don't even use our kind of letters."

"Better ask dad. He knows. Ya hafta take this stuff to be a minister."

"How come?"

"T'read the Bible the way they wrote it."

"Why'd they write it in Greek?"

"That's all they knew."

"Tough!"

Igoumenitsa has a gas station and one modern little-used motel for people awaiting the ship. Beyond that, inland, begins the Epirus region, "wild and beautiful . . . fierce ruggedness . . . swift-flowing rivers . . . full of folk art." Someone wrote a good tourist folder. We had the highway to ourselves except for a few road crews who waved and shouted as we passed. The terrain was mountainous and the little isolated settlements were of stone, houses as well as fences and corrals. This rugged area bred people of spirit to match the land. Here are "the villages of Souli which resisted the Turks until the tyrant Ali Pasha destroyed them, and the villages of Zalongo whose women chose to leap dancing to their death from the cliff tops rather than surrender to the troops of Ali Pasha." More tourist folder.

Far below us the Kalamus River snaked along like a twisted bronze ribbon. Another day of turning, twisting, climbing, and of shifting gears!

Joanina is a bustling army-post city with a stork's nest on every chimney. Here on the island in the lake Ali Pasha was murdered in a monastery. He was the last ruler of Epirus under the Turks. Today the old Epirus area is sliced by the Greek-Albanian border which Albania keeps tightly sealed.

A curious little boy accepted some of our molding Dutch cheese while we ate fresh *psomi* and oranges under a shade tree. Hay wagons passed, and a friendly man posed for a picture, riding side-saddle on a fine horse with a red blanket thrown across the water jug and grain pouch. And there was also a traveling troupe of two men with a guitar and two monkeys. One monkey wore a bedraggled white net skirt.

The road turned south along miles of stone fences to Arta where there is a long stone bridge over the river Arachthos. The chief mason of the bridge built his wife into the center span to make it stronger, says a tourist folder.

"Did he put her in dead or alive?" Clark wanted to know, but the folder did not say.

Some alive women were washing clothes in the river. Others carried on their heads pans of dough to be baked in outdoor ovens. All of them wore black, with black head coverings.

West of Arta at the coast was the old city of Nicopolis, of which Paul wrote in Titus 3, "When I send Artemas or Tychicus to you, do your best to come to me at Nicopolis, for I have decided to spend the winter there." Apparently this occurred between the apostle's first and second imprisonments in Rome. Titus was working with a weak corrupt church in Crete when Paul wrote to him.

In Agrinion, its red dust settled after a brief shower, we joined the men at tables on the square for an orange-lemon drink. A company of gypsies in battered wagons rested outside the town, and at Mesalongi on the coast two policemen were driving another group of gypsies out of a field.

One final mountain and then the road descended to the ferry that crosses the western end of the Gulf of Corinth to reach the Peloponnesus. Somehow we had managed to avoid every goat, donkey, horse, sheep, and barefoot child in our path and we had spent most of the day doing it. The mountain descent was beautiful, the bay spread out shimmering below. At the water's edge the children skipped stones and ate oranges while we waited to board the ferry, an LST of World War II vintage, with its jaw down to receive the variety of animals, hay wagons, old trucks, and people waiting to cross. The people, mostly men, climbed to a catwalk along the sides of the ship. After they had inspected us and befriended the children, they leaned gratefully into the fresh wind that blew across the water.

T WO CAMPSITES are listed in *Camping Europa* between Patras and Corinth along the north coast of the Peloponnesus. One we could not find. We did find a little black steam engine pulling its load along narrow gauge track, and a glorious sunset spilling across the bay. Standing beside the road to enjoy it, we had an hors d'oeuvre of canned hot dogs to satisfy our hunger until supper at a camping site.

Camping Lambiri, says the sign on the road. This is the second name in the book. A bad dirt track leads to a small restaurant at the water's edge.

"Camping Lambiri?" asks the Rev of the fat man who comes out to greet us.

"Cumbink?" the man repeats, his face blank.

While we pause uncertainly, a young woman dances out in a billowing skirt with an aqua band in her long hair. She waves a half-peeled banana and her approach resembles something from the South Sea islands.

"Take notes, Nan," says the Rev as he gets out to speak to the lady.

No, not to speak, but to gesture. The lady speaks French for our benefit, but it is no benefit. She does not understand German or shreds of Italian. No matter. Pantomimes are more fun, especially for the audience.

The Rev draws a tent in the air, lays his head on his hands, and points to all of us. Of course, she nods with her whole body. See how flat the ground is. Flat flat flat. And dry. Pound one stake here and one here and another here. The banana skin flops as she pretends to hammer. Bowing, swaying, wheeling, she points out the well for water and the W.C., a four-by-four shack some distance behind the restaurant.

But the flat flat ground is small, not large enough for more campers, gestures the Rev. No more are coming, sir. In and out, in and out, in and out — that is what most visitors will be doing. They come to the restaurant to eat and dance. She does not or perhaps cannot add that the guests will be in-and-out-ing most of the night directly past the campsite. The Rev counts out *drachmas* to pay for camping and the girl gyrates off. When she is inside, the Rev does his own jig version as he returns to the redbus.

For the restaurant, the day begins at sundown. The jukebox erupts raucously and men set up tables along the water. Behind the restaurant, close to us, a girl fans charcoal embers under lobster and fish.

The girls and I set out for the shack. At first glance we find nothing in it. Nothing but the odor, which is a special trial for Emily who has inherited her grandfather's nose and can always smell cows a mile before the rest of us do. Closer inspection with a flashlight introduces us to the non-Western style of W.C. which we somewhat indelicately named the S.Q., from the word "squat."

The S.Q. is a hole several inches in diameter. Better models are surrounded by tile or cement with two raised places on which to plant one's feet. Primitive ones, like this one, are just holes. This hole is overflowing. Emily rushes back to the half-erected tent to describe the facilities.

Well, it is still cozy to sit around the camping gas stove, eating bowls of beef stew mixed with string beans. The children are in their pajamas, washed clean in the yellow pail, sitting crosslegged in the open entrance to the tent or on the ends of the redbus seats whose doors are open to the warm night air. We are talking about Epirus today and Corinth tomorrow and about a hotel in Athens for the weekend. And we are giving thanks.

"If anyone bothers you," says the Rev to Clark, whose turn it is to sleep in the front seat of the redbus, "blow the horn and I'll come."

The two of us go down to sit at a rickety table on the fringe of thirty or forty laughing eating guests. It is a beautiful balmy night. We drink strong Greek coffee and a chaser of the now-familiar orange-lemon drink. The gyrating lady is supervising two waiters and charming her patrons. Cinderella sits behind the restaurant fanning the embers under the lobster. A middle-aged Belgian joins us. He plans to sleep overnight in his car, having come to enjoy the *langouste,* the special lobsters of this area. It is Friday night and the guests will be gay for hours. As the Rev hangs a maroon towel to dry on the side-view mirror of the redbus, Clark rears a sleepy head and blows a blast on the horn.

Refreshing quiet surrounds us early in the morning. Two fishermen sit beside the placid blue water baiting their nets. A man on a donkey and two women on foot arrive to draw water from the well. Chickens scavenge for bits of food where the tables stood. The Belgian has set up a portable table to wash and shave in the shade of a tree. He is grateful for a cup of chocolate left from our breakfast. Sipping, he philosophizes about the Greeks.

"They have a great past," he says, "but they are not a great people. No,

they are not even an interesting people today. Ah, but the *langouste* —
this is worth coming for."

The fishermen share one cigarette between them. They watch the
children wading and they look contentedly across the quiet water to see the
mountains emerge from the haze.

Suddenly the juke box blares in the stillness. The sun seems unbearably
hot. At my urging, Clark gives the comic books acquired at Vesuvius to
some boys fishing on the dock. We are glad to go.

After half an hour we are back again, hoping to find Clark's watch,
which he left lying on a table when he went wading. The fishermen know
about it. So do the boys on the dock. Inside the restaurant a man unlocks
two padlocks on a chest and takes out the watch. He handles it carefully and
wants to give it directly to the Rev. No, he will take no *drachmas* in
reward, but he obviously questions why a boy should own so valuable a
thing. Pantomimes cannot explain that Timex watches are not expensive
in dollars. Americans always look rich, no matter how poorly they travel.
And, in comparison, they are rich indeed.

A second time we begin the sixty-five miles to Corinth, riding with
bright blue water on our left and piles of plump yellow lemons gathered
beneath the small trees on our right. There are few people on the sandy
beaches or in the raised wooden pavilions. Time, time, go away, give us here
another day.

Soon after ten one gets *psomi* warm from the ovens. We buy some at a
place where the open hearth and wooden mixing bowls are in plain view.
The bread here is round, the crust a challenge, and the inside the color of
baked meringues. Lemons are a penny each. Let's eat at Corinth, overlooking the ruins.

"What do you remember about Corinth? Dave, take the Bible from the
map shelf and check Acts 18. What happened to Paul here?"

"Well, he came to Corinth from Athens. We're doing his missionary
journey backwards, huh? He made tents with Aquila and Priscilla. He
argued in the synagogue every Sabbath until they threw him out. But the
head of the synagogue believed. Other people did, too. Then God told Paul
in a vision to keep on and Paul stayed there a year and a half. Long time.
But the Jews were angry and brought him before the proconsul Gallio."

"What's a proconsul, dad?" Clark.

"I'm very hungry." Dicker, naturally.

"And the proconsul wouldn't take sides," Dave continued, "because he
said it was about the Jews' religion and laws. So he ordered them out.
Paul stayed a while longer and then sailed to Syria from Cenchreae. Where's
Cenchreae?"

"I'm very, VERY hungry." Dicker.

"Will we see any ruins of the synagogue or the judgment place?"

Before entering the walled-off ruins of Corinth at the museum gate, we find our hill for lunch. Behind us, on the south, rises the Acrocorinth, 1,750 feet of mountain which was Corinth's acropolis, its rock city once templed and fortified for defense. The noonday sun beats down, but there is solution for this. Into a pan of lukewarm water from the water jug the Rev squeezes the lemons, adding a minimum of sweetening. Sitting on a rock, he doles out the liquid and soon we are all shivering from the sourness. From my rock, tomatoes and bread with jam are dispensed. Please, no cheese.

The menu is not important when one can see against the backdrop of the emerald bay seven massive pillars of an Apollo temple begun six hundred years before Paul. The boy who comes selling coins finds us very gullible. We have not yet learned that there are many boys selling coins at every ruin.

What a city this Corinth was, with deep water ports on either side of the isthmus, a crossroads city facing west and east as no other city of its day. We walk where the South Stoa stood, the longest *stoa* in Greece, with a colonnaded porch running five hundred feet. On this promenade men from everywhere met and talked, jested and caroused. The shops with marble gutters and mosaic floors opened onto the promenade. Each had a storeroom behind it and an open shaft down to an underground refrigeration system supplied by the cold waters of the Peirene Fountain. Thirty-three taverns have been excavated here, says a guidebook. This cosmopolitan port was known for its great wealth and great corruption. Even the Christians fell back into gross living. We ought to reread what Paul writes them in First Corinthians, especially the middle chapters.

A tall man shouts at us from the far end of the *agora*. We are standing at the ruins of the *bema,* the proconsul's judgment seat in Paul's day.

"Ignore him," says the Rev. "He only wants money for watching the car or something."

"Look, the tall man is coming here," says Em. Squinting against the sun, we watch the man in the blue plaid shirt stride toward us. He calls our names. Dumbfounded, we recognize the professor-friend from Michigan who is supposed to be excavating in Dothan and lecturing in Jerusalem.

"When I saw that microbus and all those blonde children," he says, "I knew it had to be you." He has driven from Jerusalem to Athens with two students in their Volkswagen convertible and will return by ship from Piraeus to his assignment.

Together we explore the Peirene Fountain and its reservoirs, the elaborate baths, and we find stones carved with Christian symbols like the rooster and various cross forms. We walk as Paul did on the flat stones of the well-preserved Lechaeum Road, beside which excavators found the lintel of a synagogue.

It is hard to choose from the pieces of hand-painted pottery in the shops outside the Lechaeum Gate. The geometric patterns and the figures of Greek gods are done in intricate combinations of black, beige, red, and white. There are plates, bowls, and pitchers of every size.

The Volkswagen cavalcade departs for Athens as the daily tourist bus arrives from there. The girls ride with the student couple in the open convertible while the professor exchanges news with the Rev in the redbus. First stop is the bridge over the narrow Corinth Canal where ships pass beneath us at a dizzying depth. Slicing down through a hundred feet of solid rock was too much for the emperor Nero who began the canal project in the 60's after Christ, using hundreds of Jewish slaves. The work was completed in 1893, cutting loose the Peloponnesus from the mainland of Greece.

We make a stop for swimming, too, in the calm blue water along a beach of white pebbles matched by a white sailboat drifting by. Then, disheveled and salty, with Dicker standing like a hero in the rear of the convertible, we make our entry into the glorious city of Pericles, Plato, and the Parthenon.

M EETING A CITY is like meeting a new person. Some you like instinctively, some you learn to like, and some make no impact at all on your heart. Athens fell into the first of these categories for us, along with Istanbul and Jerusalem-Jordan.

In April the official Athens tourist agency had written that hotels were booked solid for the summer and no space was available. So we tried again from the Netherlands. The AAA guide, *Motoring Abroad,* 1962 *Travel Guide to Europe,* listed among many others the Hotel Nestor, a fifty-room hotel on Agiou Constantinou, a street near the middle of the city. Here a double room cost $3.20 in comparison to $18.45 at the Hilton. The Nestor confirmed our reservations at once and in good English.

Ready for us was a mammoth room with seven beds, two balconies, and high cool ceilings. Though the hotel served only breakfast, breakfast-like foods and snacks were available all day. Three nights and breakfasts cost us 535 *drachmas.* Figuring a *drachma* at 3.3 cents, this was $17.65 for the seven of us.

The children enjoyed scrambled eggs at the hotel the first night, and later the two of us joined the professor and the student couple for dinner, main course in one sidewalk café, fresh strawberries and coffee in another. We dallied at the fountain in Omonia Square, two blocks from the hotel, and ended the evening on one of our balconies, exchanging information since we were traveling in opposite directions.

Sunday morning we worshiped in Saint Andrew's American Church, one of many American Protestant community churches around the world staffed by American ministers of varying theologies. This church had been built by German Lutherans. Paul on the Damascus road and on the Areopagus shone down from the stained glass window in the chancel. It was first Sunday after Trinity, the feast of John the Baptist. At the Greek church dedicated to Dionysius the Areopagite, Paul's Athenian convert, a small procession was entering the main doors. In honor of the feast day, probably.

"What do processions remind you of, children?"

The best time to evoke the old glory of the Acropolis is at night. During full moon the Acropolis is open in the evening. Every night from April to September there is a Sound and Light Spectacle, with performances in English and in French. Spectators are seated on the Pnyx, the hill where the first parliament of free citizens met for open-air discussions. Changing lights flood the Acropolis, which looms across a valley of low buildings. Stereo sound in music and voice tells the story of an illustrious past.

By the time the Persians attack, Dicker is asleep in the arms of a student. It is 480 B.C., after Marathon and before the great Greek victory in Salamis Bay. The Persians are burning and plundering the Acropolis. A red glow climbs the west side, only access to the rocky fortress. Now it is all a mass of red. The Rev is taking time exposures on a tripod.

But greater glory rises from the ruins. Themistocles, leader of the rebuilding, erects the Long Walls from Athens to Piraeus port not long before Nehemiah and the Jews rebuild the walls of Jerusalem. Then comes the helmeted statesman Pericles, hero of the Golden Age, who declares in an eloquent funeral oration, "Our form of government is called a democracy because it is placed in the hands, not of the few, but of the many. All have equal rights under the laws."

The Athenian Golden Age, unmatched in history, lasts from the Persian defeat of 479 B.C. to the Peloponnesian War of 431. It is a short full flowering. On the Acropolis plateau temples rise. They are flawless in sculpture and majesty, the Parthenon for Athena, patroness of Athens, with her sacred owl, and the Erechtheum with a caryatid portico — six stately virgins supporting the marble roof upon their heads. Up a zigzag road on the west, chariots arrive at the steep steps of the Propylaia, the pillared entrance hall to the temples. Beside the entrance steps, in smaller elegance, stands the Temple of Athena Nike.

The theater of Dionysius is carved into the south side of the Acropolis hill. Here the Greeks sit enthralled at the plays of Euripides. Socrates conducts his dialogues in the *stoa* given by King Attalus of Pergamum. After him come Plato and then Aristotle. Every day the cultured curious walk and talk of new wisdom in the *agora,* certainly the most learned marketplace of its day. Here, in a burst of creative energy, the Athenians embrace democracy and learning and the arts. Here, as the poet Pindar said more eloquently in his native Greek, was

> . . . the gleaming and the violet crowned, and the sung in story; the bulwark of Hellas, famous Athens, city divine!

The spell of the sight-sound spectacle is broken. The student gathers up Dicker. The Rev gathers up his tripod and camera and the usher's flashlight motions us along to make way for the French-speaking audience. Over our shoulders we glance again at the temples bathed in light and mellowed by centuries to a luminous cream color.

These are the temples to which Paul raised his eyes when he walked between the Long Walls from Piraeus to Athens. They were there in full view and glory when he spoke to the Athenians about the God who dwells in temples not made with hands. They towered over him as he spoke with the Stoics and the Epicureans looking for new wisdom in the marketplace.

Many think that Paul did not make his formal speech on the Areos Pagus rock, a lower hill beside the Acropolis where the supreme court met at two unhewn stones, one for the accused and one for the accuser. Paul was not on trial, though his speech is recorded on a bronze plaque on the Areos Pagus. More likely he spoke in the royal hall of the Areopagus Council which met on the *agora* where anyone could come to listen.

"Men of Athens," Paul said, using the words of Socrates in his defense. And then he quoted from a Greek poet of Cilicia who had written an invocation to Zeus. "In him we live and move and have our being," Paul said, but not of Zeus or of the Acropolis statue of Athene Promachos, whose gleaming golden spear and helmet were the first objects visible from the sea. Paul spoke of "the God who made the world and everything in it . . . who gives to all men life and breath and everything . . . who commands all men everywhere to repent because . . . he will judge the world in righteousness."

The Acropolis has many moods, and its marbles change with changing light and sun from gold and amber to rose and gray. We walked on it at several times of day, hoisting Dicker up the giant steps of the Propylaia, standing dwarfed beneath the Parthenon pillars which taper slightly inward and the immense caryatids holding up the portico of the Erechtheum. The whole Acropolis is about nine hundred feet long and five hundred at its widest point. Considering the harsh treatment it received after Pericles' Golden Age, the wonder is that anything remains on it.

The Parthenon, for example, was finished in 432 B.C. It was Athena's temple for nine hundred years and in one of the two rooms stood Phidias' statue of Athena the Virgin, wood overlaid with gold and ivory. Then the Parthenon became a Christian church for a thousand years, after which the Turks made it a Moslem mosque and the Turkish commandant kept his harem in the Erechtheum while he himself lived in the entrance hall, the

Propylaia. The Venetians lobbed a shell onto the Acropolis when they attacked Athens in 1687 and that exploded a powder magazine in the Parthenon, destroying much of it. Lightning had exploded gunpowder in the Propylaia, and the Turks took down the Athena Nike temple to strengthen a fortress. Subsequently Acropolis marble was used to rebuild walls, collectors carted off treasures, and the Turks paid no attention to the temples of the land they subdued for four hundred years. Before the last siege of Athens in 1826, the British ambassador, Lord Elgin, removed many Acropolis statues to England where they now fill a hall in the British Museum in London.

From the Erectheum there is an excellent overall view of the ancient *agora* where Paul walked and discussed. Explored at closer range, most of the *agora* looks like orderly rows of marble blocks. In the center a headless Hadrian casts a long shadow. But on the edge of the *agora* is a splendidly preserved temple. It was a temple to Hephaistus, patron god of the craftsmen and metal workers who lived in the Keramaikos quarter nearby. Today a little museum, it was for centuries a Christian church. Its front portico is an excellent place from which to view the Acropolis.

Paul must have seen the Roman *agora,* too, the one Julius Caesar built in the first century before Christ. It is connected to the old Greek one and has an eight-sided Tower of the Winds with a figure personifying each breeze. The ruins of Hadrian's library are here, too. We met Hadrian many times more in our progress through the Mediterranean area. He was the emperor who finished the temple of the Olympian Zeus whose towering Corinthian columns are the tallest in Athens. Only eight of a hundred columns are standing today. I sat on a piece of fallen cornice the size of a park bench, making notes and wondering how the Greeks ever hoisted those tremendous pieces into place at the top of the columns.

Keramaikos — does the word "ceramics" come from this? It is the name of an old cemetery, named for the potters' district in which it lies outside remnants of Themistocles' wall. The graves are tightly spaced and topped with unusual statuary. There is a large horse on the tomb of a Dionysius and a bear on another. There are many sculptured reliefs like the one of Hegeso Proxenou looking at her jewels which are held by a maidservant. On another relief a seated lady with her husband at her side bids farewell to a manservant in a loincloth. Demetria and Pamphile sit devotedly together on still another stone.

Our most interesting meal in Athens was not first of all delicious. For delicious food we went to the Ideal Restaurant near the hotel and inexpensively ate foods like beefsteak, french fries, string beans, sliced tomatoes, fresh strawberries, with many glasses of cold water. But one noon we asked the salesgirl in a woolen bag shop to suggest a place. She directed us, in

French, to the restaurant of the seven brothers, Les Sept Freres, and came there later to see whether we had taken her advice.

It was a little place, one wall hung with paintings, the other holding eight casks on a high shelf. Why eight, we asked, if there are seven brothers?

"Aha!" replied one of the brothers in a big white apron, holding up a stubby finger. "Mama."

"Ah-HAH, Ma-MAH," repeated the Rev to the merriment of all.

A large piece of waxed paper covered the tablecloth and small squares of the same served as napkins. There was no menu, we could not understand French or Greek, so the Rev went to the open kitchen at the back of the restaurant and, guided by sight and smell, pointed to what attracted most in the fifteen pots lined up there. This we ate, sampling from each other's plates, with chunks of bread laid on the table paper. The experience cost us forty cents each. The whole staff, brothers or whatever they were, and the shopgirl lined up to shake hands when we left. *"Au revoir,"* we said, and, *"Merci,"* and, *"Ef caristo,"* in a lovely French-Greek mixture.

Before the professor boarded ship, he and the Rev wanted to browse in the South Stoa, part of the ancient *agora* which has been restored by the American School of Archaeology to house up to fifty thousand Athenian antiquities being unearthed. The gate to the *stoa* is off a narrow street lined with dark little shops. Nan and I stayed there to look.

It was siesta time. An old man slept half in and half out of a battered bathtub mounted to serve as a wheelbarrow. Through a basement window we watched a man stretching dough to cover his whole working table. Brass and copper pieces stood on the sidewalk. One of them was a large tray about three and one-half feet in diameter. It was very heavy copper, patched in two places with brass, and its primitive designs showed it to be old. Tarnish had turned it greenish black.

In English, then in German, I inquired the price from the man inside the shop. He understood neither language but he wrote the price on a piece of dirty cardboard. One thousand *drachmas*. "Epirus," he said, imitating the hammering and etching to decorate the tray. Very old, he explained by pointing back over his shoulder. In pantomime I promised to return with someone as tall as I, belonging to me — in words, a husband.

This was more easily promised than accomplished. It has been the bane of several trips that I found a cumbersome souvenir to transport home — a big driftwood piece from Maine, from a Dutch art fair a heavy pottery bowl that pushed the luggage weight over the airline's limit. And now a monstrous old tray. Too much money. Why this one? Where would we carry it? There will be better ones in Istanbul and Damascus. It's time to bring the professor to Piraeus. On this unhopeful note we left the tray on the sidewalk.

Because of my pleading, we returned a second time to consider the tray. It is expected procedure to haggle over price, but this shopkeeper would not budge one *drachma*. He made it plain with pantomime and paper that on the main streets in better shops the tray would cost three thousand *drachmas*. He found some more cardboard on which to write 175-200 and with back motions indicated that this was how old the tray was. Epirus — that was where it was made. When the Rev shook his head, the shopkeeper produced a smaller tray for our inspection but it did not appeal.

This was our last evening in Athens. We walked a while after dinner and the children decided to spend some of their own money for silver rings with geometric designs on them. We found a *lepeltje* with the Parthenon in its bowl and the head of Pericles on the handle. After the children slept, the two of us sat on the balcony, talking and wishing. The Rev wished to stay a year. I wished, more realistically, to own the copper tray.

The hotel staff gathered to say farewell. The desk clerk asked about American stamps. One of the porters refused a tip for filling our five-gallon jug with ice water. They stood on the sidewalk to wave as one does for good friends.

There were a few slides still to be taken — the brass plaque with Paul's sermon in Greek letters on the Areopagus Hill, the Acropolis in morning light. We bought a sticker for the car window and a pottery plate with geometric patterns painted on it. I left my leather-and-linen travel purse on the floor beside my chair in the restaurant where we ate lunch and the waiter came running after us to return it. *"Ef caristo,"* I said fervently, thinking of all the essential things that were in it. This man did not want a reward, either.

At the very end we went back to the copper tray shop.

"I can pay for it with three or four speeches at home," I pleaded. "We can stand it up and tie it behind the front seat. Think what a coffee table it will make. And from Epirus. Much more interesting than a new one from Istanbul."

Once more the Rev bargained. In the end we paid the thousand *drachmas* but the man agreed to include a heavy old mortar and pestle that I admired and a handful of coins, probably worthless. And his card, greasy and bent, in Greek and below in French. Mishel Pelecanos was his name and at the bottom of the card were the words, *Prise small.* A boy carried the tray on his head to the microbus — it weighs forty pounds — and we roped it in place against the back of the front seat, stuffing in two maroon towels to keep it from scratching. Here it rode to Jerusalem and from there back to Amsterdam where we packed it in the foam rubber sleeping pads with cardboard and rope over that. Today the copper tray from Epirus, polished to the warm glow of antique, is the focal point of our living room.

AT LEVADIA the main highway continues north and a smaller road branches west to Delphi, where an ancient oracle governed the destinies of kings and kingdoms. The road climbs continuously, past clumps of purple thistle flowers, alongside the range called Parnassus, eight thousand feet of grey rock sacred to the early Greeks as the home of Apollo and the Muses.

We worked our way through a flock of black and white sheep with bells around their necks. A boy threw stones at them to keep them moving and out of our way. Next on the road was an old woman leading two loaded donkeys and driving a flock of brown and white goats. And lest she waste time, she carded fluffy wool as she walked.

Arachova, the wool village, is known also for its black wine and cheeses. Old women sat in doorways carding and weaving. The shops were full of scarves, shoulder bags, skirts, and table coverings in colorful patterns which somewhat resemble those of the American Indian. For sixty *drachmas* we bought a covering for our hi-fi. Thirty *drachmas* — ninety-nine cents — purchased a shoulder bag of the kind sold in the Greek pavilion at the 1964 World's Fair for five and six dollars.

The ruins of Delphi are only minutes beyond Arachova. They lie on a slope to the right of the road. Beyond the ruins a modern settlement of hotels and shops has developed to accommodate tourists. Large shiny busses from Athens and shabby local ones stood along the street. The camping place was still farther, well beyond the town and noise. It adjoins the Pavillon Saint Lucas, a rustic eating place with walls of windows facing toward the Gulf of Corinth. What a location for a campground, we said, looking off the edge of the small plateau, down to the switchback road that led seven miles to the bay. There was room for eight or ten tents, though Dave bent many stakes trying to pound them into the rocky ground. Pink phlox grew among the rocks and low green bushes added color.

The *pavillon* was not yet open but the immaculate W.C. on the outside of the building was. A bus driver with a rattling local bus drove up and parked nearby, waiting until the time to make his return trip down the valley. He played ball with Clark and Dicker and for atmosphere turned his phonograph to full volume to play American hit tunes of the 1930's on scratchy records. So we pitched camp to the strains of "Deep Purple" and "Alexander's Ragtime Band."

When it became dark, Dave and Nan and we walked over to the *pavillon* where a white-jacketed waiter seated us at a table with wooden stools and a flickering candle. Looking out through the window wall into the valley, we saw the twinkling lights of the port of Itea. That was one way the Greeks used to come to Delphi for the festivals of games and plays.

The only other people in the *pavillon* were a black-haired man and a platinum blonde woman who called the man "George." She was obviously a tourist and he seemed to be a local guide. They spoke in English, she well, he poorly.

A light breeze blew from the bay. We sat a while on the stone benches near the tent. Behind us a rough black rim of mountains rose into the star-filled sky. What a place to remember, we said.

Voices pulled us out of that first deep sleep. Midnight, maybe. A woman was protesting. "George, you promised. Where are the *caballeros* you said would sing for me?" It was the platinum blonde, no doubt, whom we had seen in the *pavillon* with the man George.

There was the sound of a car door and the coughing of an old motor. George's, apparently. We were trying to go back to sleep when the old car returned, followed by a second. George had brought the *caballeros,* who began to sing lustily to the accompaniment of a banjo.

Between songs the village clock sedately struck three. The singers left, and finally George and the Platinum departed also. One more group came to stand on the little plateau overlooking the valley. We even heard the sound of tent stakes being driven. And then we heard the far-off music of sheep bells and the first streaks of dawn filtered in before we slept. It *was* a place to remember.

At seven the children woke us, bright-eyed and rested.

It was a beautiful morning. On the road sheep herders drove their flocks with bells tinkling. The bay lay in a haze, the sun was not yet oppressive. The *pavillon* was locked, also the W.C. It was, after all, a night spot, and revelers of the night hours were all abed. Also the Platinum. Only natives and simple folk like us were up and doing. The hotels and shops were still as we passed through the town on the way to the ruins. People and donkeys went up and down the road, quiet orderly people doing their daily work.

We parked where the stream from the Castalian Spring runs beneath the road and on down the mountain. In the gorge where the spring originates, the priests used to purify themselves before they interpreted the voice of the priestess, the *Pythia,* who sat on her tripod chewing laurel leaves above the steaming fissure which was the oracle itself. No one in the whole Greek world made an important decision without consulting the oracle and bringing offerings to fill the treasuries of Delphi.

So here we were, washing faces and brushing teeth in the same waters. Nearby stood the music-playing bus driver of the previous evening, his empty bus ready for passengers. Several more local bus drivers arrived and came forward to be friendly. The Rev had gone below the road to photograph the Marmaria area and he found a wizened little woman chopping wood. She gladly posed for a picture and the few coins given her she tied up in a cloth and put away in a hidden pocket as if she were handling pure gold.

Meanwhile the bus drivers converged on us. They tapped the copper tray, investigated the redbus, and one held Clark up to pick blackberries from a tree. I was wary of any George-like qualities but they were quite courteous. They also advised the Rev about the route to Lamia and north.

"Non good," said one about the shorter route we planned to take via Amfissa. *"Non* good, *non* good, *non* good." Pointing in the direction from which we had come, he said emphatically, "Levadia Lamia, Levadia Lamia."

The ruins were deserted so early in the morning. Following a map, we walked the Sacred Way past the offerings and treasuries to the five pillars of Apollo's temple from the fourth century before Christ. There was an Athenai inscription on its base in the south porch area. The Athenian treasury building is better preserved. Nan and Dave posed beside a headless statue.

From the amphitheater the view is spectacular, down across the temple area and out into the broad valley full of century-old olive groves. What a spot for an oracle and for the famous Pythian games held every four or eight years with laurel wreaths for the winners! Dramas in the theater, games in the stadium, chariot races in the plains below. The children tested the amphitheater acoustics. From the circular stage they spoke with ease to the top row of stone seats.

Per advice, we returned to Levadia, stopping in Arachova to buy several more shoulder bags. Men with ox-drawn wagons were working together on a common threshing floor in the valley. High, high above them there was snow in the crevices of the Parnassus.

The road north between Levadia and Lamia is rugged with curves and climbs. At the top of one ascent we traded two cigarettes for a dozen big lemons from a Corinth truckload. The driver would not take money. These lemons were the size of small grapefruit. At last the road relents and, tree-lined, runs straight as an arrow into Lamia. While we ate ice cream on the square, the lemon truck caught up to us and the men waved as to best friends.

North of Lamia the road is excellent. For forty *drachmas* one rides a national highway from Larisa to the coast along blue beaches, golden grain fields, and salt works. Mount Olympus and its range rose in the clouds to our left. At Alexandria we left the national highway to go to Veria, the old Berea, where Luke says the Christians searched the Scriptures daily. This route covers in reverse the second missionary journey of Paul. When he was forced out of Berea, friends escorted him to the coast and he went by boat to Athens, then to Corinth.

Clark read in Acts 17: "The brethren immediately sent Paul and Silas away by night to Berea; and when they arrived they went into the Jewish synagogue. Now these Jews were more noble than those in Thessalonica, for they received the word with all eagerness, examining the scriptures daily to see if these things were so. Many of them therefore believed."

Berea today is nondescript. A level road, dusty wagons, a few chickens, a bridge over the Aliákmon River, two men leaving town leading two bears. In the city the square is dusty, too, faced by a shabby church. A Greek Orthodox priest in his flat-topped black hat sat fanning himself with a newspaper in a sidewalk café. As we left, we took a slide of the sign at the edge of the town. It was the only distinguishing mark about the place. BEPOIA, it said in yellow on blue, in the Greek spelling. And below, in white on green, was the Roman spelling, VERIA.

Thessaloniki was better, even though Paul received rough treatment there. The Jews used modern-sounding methods and induced "some wicked fellows of the rabble" to create a riot and to drag Paul's host Jason before the authorities.

Today this second largest city of Greece is attractive. It lies at the head of Salonika Bay against the lower slopes of mountains piled high behind it. Along the waterfront the street is broad. Khaki-clad soldiers and well-dressed people walked on the cement promenade at the water's edge. White and cream-colored buildings face the harbor. Thessaloniki is named for the half sister of Alexander the Great. She was wife of King Cassander of Macedonia. Alexander himself was born at Pella between Veria and Thessaloniki. Now the old and new stand side by side. Through an arch of Galerius, erected about three hundred years after Christ to commemorate victories in Asia Minor, one sees the balconies and shutters of modern apartment buildings.

Thessaloniki is also the gateway to the peninsula of Chalcidice. The peninsula has three fingers and at the tip of the easternmost one are the monasteries of Mount Athos, which are a thousand years old and have never allowed a woman to enter their gates even as a visitor.

The main street of Thessaloniki is Via Egnatia, part of the important road built by the Romans after they conquered Macedonia. The Roman highway ran the width of the Balkan peninsula as part of the road connecting Rome with Asia. A German from Frankfurt came to talk with us about moving to Montreal. In an open butcher shop a pig hung, intact to his tail. NATO has offices in a big well-shaded house, and someone important lives in a white mansion with guards at the gate. Like Athens, Thessaloniki is a modern city — two wrecked cars were mounted on the Via Egnatia as warning to a city of cars, not donkeys. And there was Uncle Gerry's Pfizer, Pfizer Hellas, in offices under a blue awning.

Camping Neon was on the bay in the Nea Krini section of Thessaloniki. It was a good campground, large, fenced, grassy, with ample facilities including two outdoor showers in the middle of the campground. The beach was not good for swimming, but it was fine for watching small boats in the sunset. Supper menu featured instant mashed potato, green beans, and Spam, with a big pan of orange lemonade. We all showered after dark. The tops of the unlighted shower stalls were open to the stars, clematis twined fragrantly around the shower pipes, and the air became pleasantly cool.

In the morning we met some of our neighbors. Next to us was a Volkswagen from Austria, whose owner asked, among other things, what the Rev's occupation was. When told, he replied with cheerful nonchalance about his own religion, "Well, you see, I am nothing." Most Americans would have claimed some church connection. Europeans are perhaps more honest. If they do not have a meaningful relationship to a church, they say so.

On the Athens-Istanbul highway we bought bread at a blue bakery. Blue is a favorite color in this part of the world. The Greek flag is blue and white. Turks love blue, too, especially in mosaics. We took a slide of this bread because it was long and white and soft inside, unlike the round dark sourish hard ones we had been eating. At a gas station a girl pumped the gasoline by hand while an old man held the funnel and hose into the tank.

"Now when they had passed through Amphipolis and Apollonia, they came to Thessalonica." We had memorized these strange names in school. Now we saw them. First there was Nea Apollonia, off the road to the right, and then, two miles farther, Apollonia itself, a small cluster of red-tile roofs on the edge of a dry stream bed. A group of turtles was sunning on a half-submerged log in a sinkhole.

The road approaching Amphipolis was ripped up. The procedure seemed to be to rip up the entire section intended for repair and then to repair it bit by bit. There was a great deal more under destruction than construction. A thirty-foot stone lion sits on his haunches, teeth bared, guarding the Strimon River at the site of old Amphipolis, local capital of Macedonia in Paul's day. Greek military men and vehicles were practicing fording the river, a reminder that the Bulgarian border is not far north.

F ROM THESSALONIKI TO PHILIPPI is seventy miles. To reach the Philippi ruins, one turns north off the highway before the port of Kavalla. We thought the ruins unimpressive, considering Luke's description of Philippi as "leading city of the district of Macedonia, and a Roman colony." To the east of the road is the acropolis and near its base an amphitheater with a stony wheat field where the stage had been. On the west side of the road lie the ruins of the city rebuilt in the second century after Christ and the three crumbled towers of fourth- and fifth-century churches. Finegan says, "It is probable that the archway ruins on the northwest of the city date from Paul's time. Beneath it, running west, the Via Egnatia left Philippi. Probably the arch was the line within which foreign deities might not be worshiped. It is the gate of Acts 16:13 and the women were praying at the Gangites River."

The river is still there. French archaeologists were sitting in the shady grove along its banks. The river had been wider, they thought, and its bed has changed, but the general area is the same. The water still flows dark and cool. It was easy to imagine a group of Jews gathered there on a Sabbath because their religious practice was outlawed in the city where only the emperor and the Roman gods might be worshiped within the gates. Lydia, the seller of purple from Thyatira, was converted here. Here Christianity entered Europe.

Many triumphant emperors and commanders, many merchants and fortune seekers, traveled the Via Egnatia from Asia to Rome. None made a greater impact than the man who came on foot in answer to a vision. Of him and his companions the proud folk of Philippi complained, "These men are Jews and they are disturbing our city. They advocate customs which it is not lawful for us Romans to accept and practice." And after this "the crowd joined in attacking them; and the magistrates tore the garments off them and gave orders to beat them with rods. And when they had inflicted many blows upon them, they threw them into prison. . . ."

"About midnight Paul and Silas were praying and singing hymns to God, and the prisoners were listening to them, and suddenly there was a great earthquake. . . ." Everyone's chains fell off and the doors burst open. The jailer, about to kill himself, believed in the Lord Jesus Christ of whom Paul testified, and was baptized with his household. But the magistrates, when they sent the police to release the missionaries, discovered to their chagrin whom it was they had mistreated. For Paul said to the police, "They have beaten us publicly, uncondemned, men who are Roman citizens, and have thrown us into prison; and do they now cast us out secretly? No! let them come themselves and take us out." "The police reported these words to the magistrates, and they were afraid when they heard that they were Roman citizens; so they came and apologized to them. And they took them out and asked them to leave the city. So they went out of the prison, and visited Lydia; and when they had seen the brethren, they exhorted them and departed." This Luke tells us in Acts 16.

Kavalla is the seaport called Neapolis in Acts 16:11. We looked down on it from the top of Symbolum Mountain, remarking about the steep climb Paul had to make when he disembarked from Troas and set out for Philippi in the plain behind the mountains. A little Volkswagen stopped at the lookout point with us and three Indian students got out. They were driving home from study in Europe. Yes, sir, indeed the roads are passable through Iraq and Iran to India. We filed that idea away for future reference.

Kavalla's campground on the beach was crowded and bad-smelling, so we drove on to Xanthi where we saw our first mosque and veiled woman.

In the area near the Turkish border there are more mosques in Greece than there are Greek Orthodox churches in Turkey. What was really the difference? Dave wanted to know, and involved his father in considerable discussion about Islam as we drove toward Komotini. Clark and Dicker were more interested in all the military vehicles and installations along this road close to the Bulgarian border.

We were back in poorer country again. Women wore heavy black shawls over their heads. In every village one or more Greek Orthodox priests sat in the café on the square, their long hair in ponytails or neat little knots, their beards flowing. Judging by the time they spend supervising their flock from the village square, one might deduce that they are better pastors than preachers. And of course their worship services have a substantial amount of liturgy on which to fall back.

The people were friendly here. Even in poverty, their faces reflected dignity and contentment. A pretty teen-ager waved as we passed the wagon in which she was riding with her family. There was a tranquillity here that we of the frenetic American pace have lost.

At Alexandroúpolis the old and the modern meet again. A trim young lady wearing white high-heeled shoes and lipstick trips down the street followed by two barefoot women wearing long dusty clothes and head coverings, bent under heavy sacks.

Camping in Alexandroúpolis depends on whom you ask. Despite the *Camping Europa* notation, the policeman on main street says there is no camping. To him foreigners are those whose yachts dock in the harbor. The Shell station attendant, more geared to common tourists, reports that there is camping behind the Astir Motel on the edge of the city. This is a beautiful motel on the beach with modern units connected in a U-shaped complex. But the motel proprietor denies that anyone camps in the pine grove behind the motel. Naturally, he would rather rent his motel rooms.

So we drove back to the city, inquired at the tourist office, and were directed a second time to the motel. This time the caretaker helped us willingly and the proprietor was — purposely? — out of sight. At a respectful distance from the modern units we set up camp on a floor of fragrant pine needles. The army shovel served for sanitary purposes and the caretaker showed us how to get water from a hose. Another employee assured us someone had camped there the previous night also. After the children played on the beach we had a meal of meat ball stew with a can each of corn and beans mixed through it, plus fresh tomatoes and apricots. These camp meals were simple, basic, unadorned with sweets or frills. By the end of the trip we were all lean, brown, and healthy from daily walking, sensible eating, and unbroken sunshine.

I awoke first in the morning with the feeling that someone was watching. Sure enough, behind the wire fence around the motel property stood a man and his dog, both surveying us intently through the open tent flaps. When we sat up, he moved on to observe the redbus with equal concentration. From the city came sounds of a band. Another feast day, this time Saint Paul's, quite appropriate to our travel in that part of the world.

At the Shell station where the attendant had directed us to the motel for camping, we exchanged money to get Turkish currency. The official rate is nine Turkish *kurush* for a dollar. The Shell station offered eleven and we bought ten dollars' worth. This is a courtesy done in a number of establishments close to the Turkish border, and the benefit is mutual.

Dealing in Turkish money is a fussy business. One gets more *kurush* for a dollar outside of Turkey but may bring only a hundred dollars into the country this way. Within Turkey it is a crime to deal in anything other than *kurush*. Unlike most countries, Turkey forbids the use of a dollar bill in a store even if one accepts his change in Turkish coin. Places like the YMCA accept payment in nothing but *kurush*. Neither will Turkish banks convert *kurush* into any other currency for the tourist leaving the country. Areas adjacent to Turkey therefore have been accepting *kurush* from tourists leaving Turkey and businessmen like the Shell station man get rid of it cheaply to tourists entering Turkey.

It is eighteen miles from Alexandroúpolis to the border. Dicker surprised us at morning devotions by singing all of Oom Bee's *"Klokje klinkt."* He sings less and less about "Winston tastes good . . ." and "fresh from the Kraft candy kitchen."

Two policemen in trim green uniforms were stationed in every village, one officer at each end of the town, no matter how small it was. A one-legged shepherd paused in a field to wave. A motor scooter cut across our path and we also narrowly avoided collision with some sheep loitering on their way to drink with the rest of the flock. They drank from a cement watering trough. All the river beds were dry.

A priest was riding his donkey along the road, urging the animal on with a stick. We stopped to converse in Greek and German. Where are you from? Where are you going? This he asked. No, no, do not say Istanbul. Say Constantinople, please. We understand his preference. The city on the Bosporus has been called Istanbul only since the Turks took over this citadel of orthodoxy. The chief prelate of the Eastern Orthodox Church still makes his headquarters there despite the Mohammedanism of Turkey. The priest pulled out his silver chain and cross so that they would show to advantage on a photo. He was happy to accept some cigarettes.

We entered Turkey at a new border crossing, the one at Ferrai-Ipsala. Ferrai is the last Greek town, then comes the Ergene River which is the actual boundary, and the first Turkish town is Ipsala. This is the southernmost entry point in European Turkey, and it is on the road leading to Istanbul via Tekirdag. At the Greek border everything was blue and white

— the bars across the road, the customs building, and the flag flying atop it.

"Do shepherds get lost, too?" Em wondered when several shepherds passed with bells in their clothes.

"That's so the sheep will know where the shepherds are, huh, mom?"

"Be easier if they'd just look where they're going," said Clark as we watched the flocks pass, all heads down, bodies pressed close together.

"Maybe sheep are nearsighted. Are they?"

One laggard stood baa-ing plaintively. He hurried to catch up to one flock, discovered that it was not the right one, and rushed frantically to reach the dogs rear-guarding his own flock.

"How does a sheep know his own flock?"

"Maybe by the smell."

"They all smell the same — bad!"

Several small boys arrived with a flock. Each boy carried a stick, and a cap and coat folded neatly over his arm.

At the end of the long bridge flew the Turkish flag, a white crescent and star on a red field. The flag has an interesting history. Mohammed II adopted the moon and star device when he conquered Constantinople in 1453. Originally these were the signs of Diana, patroness of the city. More than three hundred years before Christ, Philip of Macedon, father of Alexander the Great, laid siege to Constantinople but his night attempt to undermine the walls was betrayed by the light of a crescent moon. In gratitude for their escape, the Byzantines raised a statue of Diana and made her badge the symbol of the city. And so the special emblem of Constantinople, greatest of cities, became the flag of modern Turkey.

A blue Plymouth with Michigan license plates stood in front of us at Turkish customs. In this setting it looked large and luxurious. There were only three vehicles in the line. Their owners entered a yellow quonset hut along a walk lined with Mobilube oil cans sprouting flowering plants.

Customs takes time in the Middle East. Any effort to speed the process only makes the officials suspicious. Why should one hurry? No one does in this part of the world. The owner of the Michigan Plymouth was a young Turk who had studied at Wayne University in Detroit. Customs men gave him a grilling to determine how a student could return home in such affluence. No one checked our luggage, men smiled in approval when we photographed the flag, the oil can plants, and the bridge. On this congenial note we entered the country about which we had received strenuous warnings from an air force colonel who had been there.

"I can see that you will save a lot of money driving to the Holy Land instead of flying," the colonel had said. "But let me warn you. Turkey is hot, dirty, dusty, smelly, full of animals and most primitive conditions. There is nothing interesting to see. The people are the world's most curious. The laws are from the Middle Ages and if you hit so much as a goat you will be in real trouble. Be careful and drive through as fast as you can. I don't envy you."

Not a very encouraging introduction. We have often laughed about it. Anyone who asks the children what they remember most about the trip and to what country they would like to return will receive the unanimous answer: Turkey. Not because it was easy there or even pleasant most of the time. But because this country holds so much Biblical and secular history within its borders and because, until it is spoiled by tourist influx, it is a land of one unbelievable experience after another.

East

WE CAME BOUNCING INTO KESAN just at noon. A policeman wearing a white helmet with a red band stood in the middle of the town. What's bread in Turkish? Look in the army phrase book. Not *psomi* anymore. The word now is *ekmek,* accent on the second syllable. Everyone in town dropped what they were doing to watch us. They gathered around the redbus in silence except for one child who knew enough English to say shyly, "Touris'?"

At that moment, as we sat surrounded by the silent audience, the *muzzein* mounted the minaret to wail his call to prayers. Facing in each of four directions he repeated the minor plaintive call. Nothing else stirred in the hot air. The sensation of that moment was our introduction to Turkey. Everything stood still in a sort of a spell until the Rev came out of the shop with *ekmek,* cookies, and peanuts, the latter two in bags made of newspaper and flour paste. He shook hands with the man nearest him and others crowded forward to be greeted.

"Think what you missed," he told us. "The man in the shop was really disappointed I didn't buy some lard from a bucket and some yogurt from a pail."

The way to Tekirdag is forty miles of bad road and primitive villages. But every village had a policeman sitting in a raised booth at the main intersection. At the uncommon sound of a motor, he sprang to his feet, stepped out into the street, put on his helmet, blew his whistle for no observable reason, and grandly signaled us on to Istanbul.

Water buffalo lay partly submerged in muddy water holes. A herd of goats crowded precisely into the shade of a tree. Not one had so much as a tail or nose in the sun. That first day we thought how nice it would be to eat lunch under a shady tree. We soon realized that at every tree the goats either were there or had been there, and all trees were thereby rendered unfit for picnicking. So we ate lunch in the noon sun and it was hot hot hot.

We were being waved on through shabby villages with white minarets piercing the blue sky when the redbus began to protest. Gas was not coming through the line. Even with the gas pedal pushed down to the floor and the motor shifted into first gear, it moved by spurts and starts. Dirty gas, probably, the kind we had been warned about, mixed with kerosene or flecked with dirt. Coughing and jerking, the redbus fought its way along and halted precariously on a long hill. After Tekirdag it was better.

About thirty-eight miles from Istanbul we met the good highway from Edirne, which is the usual Greece-Turkey border crossing, farther north and near the Bulgarian border. Returning from Israel, we would go that way into Bulgaria. "D.V.," added the Rev, *deo volente,* the Lord willing. Much could happen in the five weeks intervening.

Beside a watering trough was a picnic table, the first we had seen since the road to Berlin. At Silivri, there is a beautiful beach campground and fifteen miles farther a roadside *parki* with brick stoves. All the blue water on the right is the Sea of Marmara which opens in the south through the Dardanelles into the Aegean and in the north through the Bosporus into the Black Sea. People have summer homes here, little pastel-colored buildings along the water's edge. There were two more campgrounds before we reached the populated suburbs of Istanbul.

The walls of Istanbul secured it a thousand years until the cannon of the Turks broke through in 1453. Four miles long and fifteen feet thick, they were begun in A.D. 413 and today's visitor still enters the city through them. Istanbul, with two million people and five hundred mosques, stands at the meeting of two continents which has always been the world's crossroads. It is the most intriguing combination of history and modernity, of Orient and Occident, to be found anywhere.

Like Rome, Istanbul is built on seven hills, but the name is Greek, from *Stamboul,* meaning, "into the city." Istanbul has three parts, two European and one Asiatic. The European parts are separated by the blue finger of the Golden Horn. The southern part is Old Stamboul, while the northern one, Galata or the Beyoglu district, is more recent and houses embassies, hotels, and business centers. The two parts are joined by the old Galata Bridge made of floats and by a modern bridge named for Ataturk. The Asian part of the city is reached by a ten-cent ride on one of the ferries which cut across the lower end of the Bosporus at right angles to all other water traffic, including Russian ships that pass at the rate of a hundred a day between the Black Sea and the Aegean-Mediterranean.

We were looking for the YMCA, whose director, named Glenn, had written that he would be glad to select a small clean hotel for us because the Y housed only men. But Mr. Glenn had gone to a Turkish bath to relieve an aching back. We explored while awaiting his return. A cool breeze made all the smells and sounds and sights intriguing. In the cobble-stone streets near the waterfront, haunting minor music mingled with shouts, boat whistles, creaking wagon wheels, and insistent car horns.

We saw the Hagia Sophia, which means Holy Wisdom. Built by Constantine as a Christian church in 347 after Christ, it is Istanbul's most historic building. And nearby is the Blue Mosque whose six minarets aroused the envy of Mecca whose mosque had only four. Near the fountain of Sultan Ahmet we sat reading more about the city around us.

The Greeks founded Byzantium in 657 B.C., a few years after other Greeks founded Chalcedon on the Asian side of the mile-wide Bosporus. The city was captured, razed, and rebuilt by various emperors. Pirates plundered the coastline until Constantine, converted by a vision of a cross near Rome and acting, he said, "on the command of God," set up his Roman capital here. It was dedicated and named Constantinople in A.D. 330 and was stocked with treasures from all over the world. This became the cosmo-politan city of which Herbert Muller says in *The Loom of History* that it was "populated largely by assorted Asiatics who alike professed Christianity, spoke Greek, and called themselves Roman."

Within a hundred years Constantinople had a population of a million and for a thousand years it stood as a Christian citadel, repelling barbarians and Arabs until it fell to the Turks in 1453. Strange as it sounds to us of the civilized Western world, Constantinople and its Byzantine Empire held on to civilization through the Dark Ages of Europe, Rome having fallen in 476, and held back the Moslem Arabs in their drive to defeat Christendom. Here in the eleventh century the Holy Orthodox Church, which we know as the Eastern Orthodox Church, formally terminated communion with the western Roman church. The Eastern Orthodox patriarch officiated in the Hagia Sophia where he crowned emperors and served as spiritual ruler. In these centuries Byzantine art flourished, especially in mosaics, influenced by ideas from the lands still farther east. And though in its Christian orienta-tion, Constantinople reeked of graft, intrigue, profligacy, and superstition, yet for centuries it was the greatest city in the world, defended by three walls and bulging with treasures.

Then came the gradual decline as the Arabs and Seljuks subdued the Asia Minor peninsula. The armies of the Fourth Crusade, en route to "rescue" the holy places from the infidels, plundered and captured the city in 1203. Finally, in 1453, after a seven-week siege — the emperor receiving communion on the last night in the last Christian service in the Hagia Sophia — Constantinople fell to the Ottoman Turks under Sultan Mohammed II. Islam replaced a decadent Christianity. The mosque and the Koran took the place of the church and the Bible. The sultans ruled and their Ottoman Empire at peak power reached from the Persian Gulf to Poland.

In our century, during the twenties and thirties, the Turkish people enjoyed peace for the first time in six hundred years. It was Kemal Ataturk, whose assumed name of Kemal means "perfect," who brought progress and fundamental reforms to his country and held together the shrinking Ottoman Empire after World War I. He removed the Ottoman palace and the Moslem state church and recreated the Turks as individuals and as a nation. As signs of emancipation, the fez and veil were abolished and people assumed family names for the first time. Polygamy was legally prohibited and Roman characters replaced Arabic. To the Turks Ataturk is their Abraham Lincoln. He served the Ottoman Empire during twelve years of steady warfare and ruled the new Turkish republic as president for fifteen years until his death in Istanbul at the age of fifty-seven from cirrhosis of the liver.

Ankara was made the Turkish capital in 1923. But it is Istanbul that speaks of centuries of history. The Hittites of Abraham's day, Xenophon's march to the Black Sea, Alexander the Great's world conquests, Paul's missionary churches, Constantine's Christian capital, the misguided Crusades, and the Moslem conquests — it is all here in Turkey, summed up in the crossroads city that symbolizes the conflicts of East and West.

Resolved: to spend some winter evenings reading all about this Eastern empire, this fabled city. Questions crowd our minds. The Rev wonders whether the ascendancy of Arianism did not make acceptance of Islam easier because it reduced Christ to someone less than total God, an acceptable parallel to the relationship of Allah and Mohammed and to the Mohammedan concept of Jesus Christ as a lesser prophet.

M R. GLENN STAYED LONG in his Turkish bath but he was worth waiting for. First he sent us to the Atlas Oteli. "In the middle of picturesque old Istanbul moderate prices," said the brochure with a map showing the bazaar, the Blue Mosque, the Hagia Sophia, and Topkapi Palace all within walking distance. Halid of the Y staff went along as interpreter because no one in the hotel spoke much English. Halid also explained that the hotel management requested us to park our redbus in front of the police station each night to guarantee its safety from theft.

Three rooms were ready. Each had a sink with cold water and a double bed with four hard pillows, double the usual number. Dicker slept on a cot in our room. The children discovered that our floor had an S.Q. and the floor below us a W.C. A shower, locked, was at the end of the hall. It could be used at cost of twenty-five cents per person. Breakfast was included in the price of the rooms. On the way back to the YMCA we stopped at the police station where Halid explained to the officers that the redbus would be parked in front of their door for three nights. "Here nobody will take your tires," said Halid solemnly.

The Glenns invited us to supper in their apartment which was across the Galata Bridge, through the Beyoglu section, and up a perpendicular street near Roberts College. Creamed tuna over rice and peas with a view of the Bosporus. Clark spent an hour with the Glenn daughter his age who taught him how to count from one to fifty in Turkish. *Bir, iki, üc, dört, bes, alti, yedi, sekiz, dokuz, on* — this is one through ten. All the way through Turkey we depended on what Clark learned in that hour. Like his father, he picks up languages easily and he dares to try them. The rest of us never got beyond Dicker's chants of "beer, icky, ouch."

The Glenns had lived in Montevideo before being assigned to Istanbul. Mrs. Glenn's parents, long-time Y people, had been in Russia during the revolution, before that in China, and later spent three years in Germany and many more years in Paris. Glenn was leaving the next day to conduct a Boy Scout camp on the Black Sea. Did our boys want to come, too? While he was gone, Halid was available as guide or for anything we needed. And Mary Glenn would meet us in the American church on Sunday. How can one thank such hospitable people?

On the way back to the hotel we stopped at the floodlit Fortress Rumeli Hisar, built by the Turks in four months for their 1453 siege of Constantinople. They first assembled it on the Asian side of the Bosporus and then brought it across piece by heavy piece. It has three main fortresses and many smaller ones, the whole stone group of which stretches down a hillside to the water north of the early city. The Turks called it Boghazkesen, "cutter of the throat," and it was the springboard for their successful assault.

A little farther south is the waterfront Dolmabahçe Palace where Ataturk died in room 71 at 9:05 one morning. All the palace clocks are set to register the precise moment of death. The last cigarette Ataturk smoked is in the ashtray where he laid it.

The hubbub on the Galata Bridge had subsided when we recrossed it and the city noise was subdued. But the music never ceases. Voices sing or radios wail plaintive minor melodies with plucked accompaniment all through the night. Beneath our hotel window this music cajoled men pounding on metal until dawn.

Turkish coffee is good for eliciting grit and determination, for setting a man up to face a bracing day. We felt more like tea for breakfast and it was served in the breakfast salon with two squares of butter swimming in amber fig jam, white cheese, and bread with the name of the baker stamped in purple ink on the crust. We walked to the police station and drove to the Y to discuss the day's itinerary with Halid. At the Y a Dutch boy with the predictable name of Jan attached himself to us for the day. Unlike the Dutch student who spent Sundays with us at home, Jan had no interest in children, he knew all the answers, and he was out of money. Three strikes against him, though it was the first two that bothered us.

With Jan as self-appointed guide, preceding us except when there were entrance fees to be paid, we first admired the wonders of the Archaeological Museum. Its most famous piece is the sarcophagus of Alexander the Great, ten feet long with lions guarding its corners and his Persian victory carved on one side.

On to the Topkapi Palace, once the Old Seraglio of the sultans. It stands magnificently on jutting Saray Point where the Sea of Marmara, the Golden Horn, and the Bosporus meet. The palace buildings are grouped around three courts, each with its own gate. At the first gate the executioner functioned, washing blood from his hands and sword in the spring. The Old Seraglio was built by Mohammed II in the fifteenth century and added to by his successors for another century and a half. The harem area has little courts, gardens, and suites, each in different decor, and was once filled with beautiful women who played decisive roles in court intrigue. The royal kitchen is full of rare porcelains, crystal, and silver. And the portico offers a view unexcelled.

We stayed longest in the treasury section which is heavily guarded and wired with alarms. Here in glass cases are flaming rubies and the greenest of emeralds, scimitars and chalices covered with jewels, diamonds, gold, and pearls to dazzle the eye. A giant emerald hangs over the throne of Ahmet I who built the Blue Mosque. One throne is set with eighteen thousand pearls. There is a gold and jeweled baby cradle and a gem-encrusted reliquary claiming to hold the hand of John the Baptist. In another gold case is the mantle of Mohammed, hidden under a cover with its own abundance of rubies and emeralds. It is a fabulous collection of riches. How these sultans and their favored few must have lived!

What Saint Peter's is to the Roman church, the Hagia Sophia was to the Eastern Orthodox. But in the fifteenth century the Turks added four minarets to adapt it to Islam and it became a museum in 1935. Fire destroyed the first Holy Wisdom Church of Constantine and a second one built soon after. The emperor Justinian rebuilt the Hagia Sophia in five years and dedicated it on Christmas Day, A.D. 538. It shares the first hill of Istanbul with the Old Seraglio, which was built much later on the site of the early acropolis. As we approached the ochre-yellow walls of the Hagia Sophia, Dicker stopped to watch one minaret intently. It had a wire scaffolding around it for repairs. The question was logical from a boy geared to Cape Kennedy. "When's it gonna blast off, dad?"

When the Hagia Sophia was converted into a mosque, the priceless mosaics fortunately were covered with a matting before they were plastered out of sight. Today they are restored to view, gold and multi-colored, a compelling reason for every student of art to visit Istanbul. Most famous is the fifty-foot one above the lateral entrance. It depicts Mary holding the infant Jesus, flanked by the emperors Constantine and Justinian presenting models of the church as each had it built.

The marble floor of the church has nothing on it. Low-hanging chandeliers hold glass cups for oil. Above is one great dome with a half dome at each end and two stories of pillared arches, the upper story formerly used by women. Twelve colossal pillars hold up the domes. One is from Diana's temple in Ephesus, another from Baalbek, and at the southwest corner is the Weeping Column, encased in bronze, always damp, and touched by those who want to make a wish. Around the balconies and in the domes are more mosaics. Four angels and the twelve apostles line the first balcony.

Many superstitions surround the Hagia Sophia. One of the most interesting has to do with the coffin-like metal section over the King's Gate. This, it is said, is the burial place of Constantine's beautiful daughter, for whom he built a tower in the bay after soothsayers predicted that she would die by snakebite. Despite the protection of her island tower, she did die this way, from a snake hidden in a basket of fruit. To protect her body, she was buried above the King's Gate with a guard posted below. But if you look carefully you will see holes in the metal through which a snake entered here, too, and left, having laid her eggs inside.

Less historic than the Hagia Sophia but no less beautiful is the Sultan Ahmet Mosque, better known as the Blue Mosque because its mosaic interior is predominantly blue. It is the only mosque with six minarets, four around the mosque and two a short distance in front of it. As in any strict mosque, worshipers must enter with heads and arms covered and they leave their shoes at the entry. We chose to enter barefoot in preference to the dirty tattered *mukluks* offered by an attendant. The mosque was carpeted with oriental rugs. People cleansed themselves with water before they knelt to pray, facing toward Mecca and with heads bowed to touch the floor.

In the dome, on the pillars, and in the five hundred stained glass windows, shades of blue form beautiful patterns. Sky and dome seem almost to float together. Pigeons coo and flutter and the *imam* chants in a sort of desperate wail. A family passed, heads covered with white. We sat on carpets near the wall. The Rev made time exposures of the blue dome with gold Arabic letters from the Koran around its base. Somewhere in the Blue Mosque is its treasure, a bit of stone supposedly given by the angel Gabriel to Abraham.

The blue mosaics reminded us of Dutch Delft blue, though the Turkish color is more aqua and more delicate. Could the Dutch blue have come in some way from the Turkish? Admittedly the tulip came to the Netherlands from Turkey. It takes its name from the Turkish word *tülbend,* meaning "turban," because the flower resembles the shape of a face topped by a turban. Vienna botanist Clusius officially introduced tulips to the Dutch when he came to teach at Leiden University in 1593. They became such a fashion that men paid with a house or a precious piece of jewelry to get one bulb of a new variety. How possible that the Dutch with their doughty fleet of ships also might have brought back the blue tile and ceramic which we saw in the Blue Mosque and in many museums of the Byzantine period!

"Not possible, not at all," said Jan with finality and Dutch pride. So we let the matter drop.

The perfect setting for a mystery thriller is the Kapali Carsi, the Grand Bazaar, a twenty-acre underground labyrinth of alleys and aisles with four thousand shops selling everything from medieval chalices to modern furniture. In its present form the Istanbul bazaar is recent, rebuilt after a fire in 1955, but the flavor is as ancient as 450 years ago when the first bazaar was built here. Merchandise is grouped. Weapons, antiques, rugs, clothing, jewelry, foods, furniture all have their own areas. Stacks of gold bracelets, stalls hung with copper and brass, plates and tiles, and men unfolding the reds-browns-golds of oriental rugs. In the center is a vaulted room called the Bedestan where the best of ancient brass, copper, weapons, and jewelry is sold. One's nose, eyes, and ears are overwhelmed.

I found a chance to return alone to the brass and copper section. Pointing to a new brass tray a little smaller than our Athens antique, I asked the price. One hundred fifty dollars, said the man firmly, writing it down on paper to be sure I understood. Even with success in bargaining, this was far more than thirty dollars for our aged copper piece from Epirus. I must have looked perplexingly happy as I thanked the merchant and said I would speak to my husband. Which I did, without delay.

We ate lunch in the bazaar, in a dim small place where eight of us posed a seating problem. Bottled mineral water, shishkabob, rice, and stewed tomatoes. On the way back to daylight we bought a *lepeltje* with a star and crescent on it and two records of the "sick music" that conjures up instant visions of Istanbul and the Atlas Oteli.

Jan thought it would be nice to see the Black Sea, "only twenty minutes away." He was reluctant to part with us before the day was over. For once the Rev did not consult his own map. We picked up swimsuits at the hotel, crossed the Ataturk Bridge, passed through Taxim Square which is the center of modern Istanbul, and headed north. The twenty minutes stretched into an hour and a half, punctuated by Jan's comments — "almost there now," and "just a minute more" — and by the complaints of irritated children clutching their swimsuits. So we did not enjoy the vistas of the Bosporus as much as we should have, and when we came at last to Kilyos it was six o'clock and the only access to the beach was through the hotel where guests were dressed for dinner. We photographed an array of tents at the fort on the promontory. Having looked hard across the water in the direction of the Soviet Union, we drove south again, consoling the children with a promise of hamburgs at the Hilton. Jan made no apology for his miscalculations and implied that we had taken a devious route. Had he driven to the Black Sea before? No. But he knew. We rolled up the wide approach to the Hilton in stony silence.

It is not easy for us to imagine how the Turks feel when they see rich Americans, but something of that sensation seized us as we walked past the doorman onto the thick green carpet of the Istanbul Hilton.

"Feel the rugs," breathed Clark.

"Do you think they have a bathroom here we could use?" said Nan wistfully.

Around us swirled elegantly dressed guests ready for Saturday evening cocktails before dinner. To them Istanbul was Turkey and the Hilton was Istanbul. Many of them would see nothing more of the country than this one city. And they would judge the city by short sallies forth from hotel luxury. But let it be confessed that on this Saturday evening we envied the affluence that provided soapy hot baths in private tubs, beds crisply clean and comfortable, and room service bringing up a whole pot of American coffee to drink on a private balcony overlooking the twinkling lights of the Bosporus.

For fifty American cents, paid in *kurush,* of course, we each had a deluxe hamburg and french fries in the Hilton coffee shop. Milk shakes, though thin, cost less than coffee. Dicker blew the paper off his straw and it whizzed past the nose of a paunchy man at the next table. Clearly we were not Hilton caliber.

We left Jan at the Y, politely ignoring his hints to rejoin us the next day. He did not thank us for the day that was ending but he did ask for money. His father had telegraphed money, he said, but he did not want to cash it into Turkish *kurush* because he was leaving by plane on Tuesday for Beirut. We suggested he discuss his problem with the Y staff.

The Rev carried the yellow plastic pail and dishpan from the police station into the Atlas Oteli. Try that at the Hilton. Dicker was sponged clean at the sink because he was sleepy. For the rest of us the Rev paid a quarter each to have the shower at the end of the hall unlocked, and with much coaxing, warm water began to fall from the rusty showerhead over the chipped raised tub. I took two pails of it to wash clothes in the room. Twice the attendant came up with his key and twice the Rev pantomimed him away while the showers were completed. So the room was strung with washing, the whole family was clean for Sunday, and beneath the window "sick music" lulled us to sleep. We would miss that sound when we moved on.

Nan, Clark, and Dicker awoke with diarrhea in the morning. It is said that olive oil cooking does this to the uninitiated. Probably it was the food in the bazaar. Substantial doses of Kao-Resin, recommended by a doctor at home, were not as effective as Uncle Gerry's antibiotic to which we re-

sorted after two days. Our Sunday morning pleasures were further enhanced by David's breakfast discovery of a whole moth in the bottom of the
fig jam, whose amber stuff magnified the insect nicely.

The Dutch embassy chapel, down a street too narrow for cars, is meeting place for the American Community Church which serves Protestants
among the thousand Americans living in Istanbul. The embassies have
moved to Ankara, the new capital. Today there are no Protestant services
conducted in Turkey except on embassy property or at American military
bases. No Christian missionary is allowed to enter Turkey. A few enter as
teachers of English, and we knew of two young men who ingeniously were
teaching English from pages of the Koran and the Bible side by side. But
they were in danger of being expelled from the country for doing so.

How sad that the cradle of the Christian church, the area most saturated
with first-century churches, should be closed today to the Christian message.
Even the sultans, under whom Islam was the official religion, were more
tolerant and allowed Christian colleges like Roberts College in Istanbul to be
founded a hundred years ago. Today no prayer or Bible reading is allowed in
this English-speaking college. Though the modern Turkish state has freed
itself from official connection with Islam, in practice it blocks a Christian
witness more completely than before.

The American pastor preached while peddlers competed with him from
the street. Nan and Dicker stayed in the courtyard to be near the W.C.
The pastor invited us for coffee and he furnished all kinds of information
about the area of the seven churches to whom Christ wrote in the early
chapters of the book of Revelation.

Dinner, preceded by swigs of Kao-Resin for the sick ones, was eaten at
the U.S. Army's NCO Club to which certain non-military Americans like
the Glenns hold passes. Mary and her daughters drove with us. After the
breakfast moth, mashed potatoes and meat and coke and ice cream made a
feast. The Rev was able to cash a traveler's check for dollars when he paid
the bill, a feat Jan would have envied him. Half the banks in Istanbul are
not solvent, Mary explained, a fact which sheds light on why the use of
Turkish money is so circumscribed.

July 1 is Turkish Navy Day. Boats whistled in chorus on the water and
flags flew everywhere. The Galata Bridge was crowded with people as we
drove back to Old Stamboul. Not far from the *oteli* is the blackened column
of Constantine, once a dozen blocks of red porphyry brought from Rome to
support a likeness of Constantine as Apollo on the top. It stood in Constantine's forum, the business center of his day. Fire blackened it, wire
hoops support it, and Constantine-Apollo is long gone from the top. We
also took a look at what is left of the largest cistern of old Constantinople, a
feat of Justinian's day called The Thousand and One Columns.

A large group of European students arrived at the hotel in the evening.

The peace of the place was shattered. One could not even hear the music from the streets. Confused, noisy, laughing, the students were running in the halls for hours and the W.C.'s were hopelessly inadequate. We

wrote letters while the children read from a stack of books loaned overnight by the Glenns. The Rev arranged to have breakfast at 5:30 and Dave showed him how to do a pantomime meaning "without moths."

MANY FERRIES cross the Bosporus. Before seven on Monday morning we were on one that would bring us nearest the highway to Ankara. It was a grey day. Wearing sweaters, we stood at the ferry railing, memorizing the receding shoreline from the Blue Mosque north to the Dolmabahçe Palace and the Rumeli Hisar. Turkish soldiers on the ferry wanted to practice English.

The four-lane, divided highway toward Ankara was strewn with the gory remains of three cows struck by a truck during the night. The truck lay overturned in a field. Our immediate destination was Iznik, the old Nicea, scene of many church councils, the first of which affirmed what was later formulated in the Nicene Creed. To reach Iznik we turned off the highway after fifteen miles to see whether there was room for us on the Kartal-to-Yalova ferry which shortens the distance by crossing a part of the Marmara. Glenns had warned us that the morning ferry carried only six cars and a few trucks, but there was room for us and we waited only twenty minutes. A group of men waited under a tree. One held a small string of yellow beads in his hands. Hands behind his back, he kept working the beads as he talked and listened. "Worry beads" these are called, just the thing to keep your hands busy, especially if you are a good Moslem who does not smoke. We bought a little string for the Rev though he has not found much time to cultivate them.

Fish leaped out of the water ahead of the ferry on the ninety-minute crossing. We sorted out literature for the day's adventures which we hoped would end in Akhisar, the old Thyatira. As for lodging, we would see. The Glenns warned us that no matter how desolate an area, curious people would appear from nowhere to watch for hours until we moved on. In Asian Turkey and the Middle East we saw no organized camping.

By taking the Kartal-Yalova ferry we had avoided a ninety-mile drive around through Izmit, the old Nicomedia, capital of Bithynian kings and of the Roman emperor Diocletian. Nicomedia always overshadowed Nicea and still does because it is on the main road to Ankara while Nicea is reached over twenty-six miles of bad road along the north shore of Iznik Lake. The ancient name was Lake Ascania and it opened via a navigable river into the Marmara, making Nicea accessible by water when Constantine called a council to settle the matter of Christ's divinity — in what sense is Christ God? The emperor in gold and purple welcomed three hundred bishops who assembled in the imperial palace in Nicea on May 20, A.D. 325. Over two thousand ecclesiastics arrived in the city for the council which lasted two months. Temporarily the Athanasians won out and Christ was declared "of one essence with the father" to the consternation of the Arians whose success came later. Constantine declared that "the decision of three hundred bishops must be considered none other than the judgment of God." The judgment of God was perhaps more obvious later in the same year when an earthquake toppled the city.

One must leave the good road south to Bursa at Orhangazi to reach Iznik at the eastern end of the lake. Women in baggy black pantaloons were working in tomato fields. This working costume is the same throughout the Middle East. The crotch of the garment hangs down to the knees and the whole is made of voluminous folds of material which facilitates donkey-riding, roadside squatting, as well as harder work in the fields. Ataturk notwithstanding, the women held part of their headdresses across their faces as we passed. We edged through a herd of cows, photographed a village especially full of storks' nests, and crossed a stream on its dry bed because the bridge was blocked off.

Ahead lay what is left of Nicea. The Greek general Lysimachus, who ruled Pergamum, named the city for his wife when he conquered this part of Asia. Nicea used to be an exact square with a gate in each side. Earthquake, Crusaders, and Turks have had their turns at laying it waste. The potters, who made marvelous tiles of flowers in green, blue, and to-mato-red colors, moved to Istanbul.

A road of fine deep dust leads through triple gates in the three walls around the town. The gates on the west are the Istanbul Gates, on the lake the Roman Gates, and on the east through which we departed the Yenesehir Gates. The outermost gates and wall were Roman, from the third and fourth centuries. There were remnants of a frieze on top of the arch. Next come the Byzantine and Seljuk walls with their gates. In the center of Iznik is the ruin of the Saint Sophia church where the seventh ecumenical council was held in A.D. 786 under the empress Irene. A stork sat on the mosaic floor remnant.

"The glory has departed" is an Old Testament phrase that fits many Biblical or Christian sites in Turkey. Kipling said it, too. "The captains and the kings depart. . . ." Nicea, now Iznik, is like that. A favorite slide of the city is one taken from the high hill to the east from which ones looks down on the whole area — the blue lake, the walls and gates blurred to intactness by distance. The singing words of the little creed come back, "God of God, Light of Light, very God of very God. . . ." Old disputes, wranglings, and excommunications disappear as the town in which they centered has also disintegrated. But the creed remains, a jewel of truth unaffected by the ravages of time.

86

RASPBERRY JAM DOES A LOT for fresh bread, especially when it is served in a field of cornflowers. The lunch setting was more attractive than what we saw in Bursa, a good-sized city which Hannibal of Carthage made famous by hiding there from his Roman enemies and then committing suicide to avoid falling into their hands. Tourist folders tell how emperors came to Bursa to enjoy the mineral springs and how modern skiers fly in from Istanbul to enjoy the slopes of Uludag, the mountain behind the city. We bought stamps and left, following the red line on the map west to Karacabey and then south to Balikesir.

At Balikesir we saw the first camel trains, one resting at the fountain, another coming single file into town, led by a donkey. Camels are always led by donkeys. The little wooden camel trains sold for souvenirs have a donkey as the lead animal. Months later, at home, we found a library book which told about an old camel whose dying wish was to take a few steps on his own without some dumb donkey pulling him along. It is at Balikesir, by the way, that one can go west 120 miles to the site of Troy which is on the coast not far south of the entrance to the Dardanelles.

Before Sindirgi we cooked supper at a wayside spring where an open cement shelter had been erected for travelers and herdsmen. There are quite a few of these. This one looked out over the road up which we had come and into a broad valley. It was five o'clock, end of the day's work, a magic time in the countryside with sun lying golden on everything and a breeze announcing the evening. While we set up the stove and prepared food, a farmer brought his oxen to drink from the water trough. Beneath the dirt his wagon was decorated in red and blue.

We all washed in the cool water before a stew-and-vegetable dinner with applesauce, bread, and coffee. The blue car of men who had been on the Kartal-Yalova ferry with us came puffing up the road. From every window the men waved and shouted. They nodded to each other, assuming with satisfaction that we had found the way to Balikesir from the directions they had given on the ferry. We were in no hurry. The children played, I restored a button to Clark's green Banlon shirt, we drank another cup of coffee and talked. About Constantine and the court intrigues that helped decide whether Arius' or Athanasius' doctrine of Christ would receive official sanction. About the mixed blessing it was for Christianity to become the official religion of the empire. At home we rarely had time to talk like this.

The wooded hill country approaching Akhisar, the old Thyatira, tempted us to camp, but we were uncertain about theft and unpredictable visitors. Perhaps we were too cautious. We made the long descent from the hills into the town, and Nancy read aloud Christ's letter to Thyatira, recorded in the second chapter of Revelation.

Dr. William Ramsay, a nineteenth-century authority on Asia Minor, liked to say that the seven churches to which Christ sent letters via the apostle John on Patmos were postal centers on a circular route, each city a Christian center in western Asia Minor. A map will show that the seven do lie in a circle, though an elongated one from northwest to southeast. The circle line began at Ephesus on the Aegean coast and moved north to the port of Smyrna, now Izmir, again north and a little east and inland to Pergamum. Then it rounded down to Thyatira, continued south to Sardis, and broadened southwest to Philadelphia and Laodicea, the last of which was due east of Ephesus about 110 miles inland.

We were able to visit six of the seven sites, omitting Philadelphia. Only Smyrna and Thyatira are alive today as cities, though with new names. It should not be surprising that Christ, who taught in parables and figures which the common people understood, would have written in the same

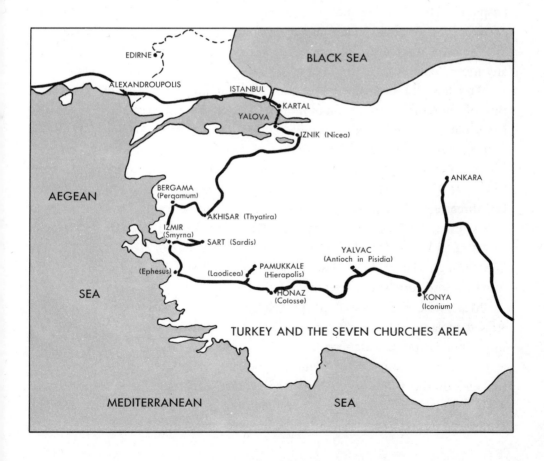

TURKEY AND THE SEVEN CHURCHES AREA

way to the seven churches. His letters speak of things distinctive to each city or area. To Laodicea he wrote of lukewarm water, to Sardis about a thief in the night, to Thyatira about broken earthen pots, to Smyrna about a crown of life, and to Pergamum about a white stone. This linking of site and Scripture was for us the fascinating and impressive thing about the area of the seven churches.

Twilight coming into Akhisar. Everything is nondescript grey and beige, the sky, the streets of hard-packed clay, the colorless buildings. There is time to locate the hospital before we think about where to sleep. On the hospital grounds is an old stone with the only remaining reference to Thyatira.

"Opital?" the Rev inquires of boys who come eagerly to the car. It takes a few minutes to communicate that we would like a boy to show us the way, no, not all the boys, no room, just one boy and we will bring him back at once. So one boy is climbing into the second seat when from the dark interior of a shop a man rushes out, yanks the boy from the car, and with his free arm gestures us on. We cannot understand his torrent of words but the fear and mistrust on his face are plain. He has just rescued his son from foreigners disappearing into the night in a high-powered car. Several by-standers try to reassure the father. Two men trace in the air the way to the hospital. The Rev reaches out a reassuring hand and says, *"Teşekkür ederim."* To the back seats he says, "Smile, children, smile and wave."

"So why does he think we were gonna steal his boy? We don't need any more." Em.

The hospital is protected by a high wall and a padlocked iron gate. But the welcome here is unanimous. Alerted by the wizened gatekeeper, every nurse and able-bodied patient comes out into the courtyard. Here are four gnarled cypress trees, green grass, and a reflecting pool with three hand-carved sailboats resting in it. At the head of the pool is the stone we want to see. It is a sarcophagus, really, with ivy growing out of the top. Rectangu-lar, three feet high, it has been whitewashed except for the six lines of old Greek inscription on one side. The Rev searches the lines for the name Thyatira. He wants one picture. "Look for the circle, the *theta,* with the line through the middle, that stands for the TH," he says to Dave and Clark, whose turn it is to get out of the redbus here.

Meanwhile the hospital people gather, barefoot patients in gowns and striped pajamas, five nurses, two orderlies, trim in white uniforms. Silently they ring the pool, watching the word search like an audience in suspense at a drama. A murmur of pleasure goes up when we find the word near the end of the third line. After the picture everyone presses forward to shake hands. Clark gets flash equipment from the car to photograph the group and reports that the girls and Dicker are suffocating, besieged by a crowd of children against whose curious hands they have locked all the redbus doors and windows.

The friendly people pose around the sarcophagus. *Evet, evet,* we will send you a copy. A nurse writes the address in my notebook: *Umit Tosun, Devlet Hastunesis, Hemsire, Akhisar.*

Is there a *oteli in Akhisar? Evet, evet,* nod the nurses and the gatekeeper. A good *oteli?* A very good one, they gesture.

The gatekeeper is not afraid to ride with us. He wears a white sailing cap and speaks a very few words of German. At the four corners where we nearly abducted the boy, we turn into a side street and stop at one of the nondescript buildings.

"Not here, dad, puleeze," comes the muted chorus from the rear seats.

"Might be something to remember," says the Rev and disappears with the gatekeeper into the doorway of the Sehir Oteli.

While we wait, a wooden-wheeled wagon jolts to a stop at the hotel. The pale glow of a dangling streetlight shows a woman sitting crosslegged in the wagon. The man fastens the reins and goes into the hotel. The woman is obviously in hard labor. She retches and rocks and pounds the wagon with her fists. As a pain seizes her, she grips the low sides of the wagon frantically. The children watch, wide-eyed.

"Mom, is she crazy?" they whisper.

I want desperately to help, to drive her to the hospital. But I cannot speak her language and maybe she does not want to go there and I am not a nurse and perhaps she will not trust me or she will deliver in the redbus. So I am watching, too, helpless. The man comes out. He speaks to the woman, slaps the donkey, and the wagon goes rattling off into the darkness.

The Rev comes out, too, to usher us up a wooden stairway into two second-floor rooms. Four single beds in one, three in the other, and each bed puffy with a feather-filled comforter of rough cotton. No sheets. A rough unbleached covering is sewn over each mattress. How often do they unsew and change these? No towels, dressers, chairs, or mirrors.

Em, the last to suffer diarrhea, needs sudden help and we are hurrying across the wide inner hall to the unmarked bathroom door when total darkness envelops us. The town's electricity has failed. But Emily cannot wait. We feel our way back to the room, Clark fishes out his pencil-sized flashlight, and we set out again, guided by a faint beam the size of a pencil point. As we reach the bathroom door, it opens from within and a bulky figure, unmistakably male, emerges. Good thing the darkness delayed us! In we go, crisscrossing the little cubicle with our light until we find the single accommodation level with the floor. Afterward we find the sink and the little metal pitcher to be filled and used for flushing. There is even a bar of grainy soap. But no lock on the door.

"Do you know how much this is costing us?" asks the Rev sleepily from beneath his puffy coverlet. "Two dollars and twenty cents for the seven of us. Fantastic. We better come back again."

But I am not thinking about bargains. Or even about bathrooms. I am wondering where the woman in the wagon had her baby.

A rare thunderstorm wakens us at 6:30. The town has been busy much earlier. A boy goes out to get our breakfast of *çay* and rolls, a safe menu, assuming that the water for the tea has been boiled. The *çay* comes in little fluted glasses carried on a round tray which is suspended with slender chains from a brass ring by which the boy carries the whole apparatus. The doughnut-shaped rolls are flat, dry, saltless. The Rev eats his. Naturally. The other rolls go into the travel purse to be improved with raspberry jam later. Fifteen cents buys breakfast.

One by one we *teşekkür ederim* the manager downstairs and he pats the children's heads. *"Güle, güle,"* he calls from the doorway as we climb into the redbus washed clean by the rain.

No one would guess, seeing the town today, that Thyatira had more trade guilds than any other city in Asia Minor. It was at peak prosperity when the book of Revelation was written. The people of Thyatira worshiped Apollo, the sun god. To this church Christ writes, "The words of the Son of God, who has eyes like a flame of fire, and whose feet are like burnished bronze." Picture that in contrast to Apollo! In those days Thyatira was known for its fabrics. Lydia on the river bank in Philippi was a seller of purple from Thyatira. The city was also known for its bronze and pottery. "And he shall rule them with a rod of iron," writes Jesus to this church about those who are faithful to him, "as when earthen pots are broken in pieces. . . ."

We want to buy a piece of pottery here. The shops are open to the street. A crowd of men, thirty maybe, gathers around while we choose a glazed red clay bowl with white and green design. It costs a nickel's worth of *kurush* and the shopkeeper is proud to pose for a picture.

Meanwhile no woman is in sight. They are on the road that leads to the river, carrying their wash in wicker baskets, their heads and shoulders swathed in light-colored cloths and a loose long-sleeved black garment over their colored pantaloons. A few are walking. Most of them are sitting in a red wagon hitched to a red tractor, the taxi to the river bank.

The road toward Bergama, the old Pergamum, is pleasant and winding. The morning air is still cool. Wagons on the road are nicely painted but all the women in them veil their faces as we pass. Cattle herds also use the road, all of it. Dicker suggests singing "Yankee Doodle" for morning devotions and when we have ended them on this light note, the rear right tire goes flat, punctured by one of many nails that drop from wooden wagons.

Some boys and a man squat close by to watch the tire changing. They finger the tools. The women walking on the road carry wooden hoes and large sifters to shake chaff from wheat. All cover their faces as they pass, except one. She comes to me under a tree, face open, smiling, takes my proffered hand and keeps holding it in hers.

"*Merhaba*," I say and can think of nothing else. But we understand each other, we look into each other's eyes and we are friends. She welcomes me to her countryside and I show her my children. When she leaves she waves, and before she disappears from view she turns and waves again. We are hoping for no more flat tires before this one can be repaired in Izmir where we will sleep overnight.

Beyond Kirkagac there are army maneuvers and then another cattle herd monopolizing the road. In Soma a shy boy drives a donkey with two wicker baskets of bread strapped across its back. The boy does not want gum, he does not want his picture taken, he hits the donkey and scurries away. The two gas stations in Soma expect gas next week. So the Rev pours in the reserve two gallons. The next town has a bank and a post office but no gas station. "*Yok*" seems to be the quick way to say, "No, there is none."

In the open country two boys in old suit coats are hauling water from a crude well. They are nonplussed when the Rev offers them Chiclets. He puts one in his own mouth, chews heartily, rubs his stomach and nods his head to express taste satisfaction, but they are unconvinced. Holding the Chiclets in their hands, they stare impassively after us when we leave.

A<small>ND TO THE ANGEL</small> of the church in Pergamum write, . . . I know where you dwell, where Satan's throne is; you hold fast my name and you did not deny my faith even in the days of Antipas my witness, my faithful one, who was killed among you, where Satan dwells. . . ."

Clark is reading and we are sitting on the ruins of Pergamum's famous library. It was once full of priceless parchments in this city where parchment was invented and given its name, *Pergamena charta*. From this library Mark Antony sent two hundred thousand parchments to Cleopatra after fire destroyed the library in Alexandria.

There is no one else in the ruins of this "Athens of Asia," no one except a watchman in a wooden tower at the top of the acropolis and another man who appeared from nowhere to collect fifty *kurush* for parking. The sky is as grey as the stones. But the view from this solitary mountain is wide, fifteen miles of green and gold plain stretching out to the Aegean.

In this fortress off the main trade routes Lysimachus, one of Alexander's generals, left nine thousand talents of gold, a mere ten million dollars' worth. The eunuch Philaeterus, entrusted with the money, rebelled against his absent master and set up his own kingdom, ruled by the Attalid dynasty for 150 years until 133 B.C. These were the years of Pergamum's glory,

> On a tall mountain, citied to the top,
> Crowded with culture.

In these years the steepest amphitheater in the world was carved into one of the three sheer sides of the mountain. On the gradual southern slope large terraces were laid out and the visitor could walk the road up from one terrace to the next, astounded at the temples, statues, and buildings on every level. On one of the terraces, facing the sea, stood the imposing Zeus altar. It was a gigantic square and one of its sculptured walls featured a carved frieze four hundred feet long, depicting the battle of the gods and the Titans.

"But who had the city when Revelation was written?" asks Dave.

The Romans had it then. Attalus III bequeathed the Kingdom of Pergamum to Rome on his deathbed and Rome kept it four hundred years. For a while Pergamum was greater than Ephesus and it was capital of the Roman province called Asia. A hundred sixty thousand people lived here. Take the diagram and let's explore. We're here now, at the library, and we came in the gate of the First Wall, the one farthest up the mountain.

This must be the Athena temple. She was protecting goddess of the city. There is still a bench and bucket at the sacred spring in the ruins. On to the amphitheater — eighty rows of circular stone rows to hold fifteen thousand people. The children find a little tunnel that descends to the stage of the theater. Beyond the amphitheater is the Zeus altar area. You can see from the steps that it was square. Two old trees shade what is left of it. The frieze was carried off in pieces to Berlin by German archaeologists. This was perhaps the Satan's throne of which Jesus wrote. Or he could have meant the cult of emperor worship because this was the first city in the Roman Empire to go all out for worshiping the emperor as a god.

What about the white stone and the hidden manna? Well, no one is sure, but it is very possible that the rich and powerful people of the city had private guilds and societies for which the entrance token at parties was a precious stone. "Don't worry," says Jesus, "my salvation is like a precious white stone, white for purity, with your name on it, and hidden manna much better than all the fancy pagan feasts." Jesus is warning them not to think that they can take in all the pagan festivities and still be Christians. That's what the verse about Balaam and the Nicolaitans means. And then he promises that what he has for them is much better than what they find in Pergamum.

Farther down the mountain is another cluster of ruins — what is left of a Demeter temple, the sport and culture center with gymnasium, baths, art gallery, and the *odeum,* a roofed theater to seat a thousand people. There are some clear inscriptions on the stones here, even though the best of everything has been taken to Berlin, where it is now behind the wall in a museum on Museum Island.

A man wearing a beret appears, speaking good German because he has helped the German archaeologists. One of them is still in residence. We leave through the gate of the Third Wall, past piles of cannon balls from Seljuk times. It is just noon. From the largest mosque in the modern city below comes the call to prayer. But there is no *mussein* to wail it. Bergama is progressive and uses a recording played through a loud speaker on one of the minarets.

The man in the beret wants to show us some things. First the Basilica Serapeion whose ruins stand over the Selinos River, as many early churches stood at a water source.

"Begun first century after Christ, time of Hadrian," says the beret man in German. That Hadrian was a traveling emperor. He walked through most of his empire, leaving behind, as Muller says, a "trail of new temples, gateways, granaries, bridges, statues, games, and festivals," all named for himself. This Pergamum basilica has been called the largest in Asia Minor, one of seven supposedly established by the apostle John. Hadrian did not build it, but he tried to rename it for the Egyptian god Serapis. For centuries it was a great Christian center, named for the apostle. All attempts to turn it into a mosque failed. The minarets kept falling down. So the Turks have done the next best thing. They leave it in ruins and give it the Serapis name again.

It is raining, dismal. Ruins, mud, and sky are a shiny wet monotony. The beret man is disappointed that we will not stay longer in the small museum and at the Asclepion, the ancient medical center dedicated to Aesculapius and built around a sacred spring a few miles from Pergamum. "In the name of the gods, death is forbidden to enter," proclaimed the entrance inscription for the seven hundred years that men came here for healing. Marcus Aurelius came to cure his lung troubles, Caracalla to soothe his nerves. In the sacred cellar dreams were induced. A library provided books, a theater drama, and sacred ponds, fountains, temples, and potions played their part. Near today's entrance is a pillar base with the snake symbol of Aesculapius repeated on it. American army doctors wear this sign on their uniforms — a snake twined around a staff. Beyond the long row of north-porch pillars is the compact little amphitheater restored and used each year in May.

Through big puddles we set out for Manisa and Turgutlu, beyond which lie Sart and the Sardis excavations.

People jump up from the roadside and gesture for us to stop. They shake their fists angrily when we near without slacking our pace and then, seeing us at close range, they laugh and wave. Finally we realize that we are being mistaken for a *dolmus,* a shared taxi. Old trucks and cars crisscross the back country of Turkey, picking up and letting off people wherever they are and want to go. The same system exists in Puerto Rico and other places. The word *dolmus* means "full," the car leaves when it is full and passengers share the cost of the ride. True, the redbus is as dirty as a *dolmus* and indistinguishable at a distance.

Dicker is obsessed by ruins. "There's some," he shouts when he sees a pile of stones. In late afternoon we come to the ruins of Sardis. The rain does not enhance this Paris of the ancient world. It looks far less glamorous than the *Christian Science Monitor* report of findings by a Cornell University team. Where is the fifty-foot-wide marble street of fabulous King Croesus?

The ruins lie on both sides of the road. On the north are the newer excavations, the street, Roman gymnasium, and other mounds waiting their turn. On the south are the temple pillars which prompted the first excavations in 1910-14, the acropolis, and the fenced-in living quarters of the American excavation team. The working day is over. Natives of the area, for whom American excavations mean as much as gold did to Croesus, are scattering in all directions to go home. At the living enclosure a professor leans against the gate, pipe in hand, happy to discuss what his team is trying to do.

The big temple pillars were protruding halfway out of the ground, he explains, and the first excavation centered here. This was the temple of Cybele-Artemis, though it had some crosses carved into its stones by Christians who used it later. Behind the pillars, a half hour's walk, rises the Sardis acropolis where the original city stood. It has been largely washed away over the centuries. A lone student goes up every day to sift and explore on the top of the acropolis but he has found little, a few bits dating back to the seventh century before Christ, but nothing significant.

What was the story the Istanbul pastor told us about the acropolis of Sardis?

King Croesus, in his passionate devotion to Greek culture, helped rebuild the Artemis-Diana temple at Ephesus and kept all the Greek oracles well supplied with gold and treasures. Unfortunately, the Delphi oracle did not reward his generosity with clear advice. That oracle had a reputation for ambiguity — hence the meaning of the modern phrase, "a Delphic utterance."

King Croesus inquired of the Delphi oracle whether he should fight against King Cyrus of the Persians. The oracle replied that if he did, a great kingdom would fall. (Cyrus, you know, ruled in the time of Daniel and Esther, and Daniel predicted the later Persian defeat by Alexander the Great, the "he-goat from the west.") Croesus confidently provoked Cyrus by attacking him, and when the battle was indecisive, Croesus retreated to his capital at Sardis. Here Cyrus attacked with Croesus holed up on his impregnable acropolis.

One night, while the Persian army lay in the plain around the acropolis, a soldier dropped his helmet accidentally from the top. He retrieved it by a secret trail down the rocky cliffs. Cyrus' sentries marked the way and used it to assault the Lydians in their fortress. This was 546 before Christ.

And so, says the story, this defeat of Croesus and his kingdom has its echo in the words of Christ written six hundred years later. "If you will not awake, I will come like a thief, and you will not know at what hour I will come upon you." The people of Sardis knew what it was to be taken unawares, which is what history books record more prosaically about Cyrus' assault — that he found entry into the city without warning and took it.

Sardis, known for luxury and loose living, had begun to dwindle and decay when John was writing on Patmos. Seemingly the church there was in a similar state. "You have the name of being alive," says Christ, "and you are dead."

T HE RAIN SLOWED to a drizzle. It did not hamper supper at a wayside spring — hash with a can of corn mixed through it, peaches, bread, coffee. Izmir was forty miles away, seen first as a sea of tiny lights on two hillsides and in the plain, with reflections in the water on the shoreline.

On the lower square of the city we paid five dollars for two bedrooms with bath in the Hotel Ginar. The Rev took the tire to be fixed and kept as souvenir the big curved nail that came from it. While he waited with the boys, the daily bus from Istanbul came snorting in. People and taxis converged, men screamed prices and jostled to serve the dusty passengers alighting from the bus.

"You'd never know it was Turkey," said Nan the next morning as we drove through the streets of Izmir. There are many American service families here, and they have brought American cars with them. New buildings, unveiled women, and Western clothes make Izmir the most Western-looking of Turkish cities. What a lop-sided picture of the country one would get by visiting only here.

The Turkish ship on which we planned to return from Haifa to Istanbul was scheduled to dock a day in Izmir harbor. We decided to save exploring the *agora* and museum for that day, and to drive on south to the ruins of Ephesus at Selçùk. A little boy shared our roadside breakfast. Across the road shyer children stood at a well where men led camels to drink. An old couple riding donkeys led their single camel from the road onto a route over which caravans have traveled for centuries. In the fields men as well as women had their heads wrapped against the sun. They had built brush shelters for shady rest or overnight sleeping during the harvest. As we rode, Dicker requested that we sing the "Star-Spangled Banner," though none of us was aware then that it was the Fourth of July.

What Bible chapter about Ephesus shall we read? Acts 19 tells about Paul's three-year stay there on his third missionary journey. "Read about the riot," urges Clark, "when the silversmiths got mad because their image business was going to pot."

Much New Testament history is connected with Ephesus. John was bishop in Ephesus in the latter part of the first century and died here. In temporary exile on Patmos he wrote the book of Revelation. Perhaps his gospel and three small epistles were written at Ephesus. Tradition tells us that in the last years of his life he was carried to the church for worship and his admonition was always the same, "Little children, love one another."

Paul's missionary travels are bound up with Ephesus. His ministry here was the longest that he served anywhere and during these years he wrote First Corinthians. Paul brought Aquila and Priscilla with him to Ephesus from Corinth on his second journey and they stayed in Ephesus. Apollos profited from their instruction here and later became pastor in Corinth. Ephesians was written by Paul during his first imprisonment in Rome. Titus may have been written from Ephesus around 65 after Christ, between the two imprisonments. And Timothy, while he served as pastor in Ephesus, received the two letters Paul wrote him.

Ephesus is one of the seven churches of Christ's letters in Revelation. And legend says Luke too is buried here. A map of the ruins indicates the "so-called tomb of Saint Luke" is located southeast of the main city remnants. Some say that Onesimus, the slave of Philemon, became bishop of Ephesus and was the first publisher of Paul's collected letters in 110 after Christ. Certainly no Asia Minor city has more New Testament history and record attached to it.

Ephesus has secular connections, too. Homer in his epic poem, the *Iliad,* compares the Greek assault on Troy to the geese, cranes, and swans flying "on the Asian mead by Kaystrios' stream," meaning the meadow along the Cayster River at Ephesus. Homer is dated at about 850 B.C. and Peter Bamm in *Early Sites of Christianity* claims that thus, eventually, the province and then the continent of Asia got its name. The early Greek philosopher Heraclitus, famous around 513 B.C. and remembered for his thesis that fire was the first principle of all things, was born and lived in Ephesus.

After Pergamum in the rain, Ephesus marbles glowed in sunshine under a blue sky. We began at the Basilica of Saint John, which is nearest the village of Selçùk whose houses are partly built with stone from the Ephesus ruins. The apostle is buried beneath the basilica, it is claimed, and he well may be. The first chapel built over the spot was already there when Justinian built a basilica five hundred feet long in the sixth century. This cruciform church is being beautifully restored today, thanks to contributions from the Ephesus Society of Lima, Ohio. Most things that get done at sites in Turkey are accomplished with American money.

Two turbaned men were digging carefully around a waist-high water pot in order to excavate it intact. Other Turkish workmen were hoisting pieces of pillar with the help of a tall tripod and the direction of an American supervisor. The marble floor over the tomb area was completed first. In the center of it is a sealed grillwork covering the narrow staircase that leads beneath. People of the Middle Ages believed that dust from this tomb cured all illnesses. On loose blocks of old marble one can find intricate cross designs. The basilica will be a magnificent reconstruction when it is finished. John would not have believed it possible when he sat in lonely exile on Patmos taking dictation from the Lord. Or perhaps he would not have cared, since the dazzling beauties of the city eternal were displayed in vision before him.

Behind the basilica is an old castle and below it on a slope the early mosque Isabey or Bey-Djami, to neither of which we paid much attention. We were looking for the site of the Diana temple, one of the seven wonders of the ancient world.

In 1863 archaeologists went searching for this temple. It took them six years to find it, buried in a malarial swamp a mile northeast of the main city ruins. We came to the site over a path worn through a farmer's field. The swamp is a giant rectangle, the same shape as the original temple and platform. Random pieces of marble protrude from the swamp grass and stagnant water.

Shut your eyes and try to imagine what used to be here, the Rev told us. A temple 350 feet long, four times bigger than the Parthenon in Athens. It stood thirteen steps up from a marble platform which was much larger. The temple had a hundred pillars, each sixty feet tall. Inside was an altar twenty feet square, and behind the altar stood the gold-ivory statue of Diana, who was worshiped as a fertility goddess.

"What's fertility, dad?"

For a long time the harbor came right to the edge of the temple platform and the eyes of every sailor who came to port were dazzled. Stories about Diana and her temple were carried by the caravans whose routes began in Ephesus and ended in Persia.

People came from all over the ancient world to worship. They brought their money and treasures to Diana for safekeeping, paying her to keep them, in contrast to today's banking system. The worshipers bought small silver statues of Diana and her temple.

Strangely, the people of Ephesus were never very brave or ready to fight their enemies. Instead the enemies were so awed by the temple and by Diana that they helped to support her worship while the Ephesians went right on enjoying their pleasures and their goddess, no matter who ruled them. Croesus, the gold king of Sardis, gave money and new columns when he captured Ephesus. Alexander the Great, who was born in 356 B.C.

on the same day that Diana's temple was burned by a madman, offered to complete the rebuilding when he came to Ephesus. And remember what the town clerk said when the people rioted and rushed to the amphitheater because the silversmiths stirred them up against Paul's preaching. The clerk told the people, "You don't have to be upset. Everyone knows that the city of Ephesus is temple keeper for the great Artemis and the sacred stone that fell from the sky." Was it a meteorite perhaps that gave rise to this legend?

Ephesus was prosperous already a thousand years before Christ when David fought the Philistines. The city was important long before Athens, and its temple was a great wonder. The many-breasted Diana was a combination produced by superimposing the Greek virgin goddess Artemis on the primitive mother goddess of Asia Minor, object of a fertility cult. And so Diana-Artemis was both virgin and mother to her worshipers. Her temple, in one form or another, lasted a thousand years until the Goths completely destroyed it 262 years after Christ. Today there are pillars of this temple in the Hagia Sophia and several marble slabs from it in Saint Catharine's church at Mount Sinai. Parts of columns also may be seen at the British Museum in London.

And what is left in Ephesus of this great wonder? Frogs croaking in a stagnant pond dotted with marble chunks. A mule wandered over and a little boy appeared with a handful of coins to sell. We walked back through the farmer's field to go to the ruins of the main city.

These are beautiful ruins. The Austrians excavated here at the turn of the century and the Turks take good care of the site so that it does not become overgrown and lost.

The marble way runs wide and gleaming past the amphitheater to the Coressos Gate. On either side of it are pillars and inscriptions and marked ruins. There is the library of Celsus, built by the Roman governor of the province as a memorial to his father. At the brothel wandered a little dog the color of the marble and he and Em sat down to become friends. The main street turns and climbs toward the Odeon where it becomes narrower. It passes the temple of Hadrian with delicate carvings about its arched entrance. A Turkish doctor discussed with us in German the meaning of Greek carvings on two blocks of marble. One showed the snake symbol of Aesculapius and the other some scenes of healing. Perhaps this was a healing shrine. The children found the word *Ephesion* on a marble piece, the PH a circle with a line through it, the line from top to bottom, not from side to side as in the TH of Thyatira.

We had climbed high enough in the ruins to approach the enormous amphitheater from the rear, where the topmost rows began. The theater is on the western slope of Mount Pion, which the Turks call Bulbul Dag, in the center of the city. It seated twenty-five to fifty thousand people in Paul's day when the city population was nearly a third of a million. Sitting in the dry grass where the top rows had been, we looked over the city, the valley, the temple-swamp, and the silted-up harbor. The Cayster River flows sluggishly toward the Mediterranean, now five miles away. On what had been the theater stage, men were cutting grass and tying it in bundles.

The Arkadiane, a marble street which led to the old harbor, is less intact but plainly visible from the top of the amphitheater. It was thirty-six feet wide, lined with colonnades and beautiful shops. Now the harbor area is green and marshy, but in Paul's day he landed here from Corinth for a brief stay at the end of his second missionary journey.

On his third journey, Paul stayed longer in Ephesus. For three years he was a familiar figure in the marble streets. In Athens one taught in the market place. In Ephesus teaching was done in schools, and so Paul taught in the school of Tyrannus. Acts 19 tells this story. Paul did many miracles here, too, "extraordinary miracles," so that the practice of magic arts was overshadowed by what the Lord did, and books of magic worth fifty thousand pieces of silver were burned by those who renounced their evil practices to believe on "the name of the Lord Jesus." There was a great transformation in the city of Diana. Demetrius, in stirring up the crowd, said, "And you see and hear that not only at Ephesus but almost throughout all Asia this Paul has persuaded and turned away a considerable company of people, saying that gods made with hands are not gods. And there is danger not only that this trade of ours may come into disrepute but also that the temple of the great goddess Artemis may count for nothing, and that she may even be deposed from her magnificence, she whom all Asia and the world worship."

Another woman has replaced Diana at Ephesus today. Mary, the mother of Jesus, might be called the modern goddess of the city. The fertility goddess who fell from heaven has given way to the virgin assumed bodily into heaven. Five miles up on the mountain called Ala Dag is a small stone shrine at the site where Mary, it is claimed, lived while John was in Ephesus. We know that John was in Ephesus. We do not know where Mary was. There is no Biblical mention of her after Acts 1, which says she waited and prayed with the disciples in Jerusalem following Christ's ascension. Paul makes no reference to Mary. No one did, in fact, for at least three hundred years. Was it perhaps the Council of Nicea which brought the question of Mary's status to the fore? If Christ is fully and completely God, then what of his mother? Was she the mother of his divine nature also?

The shrine to Mary on the Ala Dag had its origin in a nun's vision. Anna Katharine Emmerich had received revelation, she said, about a house and tomb of Mary in Ephesus. Two priests from Smyrna made a trip there in 1891 and discovered in a heavy forest near the top of the mountain the ruin of a little church that was surprisingly like the vision. Archaeologists judged the ruin to be of a fourth-century house built over ruins that were first-century. Peasants of the area, Greek Orthodox by faith, confirmed the findings by the name they had given it, Panaja Kapoulü, "the most holy of all." This is the basis for today's mountain shrine to Mary.

A church council in Ephesus had something to say about Mary in A.D. 431. The council was a rather rough affair in which one bishop died three days after being kicked in the stomach by another. It was called the "Robber Council," because one group, headed by bishops Memnon of Ephesus and Cyril of Alexandria, decided to begin the council before the arrival of the opposing group, led by bishops John of Antioch and Nestorius of Constantinople. The first group excommunicated Nestorius before his group arrived. The second group, upon arrival, met separately and excommunicated their opponents, the bishops of Ephesus and Alexandria.

At issue was the question of Christ's incarnation. Nestorius said that Christ, being God, could not be born of a human mother, and he stressed the separation of Christ's manhood and Godhead, so that Mary was to be regarded as mother of Christ, *Christokos,* but not of God, *Theotokos.* Cyril, though unscrupulous in his intrigues, defended the historic position that the two natures of Christ were united in one person, and that the Logos took human nature to himself in Mary's womb. This made her *Theotokos,* mother of God, opening the way for later Roman Church claims of Mary's sinlessness and bodily assumption, which in our day is leading toward the claim that Mary is co-mediatrix with the Son of God.

Both Nestorius and Cyril had large followings. Cyril's group won out at the Ephesus council but the outlawed Nestorians established themselves strongly in Persia and Arabia and from there spread even into China in the seventh century. The ruins of the "double church" of Mary where the council was held lie beside the Byzantine wall west of the city site. A group of boys pursued us there, pushing each other to be the first to force coins into the Rev's hand.

August 15 is the date assigned for the celebration of Mary's bodily assumption into heaven. On the Sunday following this date the archbishop of Izmir leads a procession up the Ala Dag to celebrate mass at the white altar in the rough brick shrine.

August 15 was also the date of the annual celebration for Diana-Artemis. She had a procession, too, and her statue was carried into Ephesus through one city gate and returned to her temple through another. It was the recorded route of this procession that led archaeologists to the site of her temple.

Intriguing it is that when the virgin mother of Christianity took over from the mother-virgin Diana, the day of annual procession remained the same. Change the name, clothe the goddess, but keep the procession and the people will be satisfied.

Or was this pure coincidence separated by centuries?

CLOSE TOGETHER in the Lycus River Valley lie three churches mentioned in the book of Colossians. One is Laodicea, the lukewarm church to whom a letter was directed via Revelation 2. Another is Colosse itself, which Paul never visited, though he wrote a letter from prison in Rome to the church in this city. "Remember my fetters," he writes in Colossians 4:18. Colosse is on the same side of the valley as Laodicea.

Across the valley, about five miles away, is the third and least-known city, Hierapolis, most interesting of the three today. It is at the modern Pamukkale, which means "cotton castle," the name given to the spectacular lime cliffs here. Hierapolis is mentioned in Colossians 4:13. Speaking about a pastor named Epaphras, Paul says, "For I bear him witness that he has worked hard for you and for those in Laodicea and in Hierapolis." In five other places Paul speaks of Laodicea, suggesting that the church here and in Colosse exchange letters he had written to each of them.

Hierapolis also has a legend attached to it. Finegan relates that about two hundred years after Christ two churchmen were discussing which places were important as final resting places of apostles. The one spoke of Rome because Peter and Paul were buried there. The second, called Proclus, added, "There were four prophetesses, the daughters of Philip, at Hierapolis in Asia. Their tomb is there and the tomb of their father." Polycrates, bishop of Ephesus about A.D. 190, also quoted a tradition claiming that Philip lived, preached, and died about A.D. 80 in Hierapolis.

To reach Pamukkale we drove west from Ephesus to Denizli and then turned north. Boys tending camels watched from a distance as we cooked supper along the dusty road. The tin cans of lasagna and fruit cocktail we opened neatly and set, empty, in the branches of a tree out of sight. From experience we knew what would happen, but we wanted to give boys hunting for what we left behind a little search before they claimed a new utensil for their mothers' kitchens. During the meal a jeep load of Turkish army officers came by and stopped. One who looked like Nasser's brother said that there was food ahead, at the motel, if we wanted it.

A sign indicated the Laodicea ruins up a track to the right. We took note and rode on, through several filthy mud villages, wondering how anything desirable could lie beyond.

But around a bend after Ecirliköy, the last of the dirty villages, waited the surprise. Warm mineral springs that bubble up from a huge rock terrace have been spilling down the side of the cliffs for centuries, calcifying as they fall to produce all kinds of white formations. It looked like a frozen cascade and the sight alone was cooling on a hot day. Many shallow pools hold the waters before they brim over, falling down three hundred feet of white cliffside to converge eventually in a rushing stream. This is Pamukkale, "cotton castle." On the flat terrace is a motel built in a circle around the largest pool.

By American standards, the motel is not modern. We paid the equivalent of three dollars for the seven of us and this rented one room with a tiny connected cubicle holding a single bed. Toilets and showers were separate. But one stepped from his motel door onto a promenade and into the pool.

Pink-flowering shrubs leaned over the water. Beneath the surface lay Roman pillars of centuries long gone. The water was too warm to be exhilarating but it was delightful to laze around in, soaking out the dust of the day, resting on a submerged pillar. Turquoise-colored tables lined the natural pool at the restaurant area. Nasser's look-alike was eating here with his friends. A few men and children were in the water. A row of women, skirts covering their ankles, sat on benches along the pool edge, watching. We were the only non-Turkish guests. The women returned my smile and watched me with frank curiosity as I passed them, dripping and cool in my respectable one-piece swimsuit. Funny they don't like to swim, I thought.

After the children were asleep I went out to the redbus to get something. A sliver of moon, like the Turkish flag crescent, hung in the sky. There were lights at the restaurant and in the room doorways but the pool was dark. At the steps leading into it I came upon a line of shadowy figures, all female. Each laid her housecoat on the pool edge and slid quietly into the dark waters, wearing a swimsuit similar to mine. We had read of modest Moslem women. Here they were in person, the same ones who sat by daylight with skirts covering their ankles, watching their half-clad American counterpart curiously.

A waiter with a bright red bow on his uniform served the two of us tea and watermelon at a turquoise table. We appreciated the liquids after the drying dusty heat of the day. On the map we checked the route to Konya, including a side trip to Antioch of Pisidia. It was not a night to waste in sleeping. Fragrance from the pink blossoms hung in the warm air. Mirrored stars floated in the pool and soft "sick music" wove a haunting spell around us. Midnight came and went, unnoticed.

Early in the morning all of us were in the pool again. The girls and I washed our hair in the showers and everyone felt deliciously clean and cool. After serving us a poolside breakfast of white cheese, bread, watermelon, and Turkish coffee, the staff lined up at the entrance to take leave of us. With unfeigned enthusiasm we repeated, "Çok teşekkür ederim," and shook hands down the line. "Güle, güle," they replied and the waiter with the red bow bowed and said, "You come back, yes?"

A woman was selling shoulder bags outside the motel entrance. These were made of thick nubby off-white material with colorful embroidered patterns in yarn. We bought several and made a little boy happy by buying from him a crude clay vase whitewashed to resemble the cotton castle.

In front of the motel are *agora* ruins and remnants of Roman baths. Hierapolis was a famous health resort where pagan cults used the hot springs to make a thriving health center. Commercially, Hierapolis was dependent on its larger neighbor, Laodicea. Hierapolis means "city of the sanctuary," or "sacred city." On a hill behind the motel is a perfect amphitheater. The steep stone rows are intact and free from overgrowth. From the top of the theater one has a panorama of the whole Lycus Valley and across it to mountains with snow on their peaks. The pool clusters shimmered in the sun. The cotton castle formations glittered like a fairy-land.

Cameras clicking, we descended slowly past the motel and stopped at the pools. Dicker stooped to play in one, stepped back and fell into another, so his clothes dried out of the window as we crossed the valley to the track toward Laodicea.

Laodicea was a vital crossroads city on the east-west trade route from Ephesus to Persia and the north-south road from Pergamum to Attalia on the south coast. The city was founded in the third century before Christ by Seleucid King Antiochus II who named the city for his wife Laodice. It was a rich important center of banking and commerce, fed by the fertile valley around it. But Laodicea had no water of its own. And so water pipes, hollowed out in three-foot stone cubes, stretched across the valley to bring water from the hot springs at Hierapolis. By the time this water reached Laodicea it was an insipid lukewarm, better as an emetic than for a refreshing drink. At Hierapolis the waters were hot and healing. Colosse nearby had its own cold water springs. But for Laodicea there was only the lukewarm, cooled-off liquid that Christ used to describe the spiritual condition of the church in that prosperous city.

"I know your works," he wrote. "You are neither cold nor hot. Would that you were cold or hot! So, because you are lukewarm, and neither cold nor hot, I will spew you out of my mouth."

Christ's letter made other references to the city. Laodicea was known for glossy black wool cloth. It produced powders and potions of medicinal value. To the church here Christ says, "For you say, I am rich, I have prospered, and I need nothing; not knowing that you are wretched, pitiable, poor, blind, and naked. Therefore I counsel you to buy from me gold refined by fire, that you may be rich, and white garments to clothe you and to keep the shame of your nakedness from being seen, and salve to anoint your eyes, that you may see." Not banker's gold or black wool or local salves. What you need is that which I can give you, says Christ, and "behold, I stand at the door and knock." Open the door and I will still come in, he promises graciously.

A dead-end track climbs from the sign to a jumble of marble blocks, an arch, a half-toppled tower. Nothing more is left of the proud self-sufficient city and the lukewarm church.

A farmer's family was treading out grain across from the marble jumble. The parents took turns riding on a sort of toboggan behind the horse. Round and round they went over the grain and then with a wooden fork they threw the crushed kernels into the air to let the wind, what there was of it, blow away the chaff. The woman wore red cotton with a white head-covering. The man had a cloth tucked under his cap to protect his neck from the sun. Their four children, three boys and a girl, were with them.

The man accepted cigarettes happily and maneuvered the horse into position for photos. The barefoot children also wanted their picture taken. The smallest boy, about four, wore a faded bluish dress with sleeves. Their noses were large, a characteristic some say belies Hittite ancestry. We gave the children a small black plastic cat whose limbs collapsed gradually when pressure was applied to the bottom of the base on which it was mounted. Awed, the four passed it carefully from hand to hand. They were too busy, heads bent close together, watching the cat collapse limb by limb, to wave good-bye.

The search for Colosse was strangest of all. We returned to the east-west road between Denizli and Dinar and turned south off it after six miles. Another six miles brought us up a narrow road to Honaz. One map did not show this village at all. Another showed Honaz Dag, 2,571 feet high. People gathered around the dirty redbus.

Twice the Rev asked, *"Lüften nerede hüyük Colosse?"* Please, where is the mound of Colosse?

A diminutive man, no taller than Clark, stepped forward. He wore a cap, white shirt, and tan riding pants, all frayed. The onlookers peered in as we opened the redbus doors to give the little man my place in the front seat. He motioned us out of town and onto a stream bed, dry except for a trickle in the center. On both sides the vegetation was heavy with tall bushes and trees. The streambed was an admirable way to go through. Whether or how one went in rainy season we could not ask. Along the way faces appeared in the bushes, attracted by the rare sound of a motor.

The ride was not smooth. For three miles we bounced, lurched, tipped, and each time the Rev turned questioningly to our guide, he gestured on.

"Tamam, tamam," he said. Keep going, keep going.

"Peki, peki," answered the Rev hopefully. Only a little, a little more.

By now the children were silly, rocking with laughter as well as with the car. Where were we going, guided by a man we could not understand, miles from a recognizable highway? Then we were on a rut road on which we went a few miles before the little man told us to halt. A noisy stream rushed along beside the rut. On the other side was the three-level mound that covers Colosse. The mound is about sixty or seventy feet high with gradual slopes. Bits of pottery lie in the brown grass on the surface. On top of the mound men were cutting grass for hay.

We would have been skeptical if the little man had not led us to the far side of the mound top. Here was the shaft of which we had heard. Archaeologists some years earlier sank a shaft there, digging up enough pottery from different layers to determine, along with their knowledge of the area, that this was the likely site of Colosse. The little man gestured and used the word "America." We read him easily — when more money comes from America, then more digging, then see more of Colosse.

Colosse was a substantial city of Phrygia when Xerxes rested his great armies there on the march against Greece about 480 B.C. In those days the main road north to Sardis and Pergamum branched off here from the east-west highway connecting Xerxes' Persia with Ephesus. Later the north-south road was moved west to Laodicea and by the time of Christ, Colosse, said Strabo, was "a small town." Laodicea and Hierapolis are mentioned in histories of the early church but Colosse fades out of the picture.

While Paul spent his years in Ephesus, Epaphras was the minister who worked in the three cities of the Lycus Valley. Colosse is the home of Philemon, master of the runaway slave Onesimus. About A.D. 63, during Paul's first imprisonment in Rome, he sent letters to Philemon, to the Colossians, and to the Ephesians. All three letters were delivered by Tychicus who traveled with the returning slave.

Centuries later, under the Byzantine Empire, Colosse had a resurgence of life. It was famous then for miracles that occurred in the church of the archangel Michael. Apparently the angel worship for which Paul chided the early Colossians had its revival then. But the city disappeared so completely after this that some even have suggested that Paul's Colossian letter was for the people of Rhodes, astride whose harbor stood the mammoth Colossus statue.

Here we stood on top of Colosse, whose church had become entangled in rites and ceremonies and even in angel worship. Paul in his letter set before them Christ as incomparable, pre-eminent, all-sufficient, and worthy of their full devotion. He writes about their new life in Christ and urges them to regulate all their relationships accordingly.

The little man posed proudly beside the shaft hole with the children. Dave hunted for unusual pottery pieces. Down at the stream we washed our dusty feet and dried them on the dirtiest maroon towel. Two men appeared and tried to persuade the Rev to explore a long underground passageway farther down the road. At least, this seemed the import of their gestures. The Rev declined with polite gestures and offered them a cigarette. But we had no matches handy. To our surprise, one man pulled from the pocket of his nondescript jacket a gleaming cigarette lighter. The little man guiding us declined a cigarette and seemed bothered by the intrusion of the others. He was openly relieved when we climbed back into the redbus.

"Ne kadar?" the Rev asked when we had bounced back into Honaz. Clark was ready to translate the little man's answer into an English amount. But he did not want money, only the photos we had made of him. Amazing how much one can communicate by gesture only! Yes, we would send the pictures — yes, all of them — from America when we returned home. Here were paper and pencil for the little man to write his name. More trouble. The little man was irritated. He could not write his name and we had hurt his feelings by asking. So the Rev took the pencil and paper, cupped his ear, and the little man spoke his name three times slowly while the Rev wrote what he heard: BAKI BANAR BAS. We all shook hands and *teşekkür ederim*-ed the little man. He pointed the way out of the village by another way than we had entered and stood at stiff attention while we waved. Then he turned to the people waiting to hear of his adventure and we could see him begin his story, using gestures, in the art of which we were all becoming more eloquent.

From Michigan in the fall we sent prints of the colored slides and the children's black-and-white photos at Colosse. We sent them to the name and town, confident that anyone would know, upon opening the envelope, for whom the pictures were intended. I added no message to the pictures because this seemed embarrassing and futile for a man who could not write his own name.

We were amazed some weeks later to receive an air mail letter, the address in shaky printing, and inside the following penciled letter,

Jeneory 14, 1963

Dear mr Dr

I riplyt and I riciverd your letter and I was verry glad to hiar from your and in emvolop you send mi for of your pichers verry well mr doctor thenk you — verry much I most rimember yow for long time I wisht you send mi a letter ageint of you plias froom

Backy I am in expech-
expechubul from yow pliass good by
Mr Sam Obedin I send rigards this is a man travel in michigan I us to live in Geferson st in Dittroit

The return address on the back of the envelope was

Mr Backy Bunar Bashi
Dinizli Honaz
Torky

So Mr. Backy had found a man who had been in America, in Michigan, no less, and this man had written his reply. We chuckled to see that the name we had written by ear was quite similar to the proper way to write it.

I answered with an English letter and sent one of my books, the one with the most illustrations in it and an author's photo on the jacket.

Next we received a typewritten Turkish letter with pictures of a school and children, and we sent the letter to the Turkish embassy in Washington for translation. Whereupon we received a most gracious reply in perfect English. The gist of the Turkish letter, said the embassy, declining to translate it literally, was a request for money. This was understandable, because every Turk imagines that every American lives at the level of Henry Ford II or the late John D. Rockefeller. However, we could understand, continued the embassy, that it would be highly inadvisable for us to accede to this request because it would be the first of many others. The embassy would be most appreciative if we accepted their advice and disregarded the letter entirely.

That was the end of that. But Backy himself remains a respected family figure. When we talk of revisiting Turkey before tourists overrun it, the children always say, "We'd have to stop and see how Backy is."

THE DAY FROM COTTON CASTLE to Konya we called D-Day, Dust Day. Despite the red line on the map, the road at no time improved beyond dusty gravel. After the Lycus Valley we entered sweltering barren country. Little twisters, like small tornado funnels of tan dust, eddied along the parched fields. In the villages boys rushed out holding up bottles of Turkish soda. They thought we were a *dolmus*. Other boys ran up with pails of water which they sloshed on the front windows to wash off the dust. This was a debatable service since new dust collected in the moisture and produced a muddy mess on the windshield. Old busses and trucks traveling this area kicked up so much dust that one could not see to pass them or to stay behind them. And who knew when a wagon or an animal would be there, hidden in a dust cloud? We were aiming for Konya, hoping to detour briefly to Antioch of Pisidia ruins near Yalvac before Aksehir. All the redbus windows were clamped shut and still the dust sifted in.

In the open country we had a flat tire. We heard the air escaping when we stopped to change seats. The feminine contingent stood on the roadside while the males untied the copper tray to get at the spare tire compartment behind the front seat. Then the first old truck passed. We saw the dust cloud in the distance, heard the motor, flattened ourselves against the redbus and hid our faces in our clothes. No use. Minutes later the dust was still settling upon us. Several more vehicles passed during the tire changing. Each time we became less recognizable. Each time we stood apart from one another to shake out our clothes, wipe our faces, and spit a little. When the job was finished we got out the water, lukewarm and strong with Halazone taste, rinsed our mouths, wiped our faces, cleaned our dark glasses, and leaped into the car to slam the doors before the next dust cloud appeared on the road.

During the whole day we passed one lovely spot and that was Lake Egridir, at an elevation of three hundred feet, bluest of blue to our dusty eyes, complete with an island on which stood an old fort. On the whole lake there was one little boat and no other sign of life. The shore was rocky, there was no easy access to the water's edge, and we were pressed for time, so we looked longingly as the road circled the lake and then veered off toward Aksehir.

When we turned off the red-line dusty road for a dustier smaller one to Yalvac, David wiped off the Finegan volume and began to brief us on delights ahead. It was already late afternoon.

Freely rendered, à la Dave, Finegan had this to say:

Antiochus was the name of thirteen Seleucid kings. One was Seleucus I Nicator (312-200 B.C.), who kept naming cities for himself and his father, so there are sixteen Antiochs created by him alone. This one, in the region of Pisidia in the Roman province of Galatia was a Roman outpost, very civilized in a not-so-civilized district. The emperor Augustus made it a Roman colony before 11 B.C. It stood on the lower slopes of a mountain on the right bank of the Anthius River. You can see an aqueduct that brought down water from the mountain.

A British chaplain at Izmir discovered the old site of Antioch of Pisidia in 1833. Ramsay and the University of Michigan excavated here around 1924. He found two fine city squares, an upper and a lower connected by a broad flight of steps, and three triumphal archways in honor of Augustus. Also a great temple to the god Men, whose symbol was the bull's head, and who was the local god in charge of agricultural prosperity. (He's not doing much around here these days.) Also a triple gateway in the city wall. "Nowhere else in the Roman empire has yet been discovered a better combination of . . . sculpture with . . . architecture," says a guy named Robinson. Sounds great.

Nancy added a few things from Acts 13, though she was not in a communicative mood after all the dust.

"There's a whole sermon Paul preached in the synagogue. You don't want me to read it, do you? Lots of Jews believed, some Gentiles, too. But some other Jews got together, and some women, too, and had Paul and Barnabas driven out of the district."

"The women is because around here women were important and even had jobs in the government. I read that somewhere." Dave.

"Listen to this. 'They shook off the dust from their feet against them.' That figures. And then they went to Iconium."

"Where we're going tonight." The Rev.

"If we ever get there." Clark.

"But we wouldn't want to miss seeing what the U. of M. accomplished over here," I said, trying to inject a note of optimism into the whole situation. "We should be able to find the temple of Men and the two squares."

We drove through Yalvac, more primitive than Akhisar, so there was little prospect of staying there for the night. The ruins lay in the hills beyond the city. A track in that direction was barely discernible, but next to a pile of stones there was a sign, Antioch Pisidiae. We spotted the aqueduct ruin at once and hiked a half mile over the hills to reach it. This made a beautiful picture, the aqueduct arches turned copper color by a low sun. There were chunks of stone and marble scattered in random fashion through the hills but nothing more. We walked toward the river, feeling the coolness and noting the lush vegetation along its banks. We could hear the water flowing but there was no sign of significant ruins.

A jeep came out from the village with men in it. Perhaps they thought we were lost. They motioned grandly to the aqueduct and the whole area and then pointed out the track to return to the village. We gave them the Turkish thank you and stood at the redbus debating what to do next. Certainly the men would have directed us to any other substantial ruins.

The sun was disappearing. The children were hungry. We got out a big can of pork and beans, one of peaches, and some spoons, and passed the cans around in uncivilized fashion. There was some doubt whether we could even identify the turn at the road to Konya after dark. While we stood, boys came running and one seemed to indicate he knew where there were more ruins. We seven and five boys piled into the redbus and set off down another obstacle course toward the river. Where the trail entered dense trees, we crossed one bit of marsh successfully, but the next one was too deep to risk alone at dusk in a strange place. How did we know the boys were right? The aqueduct was supposedly five miles from the temple square, so we were nowhere near it. Twilight settled.

We drove the boys back to Yalvac, dropped them off on the square there, finished our supper a mile outside the town, and like Paul, shook off the dust of our feet before we went on our way. It was dark at 8:10 when we found the main road and began the 110 miles of dust and gravel between us and Konya. It was a four-hour nightmare.

Around curves we would come upon unlighted wagons or herds of cows being driven home. Narrow bridges, several busses, two of them broken down, a few trucks, two *dolmuses* (or is it *dolmi?*), and not one other private car on the whole distance. Passengers on the broken-down busses squatted at the roadside and jumped out to hail us, thinking we were a *dolmus*. Two soldiers with guns stepped out from bushes to stop us for a ride and for a moment we thought we were under arrest. One scared rabbit was clocked at thirty miles an hour as he leaped in front of us before darting into the bushes.

The children fell asleep except for Nan who sat with her Neustadt pillow pressed against her nose and mouth to keep out dust, though the windows were tightly shut. The Rev and I leaned close to the windshield, peering into the blackness and dust to spot the next slow-moving hazard before we hit it. Does one pass a truck with visibility zero or stay behind where visibility is no better? In the middle of nowhere stood a brightly lit gas station, but long horn-honking brought no attendant, so we poured in our reserve gas and continued.

The lights of Konya twinkled like clustered stars in the valley below. At the instant we saw them we also came to blacktop after two big bumps which threw slumbering Emily from her seat onto the floor. The city was quiet. A policeman got into the redbus to direct us to the Saray Hotel.

The girls, Dicker, and I were shown into two adjoining rooms with bath. The boys and the Rev, without explanation, were demoted down the hall to what may have been a maid's room. Dave discovered a soggy banana and some silverware in a drawer. We all drank Turkish soda and crawled into bed dusty. Dicker came from his twin bed to mine and put his arms tightly around my neck.

In the process of de-dusting ourselves the next morning we discovered the voluminous white terry cloth robe provided in most decent Turkish hotels. Ours was quite clean though one could wonder how frequently it was washed. It was THE bath towel for the four of us and quite practical though a little damp by the fourth using.

When we were all seated for breakfast in a cheerful big room with thriving plants, cages of singing canaries, and a breeze blowing in dustless from the square, it was easy to imagine that the day before had not been real.

"Do you think there was any more to see at Antioch?" Nan.

"No," replied the Rev firmly. "Let's say no. After all, it was forty years ago that they excavated there. Probably the river and the woods have swallowed it all up."

Clark described the maid who had tidied up their room. With one hand she held her head covering over her face so that only her eyes showed, and with the other hand she swept and picked up things. "Real tricky," Clark called it.

The calendar showed Friday, July 6. A tire had to be repaired, money changed, and we wanted to see the new Konya museum not yet open to the public. There was also the decision about whether to visit the *hüyüks* of Lystra and Derbe, cities of Paul's first journey. Lystra lay near Hatunsaray southwest of Konya. Derbe, in a site which our professor friend helped to verify, recently has been determined to lie to the southeast near Kilbassan.

Planning a
safari for seven

The flats in Zandvoort

Fishing nets at Zoutkamp

On the dunes at Zandvoort

A story from Oom Bee

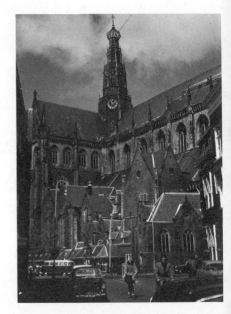

Saint Bavo Church, Haarlem

Herring cart in Zandvoort

Lake at Loosdrecht

Roofs of Heidelberg

Heidelberg Castle

East Berlin — looking
to the free world

Checkpoint Charlie, West Berlin

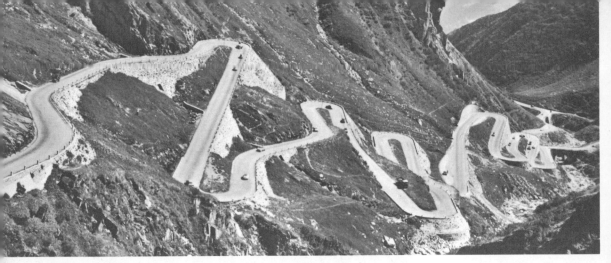

Switchbacks in the Alps

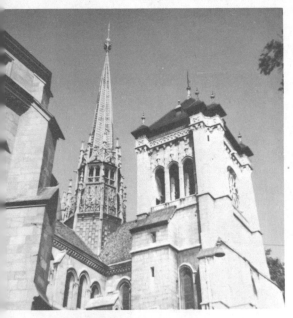

Saint Pierre, Calvin's church

Glacier seen from Susten Pass

Reformation Wall, Geneva

Swiss lakeside town

Saint Mark's
Piazza, Venice

Leaning Tower,
Pisa

Appian Way

Colosseum, Rome

Arch of Constantine, Rome

Stepping stones, Pompeii

House of the Faun, Pompeii

Campground Lambiri
Gulf of Corinth

Temple of Apollo, Corinth

Temple of Zeus pillars, Athens

Gravestone, Keramaikos Cemetery, Athens

Italy-Greece ferry

Camping at Delphi

Fresh bread, Thessaloniki

Redbus at city sign

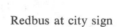

Galenus Arch, Thessaloniki

Greek Orthodox priest

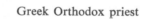

Harvesting, Philippi

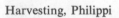

Hagia Sophia, Istanbul

Walls of Istanbul

Buying pottery, Akhisar (Thyatira)

Triple walls, Iznik (Nicea)

Wayside spring near Akhisar

Aesculapius symbols, Pergamum

Cybele-Artemis temple pillars, Sardis

Travelers near Ephesus

Amphitheater, Ephesus

Limestone cliffs, Pamukkale

Stream bed
to Colosse

Stream at Colosse mound

Threshing at Laodicea

Aqueduct, Antioch in Pisidia

Changing of the guard, Ataturk's tomb

Ataturk's tomb, Ankara

Watermelon merchant near Iskenderun

Bedouins south of Baalbek

East Gate into Straight Street, Damascus

Arab boys at Jerash

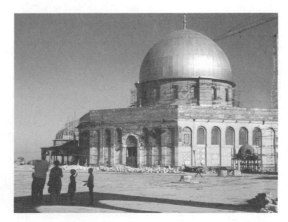

Dome of the Rock, Jerusalem

Gethsemane, Mount of Olives

The well at Gibeon

The Garden Tomb

Mosque over Cave
of Machpelah, Hebron

Elisha's stream at Jericho

Floating in the Dead Sea

Qumran Caves of
Dead Sea Scrolls

Signpost to Capernaum

Mandelbaum Gate, Jerusalem

South end, Sea of Galilee

Synagogue in Capernaum

Fishermen's steps,
Sea of Galilee

Mount Tabor, Israel

Church of Saint
Gabriel, Nazareth

Columns and statues in the *agora* of Izmir (Smyrna)

Carriage and Turkish ship in Izmir

Unloading the redbus in Istanbul

Budapest

Berchtesgaden

Salt mine train, Berchtesgaden

Lace vendor, Chartres Cathedral

Joan of Arc statue, Orleans

Chartres Cathedral

Calvin house, Noyon

Room where John
Calvin was born

Dicker in the ship's playroom

S. S. Nieuw Amsterdam

David's birthday dinner on shipboard

Stone inscriptions from both of these mounds are in the Konya museum.

"So why go to the mounds?" Dave.

"We saw a mound yesterday." Em.

"Let's go straight to Ankara after here." Nan.

It was much easier to sit there and imagine, to the accompaniment of canary song, how Paul and Barnabas in Lystra had been called gods one day and then stoned and left for dead the next. And nothing much is said about Derbe in Acts, except that Paul preached there.

"Let's look at the inscriptions at the museum and leave the *hüyük* dust to archaeologists. If we spend the morning in Konya and drive this afternoon to Ankara, we'll be there early for the weekend."

Konya prides itself on being an old city, dating back to pre-Hittite times before Abraham, when the people of this area worshiped a mother goddess served by eunuch priests. In those early centuries Konya was called Kawania.

By Paul's day the name was Iconium and the city was part of the Roman province of Galatia. Paul and Barnabas came to Iconium from Antioch of Pisidia on their first missionary journey. Acts 14 says, "Now at Iconium they entered together into the Jewish synagogue, and so spoke that a great company believed, both of Jews and of Greeks. But the unbelieving Jews stirred up the Gentiles and poisoned their minds against the brethren. So they remained for a long time, speaking boldly for the Lord, who bore witness to the word of his grace, granting signs and wonders to be done by their hands. But the people of the city were divided. . . . When an attempt was made . . . to molest them and to stone them, they learned of it and fled to Lystra and Derbe."

"And that's where they really got stoned, didn't they?"

Paul himself speaks of this persecution in his second pastoral letter to Timothy who was a native of Lystra and "well spoken of by the brethren at Lystra and Iconium." Timothy knew firsthand what Paul meant when he spoke of "my persecutions, my sufferings, what befell me at Antioch, at Iconium, and at Lystra."

Tradition tells about an Iconium girl of noble birth who was converted by Paul's preaching. Her name was Thecla and the Eastern and Roman churches celebrate her as a saint, the female protomartyr of the church. She suffered many persecutions for her faith and was miraculously spared a martyr's death by hungry wild animals who would not eat her and flames that would not burn her. Thecla, says tradition, lived to a ripe old age in a cell near Seleucia, having followed Paul to Antioch of Syria. She is heroine of a second-century romantic story included in the New Testament apocryphal writings, entitled *Acts of Paul and Thecla*. One of the two mountains behind Iconium is named Thecla. The other peak is named Philip, not Paul.

Iconium was a Christian center, site of an archbishopric in the third and fourth centuries. An early church council was held here in 235 after Christ. But the period of splendor came much later, during the reign of the Seljuk Turks who made Iconium their capital from 1073 on, decorating it lavishly with palaces, mosques, and Oriental art. The Turks have tried to restore remnants of this glory, but there is nothing in Konya to suggest its earlier Christian importance. History reminds us that in May of 1190 Frederick Barbarossa, Holy Roman Emperor, fought his last battle here leading the Third Crusade to the Holy Land. A month later "the Redbeard" drowned in the River Calycadnus near Seleucia in Cilicia.

"Man, how many Seleucias and Antiochs were there?"

Today Konya is a city of fifty thousand to a hundred thousand, depending on which literature one consults. It is the wheat center as well as the rug-making capital of Turkey. The only city of size in the whole of south central Turkey, Konya is watered by streams from the Pisidian mountains. Muller generously calls it "a garden city on the broad treeless Anatolian plain." To the latter half of that description we definitely would subscribe.

A friendly man rode his bicycle ahead of us to point out a service station. Dust billowed out when we opened the front seat to remove the flat tire. We added the nail from it to our first souvenir nail extracted at Izmir. Searching for the archaeological museum, we were directed erroneously to the Museum of Islamic Art, housed in former quarters of the order of Whirling Dervishes. It was a fortunate error and we admired the beautiful Seljuk art, which ranged from seven-hundred-year-old rugs to wood carvings, hand-written Korans, blue mosaics, and old instruments to whose music the dervishes whirled.

At the new archaeological museum the gatekeeper signaled that we would need a pass, but just then the director arrived on a bicycle and agreed to let us in. Mustafa Anbar was his name and he spoke fluent German. So did two black-bearded monks from the famous Spanish monastery of Montserrat. One of the monks had been born in Tarrasa, a city familiar to us. We talked in German and in English.

The director showed us the museum, with special pride in a heavily sculptured sarcophagus found recently in the Konya area. In a row of stones in the courtyard stood the two which interested us. One was the Lystra stone, a very clear inscription which identified the location of that city. The other is a stone formerly thought to come from Derbe. But a new inscription found on a mound near Kilbassan is more conclusive and this stone was on its way from a farmhouse where our professor friend had evaluated it. We talked about the significance of the new site.

Few people in Konya wore Western clothes. Women had all kinds of head shawls and veils. A veiled woman with two little children came to the redbus, begging, but a man walking by ordered her away. The Rev bought fruit and the shopkeeper had to ride his bike to the bank to get change for the *lira* note.

It will sound repetitious and I have consulted a book of synonyms before resorting again to the words "barren" and "blistering" to describe the 160 miles from Konya north to Ankara. A map will show how few towns and villages there are in this area. The road is paved, however. We found one scraggly tree and broke open a watermelon for refreshment.

And then suddenly, thirty-two miles from Konya, in the middle of all this bleak heat, there was Yolcu Dinlemne Parki, an acre or two of shady grassy oasis, monument to unflagging zeal in cultivation and watering. It has a big pond, roses, rows of young trees, and cement tables under a grape arbor.

Every truck driver on the Konya-Ankara run stops here to lie in the grass beside the pond, to drink at the cold fountain. We stopped two hours. Under the grape arbor we prepared a meal of instant rice, beef chop suey, tomatoes, watermelon, coffee and many glasses of cold water from the fountain. Later we discovered that the blue and white oilcloth over the table we used was the property of the caretaker who sold tea or cold drink to those who wanted it. But no one was around and we appreciated the luxury of a table covering, not to mention a table big enough for all of us to sit around.

Dicker fell into the pond before we ate. His clothes dried on a pine tree during the meal. We read the letter to Laodicea because it was about hot, cold, and lukewarm. Temperatures had acquired real meaning for us that week.

There was time to clean out the back of the car and repack it while the children made crowns and chains of grape leaves. Wearing these prickly laurels, we braved the highway again. Tiny twisters fled across the baked fields. Busses spitting black smoke threw up gravel to pock our windshield on a piece of freshly tarred road. The few villages we saw were mud-baked affairs. We had a contest to see who could say "hot" the most times in one breath.

ANKARA WAS PLANNED TO BE a rest stop and a visit with a lonely airman whom we had never met. In both respects it was a success. Mitch, the airman, we found by searching for the Ankara APO number on the subscription list of our church's youth magazine, which is sent without cost to servicemen. Mitch's was the only name, and he replied at once to our letter. Not until we saw him in person did we discover that he hadn't the foggiest idea what the Christian Reformed Church was. While working as mail clerk in a California post office, he noticed the youth magazine en route to some serviceman in the Pacific. Anticipating that he would be lonesome when he became an airman, Mitch applied for a free subscription for himself. He wrote us that he would be pleased to meet us, to reserve hotel space for us, and to help in any way he could.

In the Turkish building which housed the airmen the automatic elevator stopped between floors and the Rev was stranded half an hour before a mechanic persuaded the machine to move. Mitch was out on an errand but his roommate, Ron, hoisting barbells, also was happy to adopt a family for the weekend. We waited for Mitch in the snack bar.

"This is living," said Nan ecstatically.

"We can even talk English and they understand us." Em.

The boys had mouths only for hamburgs, malteds, and grape soda floats.

Mitch had reserved a suite of two large rooms with bath in the Monaco Hotel. It is a good hotel. The bath had lots of hot water and towels in addition to terry cloth robes. The bedrooms had big windows, desk and vanity, large closets, and comfortable chairs. For three nights, breakfasts, and patio snacks the bill was 468 *lira,* a little over $11.50 for seven people.

In addition to this inexpensive luxury, we had Mitch and Ron. It was hard to tell who was more pleased with the other, they or the children. Dicker rode Ron's shoulders. Em held Mitch's hand. Dave and Clark worked at the barbells. Two lonely fellows had a family for a weekend and we had the best of guides and friends in a strange city.

Saturday morning the males went off for Volkswagen servicing and a visit to the PX. The girls, Dicker, and I had breakfast served in our rooms — toast, eggs, juice, good coffee. Dicker and Em took long baths and then I washed clothes in a tub full of hot soapy water. The men returned with boxes of stuff — food, magazines, soap, stationery, even a new camera for Clark to replace his broken one bequeathed to Dicker. Mitch took all our undeveloped slides to mail home from the APO, more for safety in transit than for economy of mailing.

As we arrived at the air-conditioned AFEX cafeteria for lunch, a blonde servicewoman wheeled her car into the parking space for which she saw we were waiting.

"It's like that all over here," said Mitch. "Everybody for himself. It's a lousy duty spot, everybody hates it, and so it's a dog-eat-dog existence."

In the afternoon we went swimming at an Air Force recreation area on a small lake twelve miles outside of Ankara. Mitch and Ron bought king-size cokes for the children, a little too much of a good thing after our Spartan diet, and Dicker threw up on the way home, though he did it neatly into a seasickness bag left from the ship and kept handy on the shelf under the dashboard.

"We haven't been out here to swim for ages," said Ron. "Nobody to come with. No fun alone. It's the single guys who suffer most here. The Turks don't like us and the feeling is mutual. The service families all stick together, 'specially the officers. Next to Korea, this is the end." So Mitch was studying hypnosis as an escape from reality and Ron kept hoisting barbells.

The fellows talked more about this over coffee on the hotel terrace when the children had gone to bed.

"Strange thing here in Turkey," said Mitch. "The Americans use Turkish buildings and except for air bases, we have no property of our own. That's part of the deal. The billets we live in are new but practically worthless construction. We just moved in two months ago and already our inspectors condemn them as unsafe.

"We're all subject to Turkish law. All Americans are. You too. If you're in a taxi and it has an accident, get out and run if you can. Because it will be your fault since you hired the taxi. Same thing if you hit something with your own car. The Turks will try you by their law and you're always wrong. Right now there's an American newspaper guy in the hospital in Istanbul. He had an accident. It killed his wife and a Turkish woman. They sentenced him to prison for years even though it wasn't his fault. But our people keep him in the hospital and say his back is injured while they try to figure a way to get him out of the country. His little girl's waiting with a governess in Beirut. And these are the people we're defending. They're supposed to be our friends.

"Turkish men love to pick fights. Argue with one and you have a whole pack of them on you. So you fight for your rights and then Turkish law decides it's all your fault. Let an American get into trouble with a Turkish woman and he'll be sent to a back country village for six years of banishment, beaten, and made to do all the dirty work for the whole village. Nine to one he dies before his time is up. One good thing about that is we don't have trouble with women like they do in Korea.

"But the trouble is, everybody looks out for himself. You saw it at the beach this afternoon. Nobody's friendly. It'll be the same in church tomorrow morning. We tried when we first got here, but it's useless. Morale is zero. Figure it yourself. When the people of the country aren't for you and your own Americans aren't either, it gets pretty dismal for single guys who have to come here. So we just hole up in the billets and count the days.

"You don't know what this weekend means to us. We were sorta wondering what kind of people you'd be, a minister and all that. But you're not, I mean, you're okay, and the kids — man, we'll never forget it."

"Well," said the Rev, "As you say about the Turks, on this point the feeling is mutual and we don't know what we would have done without you, either."

Sunday morning church service in the theater was well attended, though almost entirely by families and couples. The senior chaplain delivered a poor sermon on not dimming one's lights, which was meant to be a modern version of not hiding them under a bushel. We were hoping that someone would speak to us, so that we could introduce him to Mitch and Ron and point out privately to the boys that things were not as bad as they thought. But we were ignored and had to concede that this was the most unfriendly community of Americans we had encountered.

Outside we did not recognize the redbus. It was spotlessly washed — and waxed! — and the two Turks who had done the job unasked were leaning against it waiting to be paid.

We drove past embassies on the hills around the city, past the white mansion of the U.S. ambassador, on to the officers' club in its elegant setting. Here, on the strength of an active reserve status, we ate steak, tossed salad with Roquefort dressing, and strawberry chiffon pie.

"Enjoy it," said the Rev to his five. "Tomorrow will be different."

Mitch volunteered that the atmosphere was grand but loyalty prompted him to add that the food was not much better than that served to enlisted men.

The gate was locked at the ruin of the temple dedicated to Caesar Augustus who ordered the census at the time Jesus was born. We looked in through the railings. Nearby, in this old part of the city, is the Citadel fortress and the new Hittite museum of rough-hewn stone. The museum is dramatically appropriate for the rare collection of Hittite treasures which it houses. A guide showed us idols, jewelry, sculptured reliefs, and dishes from the time of Abraham, 2200 B.C., to David, 900 B.C. Some were even older. Each Hittite god had his own sacred animal, with the deer and the bull prominent. Along the courtyard paths stood many stones with old carvings and inscriptions.

Dicker focused his worthless camera carefully, adjusting his stance to get his whole subject into the viewer. He photographed with unflagging diligence until we reached Jerusalem. If the Greek fisherman near Corinth was surprised to know Clark owned a watch, the Turks and the Arabs were aghast to see a four-year-old with his own camera. He was so serious about his photography that it was futile to try to explain that the camera did not work and had no film in it.

The great monument in Ankara is the tomb of Mustafa Kemal Ataturk under whose dynamic leadership Ankara became the Turkish capital in 1923. Ataturk hired a German architect to lay out the new city which now holds a million people. The transformation from a dusty primitive place to a modern Western-style one with boulevards and stately buildings was a wonder. Judging by cracked billets and stalled elevators, the progress may have been too rapid for the people to whom it has been brought.

But there is nothing inadequate about the tomb of Ataturk. It is a national shrine to which Turks flock as we do to Washington monuments and to John Kennedy's grave. The Ataturk tomb is on a hill in the southwest part of Ankara. Wide as an avenue, the approach walk leads visitors a quarter mile to the mausoleum. At the entrance to the walk stand two groups of fifteen-foot stone figures, a group on either side. On one side are three men, including a soldier and a teacher. On the other side three women dressed as the common people of Turkey. Pairs of carved lions stand along the approach avenue which ends in a promenade of polished marble, a city block long with a tower at each corner.

Here occurs the changing of the guard since the tomb is illuminated and guarded day and night. The guard marches in a goose step reminiscent of Hitler's SS troops thirty years ago. They lift their feet waist high as they march with guns over their shoulders. Dicker loved this part and tried his own version of this maneuver which was carried out in three places on the promenade.

The mausoleum is a square-pillared building somewhat like the Lincoln Memorial, though the Lincoln pillars are round. Thirty-three steps lead up to it, flanked by carvings of battles for the republic. No photographing is allowed inside. The ceiling is of gold and colored mosaic. On one wall are passages from the Ataturk speech at the republic's tenth anniversary. On the other side is his message to youth. The mausoleum was finished in 1953, and Ataturk was reburied here on the fifteenth anniversary of his death.

"And guess who paid for it," said Mitch. "Just guess who! You see, the generous American government gave Turkey six million dollars to build a new highway from Istanbul to Ankara. But the Turks thought it was more important to bury Ataturk properly. So this is the site of the six million dollars. Beautiful, huh?" We never found out whether this was truth or Mitch's version, passed along from one disgruntled airman to another.

Monday morning early we met Mitch at one of five water points where American service personnel must get their drinking water. Even in the modern city of Ankara they carry water to their apartments in big bottles on their shoulders to be sure of a pure source. We filled our plastic jug, glad to forget Halazone pills until the five gallons were gone. We were not glad to part with Mitch and Ron who seemed like old friends after the weekend. Is it cowardly, I used to wonder, to ease farewells and partings by fantasying that we will see each other again? Especially if the fantasy has remote reality in it? Mitch and Ron talked of getting leave to attend the military retreat in Berchtesgaden in August.

Our hand breakfast of sugar crisp and boxed prunes was a pleasant departure from other breakfast menus on the road. A camel train of more than twenty animals met us at the outskirts of Ankara. On the highway we ignored the first main turnoff to the east, the road leading to Kayseri. Another time we hope to go this way to see the Göreme-Urgup area where there are many caves with early Christian markings. Thirteen miles farther we left the road on which we had come to Ankara and took the one leading southeast to Tarsus and Adana. On our right lay the dry flat expanse of the Tüz Golü, the Salt Lake. In the distance snow-capped peaks of the Taurus range became visible, some of them eleven thousand feet high.

The road to Tarsus is poor, as the airmen had warned. American cars, because of their low carriage, will not make it through the loose rock on that road. A road scraper was working to clear away the larger rocks. The bus ahead of us stopped at every dubious spot, a man jumped out from the rear door and walked through the loose stuff to determine where it was most passable, and we stayed behind the bus, profiting from its explorations.

In one town there was an outdoor bazaar of cloth goods, hundreds of brightly colored bolts of material. We began to climb with twists and turns toward the Cilician Gates, that steep narrow gorge which is the only access through the Taurus Mountains to the plain beyond. In the bottom of the gorge runs the river Cakit and the new road blasted into the rocky pass has widened what was once a chasm only sixty feet across.

How many kings and armies have marched through those narrow gates, beginning with an Assyrian queen named Semiramis, who legend says came south through them to build a city near Tarsus in the eight hundreds before Christ? Then there was Darius, the Persian, leading an army north in the five hundreds, and Alexander the Great at the head of an army passing south in the three hundreds, and after Christ the Byzantines marching south to strike the Arabs, and the Moslems driving north to ravage the Byzantine provinces, and in the eleven hundreds after Christ the first of the Crusaders fighting through on their way to free Jerusalem from the infidels. More lately came the Turks and Germans retreating from Suez after the First World War. All of them passing through the same Cilician Gates. And now we. And a man on foot, carrying a pottery water jug and a Pan American flight bag!

HOT STICKY AIR rose to meet us as we descended into the coastal plain of Tarsus, which is thirty miles south of the Gates. Tarsus was the greatest disappointment of any Biblical city on our trip. At Antioch of Pisidia one could survey the hills and marble fragments and conjure up visions of Paul in that deserted place. But it is easier to relive history at a poor ruin than at a poor city which lives on in crawling, reeking existence.

We did not much care that Tarsus today exports cotton and white raisins. Or that the heavy coats of Taurus mountain goats give hair that Tarsus makes into tough thread for fabrics like tent canvas, though this was reminiscent of Paul, the tent maker. "I am a citizen of no mean city," Paul had written proudly in a day when Tarsus was a wealthy center of culture and learning, a port and junction of trade routes from Syrian Antioch and the Euphrates. Strabo called Tarsus a place where enthusiasm for learning equaled that of Athens and Alexandria, a city whose people had the rare privilege of Roman citizenship by virtue of their birth in that place. At Tarsus flows the Cydnus River in which Alexander the Great went swimming and almost died from a chill brought on by the cold waters. Here Cleopatra, sailing in a golden barge with purple sails and silver oars, arrived for her first rendezvous with Mark Antony. The whole city emptied out to see her arrive, leaving Mark Antony sitting alone on his tribunal. Turkish travel literature adds the claims that the prophet Daniel was buried in Tarsus, that Cicero was once its governor, and that Canterbury who converted the English to Christianity was born here.

Today's dirty nondescript streets do not hint at the glories of the past. We took one slide in Tarsus, of an old single arch of rough stone with yellow grass sprouting from the top. Beside it the city taxis were lined up, red-and-black horsedrawn carriages lending a rare bit of color in a drab dusty city.

Beyond Adana, which is twenty-four miles east of Tarsus, is the American air base made famous by Francis Gary Powers and his ill-fated U-2 flight over Russia. Air police at the gate of the air base examined our papers skeptically, but once we were inside the friendliness was a great improvement over the American military climate in Ankara. Perhaps on a self-contained, fenced-in base the Americans enjoy a security and identity which lessens their need to feel defensive against the Turks and competitive with one another. Yet we enjoyed the Turkish people, especially in the countryside. They were overly curious but always friendly and helpful.

The sergeant in the BOQ provided quarters for the night because he was not expecting many pilots to arrive for lodging. We all took showers and I washed what we had worn, wondering how so much dirt could get into clothes in one day. It was muggy in the BOQ, as everywhere, but it was clean. Dave and Nan lay on their bunks catching up in their diary writing, a trip assignment they enjoyed. The high-pitched whine of jets put us to sleep.

In these hot areas the day begins early. By six o'clock everything on the base was fully active. In Adana at 7:30 busses were loading for trips in every direction. Men stood on top of them piling and tying lumpy mountains of luggage. Boys already were swimming in the Ceyhan River, over which the old Roman highway ran from Syria. We crossed on a bridge originally built by Hadrian in the second century.

Some banks were open, but the only one allowed to cash a traveler's check was not. Parked in the shade of a building, we watched the people and they watched us. Horsedrawn taxis clattered by. Men pushed carts of grapes. The drink vendor hoisted a big brass-spouted container onto his back and set two little glasses on the tray resting on his wide red sash. An old woman pointed to her mouth, trying to sell us flowers to get money to eat. When we did not buy, she clucked loudly in disapproval.

The redbus needed 42.7 out of the 43 liters its tank holds. We had used our reserve can. At the roadside we ate a breakfast of frosted flakes and powdered milk but the meal was marred by a strong odor of decay.

"It's just your imagination," insisted the Rev until Dave discovered a decomposing goat nearby.

Before we could see them, we heard women washing clothes in the cloudy water of the Ceyhan Nahr. Squatting or sitting cross-legged at the river bank, they pounded the clothes with sticks. A few boys with bamboo poles waded in the water. Others swam. Dicker observed, as he was to do more often, that many children forgot their swimsuits.

For a while the highway follows the river. We began to see castles and fortresses, like the twelfth-century Yilan Kalesi on a rocky mountain and other Crusader castles on hills or peaks. The road here is old. A mighty bump threw everything to the ceiling and knocked open the tailgate. The main road south to Beirut split from one continuing east to Gaziantep and we turned south, approaching the Plains of Issus, which lie at the head of the bay of Iskenderun, most northeasterly port of the Mediterranean.

A history book helped recall the famous battle here. It took place in the year 333 B.C., an easy date to remember. Alexander the Great came down through the Cilician Gates; Darius III and his Persians were behind the Syrian Gates in the south. It seems that the whole Plain of Issus could be entered through three passes in the mountains. Alexander came down through the north one. Darius was behind the south one, but he surprised Alexander by marching around through mountains to enter the plain through the third pass, the Amanic Gates in the northeast, so that he could attack Alexander from the rear. Alexander by then was marching through the plain toward the southern pass where he thought Darius would emerge. When he discovered where Darius really was, Alexander had to turn his forces around to fight him. Darius and his Persians had by far the larger number of troops and cavalry, but Alexander was a brilliant commander. He sent his big attack not against the horsemen, hardest to defeat, but against Darius' headquarters right in the heart of the Persian lines. Only 450 Macedonians were killed, but Darius lost 110,000 of his Persian soldiers.

"Man, what a lop-sided fight!"

We stood on the empty highway, looking out in all directions over the broad silent plain. Undistracted by anything modern, we could almost see the cavalry, the phalanx forming to attack, the footmen, the spears and shields and helmets a sea of dazzling metal in the sun. On an unexpected mound in the flatness of the plain stands the ruin of Toprakkale Fortress, built during the Crusades by the Armenians of Cilicia for controlling this strategic spot.

"How far did Alexander get?"

"All the way to India."

"Where'd he die?"

"In Babylon on his way back."

"Not very old, was he?"

"Only thirty-three. Easy to remember, like the battle here was 333."

"Anything left to see at Babylon today?"

"Let's go there sometime."

"If Alexander got to India, we oughta be able to."

"Yeah, but he died doing it."

"Prob'ly didn't have any Halazone pills."

"Lucky!"

Near the port of Iskenderun we saw the Mediterranean for the first time since Ephesus. It always seems to be a brilliant turquoise blue, the more so when summer sun turns the fields and hills that frame it to shades of gold, beige, and caramel.

Many watermelon fields lie along the road. In the middle of each field there is usually a high shelter on stilts, with a roof of dry foliage. Here the field owner rests from the sun and guards his fruit. We stopped at a pile of melons and a miniature roadside shelter of four sticks and a few leaves, just large enough for the young boy sitting under it. His father, relaxing in the full-size shelter in the middle of the field, came running when we stopped. His scale used stones on one side of the balances. We could buy either a one-rock or a two-rock watermelon. The one we chose took two rocks to balance. Dicker and the dark boy his size posed at the scale, each resting a hand on the melon. The father put on the rocks and the Rev clicked the camera shutter.

We stopped for another picture, this one of a farmer in baggy dark pantaloons throwing forkfuls of grain into the air. The sea breeze blew the chaff away and the good kernels fell onto the threshing floor. What did Jesus say about the chaff? No, not Jesus, it's in the Psalms, Psalm 1. "The wicked are not so, but are like chaff which the wind drives away."

Iskenderun, the old Alexandretta, the still older Alexandria-ad-Issum, is named to commemorate Alexander's victory at Issus. Iskenderun is a busy port serving Turkey and Syria. Near the docks were large oil storage tanks, a whole field of new American jeeps, and bulging bales of cotton. The road turns inland and climbs out of the city through the Syrian Gates pass which Darius decided not to use. While there was still a good view over the city and the sea, we stopped to eat our two-rock watermelon.

In the process of much watermelon eating we developed a useful method. Having divided a melon into seven pieces, this an art in itself, we stood in a circle, backs inward, so that we could all spit pits without hitting each other.

"REMEMBER WE ARE STILL in Turkey," the Rev reminded us as we drove to Antakya, the old Antioch of Syria on the Orontes River. It is thirty miles south of Iskenderun and lies inland against the lower slope of Mount Silpius. Shortly after noon we checked in at the Atahan Hotel and booked two of its fourteen rooms for five dollars and a half. Both rooms had balconies for sitting and W.C.'s, not S.Q.'s, and even soap, a most unusual feature. The girls' toilet seat was a shade of shocking pink.

Antioch-on-the-Orontes is a clean, colorful, but unimportant city today. In many ways it seems un-Turkish. The Syrians say that historically it belongs to them and insist that the thumb of Turkish territory extending down the east coast of the Mediterranean is a bad mistake.

The original Antioch was built by one of Alexander's generals who got a big piece of his master's empire when Alexander died. This general, Seleucus I, built the city about 300 B.C. on the site of an altar Alexander had dedicated to Zeus. The city was patterned after Egyptian Alexandria. Seleucus I had some ups and downs with his part of the empire but eventually he ruled all the way from Babylon to Asia Minor where we had seen the site of his Pisidian Antioch.

In addition to sixteen Antiochs, Seleucus also built four or more cities called Seleucia. One was Seleucia Pieria from which Paul and Barnabas sailed on their first missionary journey.

The Romans took over Antioch in 64 B.C. and made it even more outstanding than it had been. It was the first city to have street lighting and it ranked third in the Roman Empire, below Rome and Alexandria. Every emperor vied with his predecessor in adorning Antioch with grand buildings. Herod the Great, ruling Judea when Jesus was born, gave Antioch a wide paved street with colonnades. By Paul's day the city was more famous for luxury, pleasure, and vice than for its learning. The Roman poet Juvenal, writing in Paul's lifetime, said he thought the people of Antioch "restless, covetous, proud, turbulent."

Perhaps ancient Antioch gave itself to garishness and license because it was a composite of many cultures. Its original citizens were Alexander's Macedonian soldiers whom he had persuaded to marry Persian women. Standing at the terminus of the Euphrates-Aleppo caravan route, the city was full of people with Oriental customs and beliefs. Even the Chinese came and reported on its sensuality. Macedonians, Greeks, Romans, and Jews were only the main groups among many peoples, languages, and religions.

When the new followers of Christ fled persecution in Jerusalem and came to Antioch, they too could be accepted or at least left alone in a city busy with its pleasures, conglomerate in its citizenry. Here for a time Christianity was free from persecution and free to make impact on a decadent city.

In many ways Antioch was the center of the early Christian church. After the fall of Jerusalem in A.D. 70 this was doubly so. The name "Christian" may have been given in ridicule, but it also evinces the fact that in Antioch the church apart from the synagogue was established in the homes of men. This was headquarters for the Gentile church and Paul spent more time here than in Jerusalem. Many church councils and assemblies were held in Antioch in a church built by Constantine. At the end of the fourth century Chrysostom estimated that there were a hundred thousand Christians in Antioch.

Forty miles east Simon Stylites sat on his pillar early in the fifth century and his body was buried in Antioch. In 1098 the Crusaders besieged Antioch nine months before they took it with the help of an earthquake and a betrayal. They boasted that they killed a hundred thousand Moslems and they established the city as an independent duchy ruled by a Latin prince until the Turks took it in the year that Luther posted his theses in Wittenberg. Today the Greek, Syrian, Roman, and Maronite branches of the church still retain a position called Patriarch of Antioch.

We spent the afternoon at Peter's Grotto and Paul's beach. The grotto is in the side of a cliff on the mountainside, a mile and a half out of the city. We had never associated Antioch with Peter, though Galatians records a disagreement between Paul and Peter when Peter visited Antioch. Clement wrote about Peter's visit to the city and said that ten thousand men were baptized within seven days and a certain rich man, Theophilus, a leading man of the city, gave "the great palace of his house" for a meeting place, "and a chair was placed in it for the apostle Peter by all the people; and the whole multitude assembled daily to hear the word."

How the palace and the grotto fit together did not become clear to us. There was persecution in Antioch later, and Saint Ignatius was thrown to the lions there in A.D. 107. So perhaps the Christians hid in the grotto and named it for Peter. Or does the Turkish guidebook speak some truth when it claims that here "the followers of Christ gathered to hear Saint Peter preach the new faith for the first time," and here, in this "first Christian church . . . the followers of Christ received the name 'Christian' for the first time?" Acts 11 links the name to the ministry of Barnabas who brought Paul to Antioch from Tarsus.

Whatever the truth, the grotto with a front of white-washed stone has some closed-off tunnels to intrigue any boy, and the terrace in front of it gives a full view of the city.

Seventeen passable miles and three impossible ones bring one to the

Mediterranean beyond the village of Samandag. Here between two mountains running down to the shore is a long cove of dark-sand beach. The harbor Paul and Barnabas used at Seleucia Pieria is now a marshy area at the foot of Mount Pieria, the Turkish Musa Dag, one of the two mountains bounding the beach. In Paul's day walls from Antioch reached twelve miles to the port just as walls extended from Athens to Piraeus. We stood on the beach imagining the tip of Cyprus a hundred miles across the water and a group of Christians bidding their missionaries farewell.

A row of flimsy wooden houses stood back from the beach and some girls came out of them when they saw us swimming. A one-armed boy on a bicycle had followed us from Samandag and he watched politely until the Rev invited him to join us. The girls had invited themselves. One in an underpants, another is a long plissé nightgown, and a third in a ripped version of voluminous bloomers, leaped enthusiastically, sometimes roughly, onto our air mattress and into a game of water keep-away. The one-armed boy wanted to play catch with Nancy. There were also several bare little boys, swimsuits "forgotten." The girls went inside when we left the beach. The boy disappeared discreetly while we dressed by turns in the redbus and then he reappeared to ride alongside on the bumpy road back to Samandag.

On a hill overlooking Antioch we cooked supper and took pictures of the city lying rosy in a sunset glow against the bosom of its mountain. It was windy on the hill, cold enough for sweaters, and this was only a day away from the sticky heat of Adana. The wind blew so briskly that it overturned Dave's paper plate of meat-ball stew and applesauce onto his sneakers. Good weather for coffee, and for blankets on the hotel beds where cool air swept in through the sliding windows and balcony doors.

The merchants of Antioch did business until nine and then promptly slammed down and padlocked the corrugated metal that covers their open shops at night. The sound was like a crashing chorus of tinny overhead garage doors. This was the signal for gay music to begin in the rooftop restaurant across the street. From our third-floor balcony we watched the guests arrive at tables. It was like a play on a broad stage viewed from box seats. We talked about everything from Alexander the Great to the large bearded man we had seen in the hotel lobby, wearing khaki bermudas and a white explorer's helmet. Just like Teddy Roosevelt fresh in from safari.

In strange places one becomes accustomed to a babble of unintelligible language. So when the girls and I walked through the second-floor salon the next morning I heard the booming voice of the safari man but did not realize until several paces farther that he had been addressing me in Dutch. He had seen the Dutch license on the redbus parked in the street and wanted to meet fellow countrymen. For this we did not qualify but we had an interesting conversation anyway. The man was a Dutch professor of geology at the American University in Beirut.

On to Tripoli — Lebanon, not Libya — 175 miles south on the coast. The Orontes was low and sluggish when we crossed it. The redbus climbed to Hariye, Daphne of earlier centuries, with groves and springs and little waterfalls. When Seleucus I made Apollo the patron god of Antioch, he planted trees on this spring-fed plateau to make a sacred grove for Apollo's temple. Here fugitives from crime were free from arrest and society's outcasts gathered. The moral laxness of Daphne became a Western proverb.

In A.D. 362 the emperor Julian arrived to make a great sacrifice to the Greek gods whom he was trying to reinstate after the years of official Christianity under Constantine and his sons. But the Apollo temple in the green groves of Daphne was falling into ruin. No priests attended it, no sleek oxen could be found for a sacrifice. Someone produced a poor goose for the altar. Julian angered the citizens by closing the great church built by Constantine and in reprisal they burned the Apollo temple and its sacred statue while Julian was debating whether to make Antioch his capital as he prepared to attack the Persians. The people of Antioch, as insolent and boisterous under official Christianity as they had been under pagan deities, made sport of Julian publicly. In answer the emperor wrote a treatise against both Antioch and Christianity and left to spend his last winter in Tarsus.

On the road to the Syrian border ours was the only vehicle. The valleys and lower hillsides were lush with tobacco. Latakya, seventy-five miles south of Antakya-Antioch, is a tobacco center. Syria has its border station in a shady valley. Overhead flew the green-white-black flag with three red stars on the white stripe.

We had not crossed a border since entering Turkey two weeks earlier. Now we were leaving it, reluctantly. And slowly. The farther east the border, the slower the procedure. Hurry and efficiency are equally unknown in this part of the world. The arrival of a car is high point of the day. Dicker climbed into an old tire swing on a tree and we got out Lifesavers and peanuts while the Rev sat inside with the officials.

Strutting importantly, two of them came out to check the number of the car motor with the number on the *carnet de passage*. Did they think we would switch cars with all that gear and all those children? One official tore off the first section of a new page in the *carnet*. The second section of each page was taken when we left a country, this to guarantee that we had not sold the car inside the border. Another official wearing clods came to check cameras, transistor radio, binoculars, portable typewriter. He spent a long time examining each item.

Inside the building an official explains that he has no more of a certain stamp which must be pasted on our passports before we will be allowed out of the country into Lebanon. You would think, to hear them talk, that they process a hundred cars a day through that lonely spot. However, in broken

English and French the man says we can pick up this stamp in Latakya, at the bookstore.

"Where in Latakya is the bookstore?"

"*Oi, oi,* zee boo-ka store."

The road continues desolate, without sight of a moving thing. The straight line on the map is in reality the opposite. It twists inland through the hills. The valleys are especially hot. In Latakya at midday it is steaming hot, dirty noisy, and the horns of old cars do not stop honking for one second. We stopped at the tourist information office in the middle of the city after looking without success for "zee boo-ka store."

The man knew nothing about a stamp. He telephoned. The person on the other end of the line did not know, either. The man could not leave his office unattended. If we waited an hour until lunch, he would lock the office and go with us to search for the stamp. Through the grillwork over the window openings we looked out on the square. Men in fezzes and ankle-length skirts were shouting their wares. None of us had a desire to brave the oppressive heat outside.

Unsmiling, the tourist agency man locked his door and rode with us down some back streets to a bookstore. No, they had no stamp. Next to the police station. They had no stamp either. This was the wrong place to get one, here in Latakya. The police thought we could go straight on to the Lebanon border. We did not need to be told twice. In all the dust and noise and broiling heat, someone of us noticed a few Corinthian columns as we drove out of town.

Baniyas had huge Iraqi oil tanks and beyond the town was a fortress, the Marqab Castle, built A.D. 1062 by Arabs, occupied a hundred years later by Crusaders as one of their bulwarks along the coast. We ate lunch over-looking the dark-sand beach of the Mediterranean. Frankly, we were home-sick for Turkey. Perhaps Damascus would help us appreciate Syria more.

People we passed were swathed in clothes. Does this insulate against the heat? In their homes they seemed wiser. They made summer bedrooms on the flat roofs of their square cement homes. Some used poles to support a roof of foliage. Blankets were strewn on the roof for sleeping.

There were a few abandoned busses. Over one mechanics hovered hopefully. Another had its crankshaft lying on the road beside it. The passengers sat cross-legged on the sand, waiting. Time is of no concern. If not today, then tomorrow, or another tomorrow.

We had to enter and leave Syria twice, once to enter Lebanon and again to get from Lebanon to Jordan. Lebanon is surrounded on all sides by Syria except for a small southern border with Israel, which no one crosses except such personages as a pope, by special arrangement. But Lebanon has few problems. It faces the Mediterranean and controls all commerce to and from the interior.

At the Syria-Lebanon border, two Swiss were ahead of us. They had painted a map on their little beige car to indicate their travel route. It included Syria, Iraq, the Aswan Dam, Alexandria, Tripoli in Libya. The map did not show clearly how they were going from Iraq to the Aswan Dam with Israel's Negev between but it was too hot to ask. Customs would be long enough in the sun without further conversation.

The official got out his big book in the customs office and began to write in Arabic, to us, backwards. I was inside too because the official sent for me to identify my own passport. He leaned back on two legs of his chair and began to practice saying our names, all six of them, each time pausing to ask me with a flirtatious smile and raised eyebrows whether his pronunciation was correct. Certainly, certainly, I assured him, concentrating to decipher which name it was.

Settling back on four chair legs, he addressed the Rev.

"You eldest daughter — how old?"

"Twelve years old."

"You bring her, too," said the official, peering out into the bright sun where the children had thrown open the redbus doors to keep from frying.

"I am very sorry," answers the Rev firmly. "She is not feeling well today." This with the protective firmness of a man who does not wish to exhibit his women.

The Arab hears the firmness. He orders coffee for the three of us. Sweet gritty mud with no glass of water for a chaser. But then, the water would not be pure. While we drank, another official emerged from the next room wearing a clean pair of pajamas, apparently his work uniform.

We were waiting to be asked about the stamp we did not get, but there was no mention of it. Would we bring inside everything we have to be declared? Yes, everything, because it must all be marked down on our papers. And it must be slowly inspected and admired by the chief official and his pajama-clad assistant.

"How you come back?" asks the chief.

Never tell an Arab that you are going to Israel. The Rev answers, with some truth, "We have not completed all our plans. We will have to see."

Smiles brighten the men's faces. "We shall hope welcome you back," says one. "You come this way, here, yes?"

"Not if we can help it," I say grimly to myself. "It is easier to get into East Berlin."

"*Shook-ran*," says the Rev, using his first Arabic word. We can now say thank you in seven languages besides our own.

A group of soldiers lolled under a tree a hundred yards from the customs building. One signaled for us to stop, and for the Rev to come to him. With a half leer on his face he inquired, jerking his thumb in my direction, who was the *dame* in the car? True, the word is more acceptable in French than in English, but the tone of voice was not.

Turkish men are not like this. They are friendly, but polite where women are concerned. Not so the Arab men, whose own women are usually out of sight, covered with clothes. Perhaps the sleeveless dress and public presence of a Western woman suggest that she is less modest than her Arab counterpart. But why the difference between the Turks and the Arabs then? This was the first of several incidents which kept us on our guard in Arab countries and made us grateful we were not escorting eighteen-year-old daughters. One of twelve was bad enough.

Intermittently, whenever the government is shaking or toppling, the Syrian border is closed. The record is something like fifteen coups in seventeen years. At least no one had engineered a coup when we arrived, and we were minded to avoid Syria on future trips.

T RIPOLI, ON THE MEDITERRANEAN, is only a dozen miles inside Lebanon. At the YMCA Director Shuhibar welcomed us in English and with cokes. We had made reservations by mail months earlier. Shuhibar was a forty-ish bachelor who had Arabicized his German name Schreiber to fit his surroundings. He lived in one of the five bedrooms in the YMCA building and was attended days by a little woman in black whom we named Yes-Missy, the words she kept chirping as she followed me around. Boys playing in the game rooms were intrigued by the presence of girls. The whole building was damp almost to dripping like the cracked sink over which Yes-Missy presided without soap.

It was mid-afternoon but Shuhibar suggested that there was still time to see the Crusader castle in the city and to drive to Les Cèdres, only stand of cedars left from the forests out of which King Hiram cut timbers for David's palace and Solomon's temple. One of the Y boys rode with us to the Crusader Castle of Saint Giles, built by Raymond of Saint Giles when his Crusaders took the city from the Muslims in 1109 after a five-year siege. The conquest included burning a great library of a hundred thousand volumes! Crusaders defended the castle two hundred years until they were starved into submission by the sultan. Large enough for several thousand knights, the castle had two escape tunnels, one under the city to the sea and the other to the Kadisha River. On one of the parapets Dave found a small stone cover or jar stopper with a Crusader cross on it.

After the castle, trustingly we set out for the cedars. To hear Shuhibar speak, they were nearby, a short ride into the hills. Next morning he told us that this was his favorite ride with his fiancée, which explained why his concept of distance was distorted.

Cedar, the king of woods, is a symbol of prosperity. Nancy read a tourist folder. The cedar tree is stamped on the coins of Lebanon and appears in the center of its flag as a green tree on a white stripe flanked by two red ones. Cedar is a pungent-smelling wood whose bitterness repels worms. Long before Solomon, this wood made palaces and coffins for the Pharaohs of Egypt as well as ship masts for the Phoenician fleet.

We found a few of the fifty references to cedars in the Old Testament. "The righteous flourish like the palm tree and grow like a cedar in Lebanon," Psalm 92 says. Ezekiel said when he described the great port city of Tyre, "They took a cedar from Lebanon to make a mast for you." And the Song of Solomon reports, "King Solomon made himself a palanquin from the wood of Lebanon . . . its posts of silver, its back of gold, its seat of purple."

"What's a palanquin?"

"It's a little chariot carried by poles on the shoulders of men."

Feel the cool air. No wonder all the rich people leave the sticky humidity of Tripoli to spend their summers in the mountains. But where are the cedars?

Fifty miles farther, that was where they were. Fifty miles of tortuous unbanked road, ascending and descending in hairpin turns. It seemed as if we were snaking through most of the two-hundred-mile range of Lebanon peaks which run from opposite Cyprus down to the Israel border.

Round and round, up and up, through villages decorated with arches of greens, past acres of grey-green olive trees in reddish soil. Groups of girls in attractive Western clothes were walking along the road. Groups of boys walked, too, perhaps to meet the girls outside of the towns. In well-to-do Moslem families there are strict attitudes about boy-girl contacts.

At the peak of the first big mountain we looked back and saw ten smaller ones between us and the sunset shimmering far off on the sea. Then, inexplicably, we began to descend. When we asked for Les Cèdres, people pointed on with broad gestures that implied some distance. The road skirted the deepest part of a gorge, the "romantic Qadish gorge." Somewhere nearby was Becharre where the poet Khalil Gebran is buried, and we would have been interested, having read his *The Prophet,* but we had to find the cedars.

The children dug under the third seat for jackets we had not used since Switzerland. The Rev's arm was tired from perpetual shifting of gears. No one thought of supper. All eyes strained into the dusk, searching for Les Cèdres.

There they were, finally, where the road widened into a parking area for all the cars and tour busses shown on the colored postcards. The only cedars left of the forests growing in the days of Solomon, said a guidebook, and they stand at the foot of the country's highest mountains. Well, if this is only the foot of the mountains! The trees remain, explained the guidebook in a rare burst of truth, because they are so inaccessible that no one could get at them to cut them down.

Dave, Nan, and the Rev jumped out with their cameras which did not record very clearly in the twilight. Shivering, we walked among the trees, several hundred of them against the sheltered mountainside. They were about eighty feet tall with foliage roughly triangular in shape. We felt their furrowed bark. In the souvenir shop we bought a little round box of cedar wood made from a small branch so that the outside of it was of the rough bark. In the cover was embedded a cedar-tree coin. The price was explained by the proprietor who said that all trees are protected by law and souvenirs may only be made from branches that fall. We also bought some cards to get a clearer picture of what we were supposed to be seeing. Apparently there was a Maronite chapel nearby. Still shivering, even in our jackets, we climbed back into the redbus to discuss where to eat and how to return to the steamy heat of the YMCA.

Shuhibar had described an alternate descent but we were not sure of it and there were no signs anywhere. We returned the way we had come. High up the air was too cold for cooking supper. Farther down, the road had no shoulders. It just dropped off into blackness. So we kept on riding. Clusters of lights hanging in midair marked villages on the mountainsides. Candles flickered in wayside shrines. A bright light illuminated a monastery and strings of colored lights hung on hotels above the road. Sometimes we heard the sound of rushing water, falling ice-cold from the snowy ski slopes advertised in all Lebanon tourist literature. Ski and swim on the same day, say the folders. It was an honest claim. We would have paraphrased it, Roast and freeze the same evening. And were these ski resorts really "easily accessible?"

Slowly we moved from one cluster of life to the next, down the cedars' mountain, along the gorge, up the next mountain, meeting an occasional car on a tight turn, descending mountain by mountain into the hot wet air on the coastal plain. Dicker had long since fallen asleep. The rest of us rated that night ride in a class with the one to Konya and the race to catch the ferry in Brindisi.

At the YMCA Shuhibar sat in bed reading, his door ajar. We told him the trip had been a real experience. (Never tell a lie, the Rev says. You can always couch the truth in gracious words.) So we said we would never forget our visit to the cedars, and how cool it was up there, and how nice it would be to linger sometime in one of the mountain resorts.

Shuhibar was satisfied. He got orange soda out of the cooler for us and said good night. We sat around a low table in the bedroom for two and ate a midnight supper of cold spaghetti, fruit cocktail, and orange soda. Over the humidity-dampened sheets on the children's bunk beds we spread our red towels to insulate against the moisture.

Yes-Missy appeared early in the morning, curious and eager to help. She took the empty tin cans, spaghetti forks, and fruit cocktail spoons. They lay in the dirty cracked sink under a trickle of cold water while Yes-Missy explained to me in pantomime that she was not a Moslem, but a Christian, and she went to church often, very often. Later, in the bedroom, I wiped the rest of the spaghetti off the forks with Kleenex before repacking them.

Meanwhile the boys were accepted in a game of pool, the girls were admired from afar, and the Rev sat in Shuhibar's office talking. Our host had worked in Gaza's YMCA before coming to Tripoli. Tripoli, he explained, is largely Moslem, though Lebanon as a whole has a Christian majority and seats its parliament according to religion, not party. The Y is the only co-educational place in Tripoli, inviting girls on special occasions.

Lebanon is so prosperous today, said Shuhibar, that girl secretaries travel to Syria with several sets of nylon lingerie made in Lebanon. They sell the sets and with the money they can pay for a hotel in Syria and for a ten-day stay in Turkey besides. Some of the world's richest people live or bank in Beirut, which is the heart of the Middle East economy. Lebanon is stable and flourishing. But America is better, yes? Shuhibar would like to come to America. In two months he would marry and then he would like to come. Later he introduced us to his fiancée who was a teacher in the commercial school run by the YMCA. What would Yes-Missy do when replaced by this lovely lady? Perhaps she could work for both of them.

Yes-Missy stood at the door while the Y boys fought to carry out our zipper bags. With one hand she held my arm, with the other the coins I had given her. There was a final pantomime about how much she liked me and the children, how grieved she was to see us go. I kissed her and said *Merci* and *Shook-ran* and Thank You. The Rev took a picture of Shuhibar with our boys under the YMCA sign in Arabic and Roman letters.

"Any borders today?"

"Nope, dad said not till tomorrow."

"How far today?"

"Dad said only sixty miles."

"Where to?"

"Beirut."

"Never heard of it."

"Ya did now."

THE ROAD SOUTH to Beirut follows part of the old Phoenician coastline, a fertile belt of level land two hundred miles long, backed by the mountains and facing the sea. From an unbroken string of ports

Phoenician ships sailed as masters of the sea. They dared to sail at night with the North Star to guide them. They brought back tin from Britain and the Far East. At Gibraltar they established a trading post eleven hundred years before Christ.

The Phoenician gods were gods of nature, first the sun god Baal and later others like the moon goddess Astarte and the fish god Dagon and Moloch who was worshiped with human sacrifice. Tyre and Sidon, among the greatest ports, held their pagan reputation until Jesus' day. He said of them, rebuking the Galileans of Bethsaida and Chorazin who had seen his works and heard his words, "If the mighty works done in you had been done in Tyre and Sidon, they would have repented long ago in sackcloth and ashes."

Somewhere on this Phoenician coast, near Sidon, it is said, Jonah was deposited by the great fish and went to preach in Nineveh. "In case you're interested," volunteered Dave, "Tyre is mentioned twenty times in the Bible and you need a special permit to go there. Too near Israel."

Though no longer worshiped, nature is still harnessed all along the old Phoenician coast. Wind-driven windmills pump water from the Mediterranean into shallow square ponds. The sun evaporates the water, leaving coarse salt crystals behind. Men rake the salt into small piles and pack it into burlap sacks. Tobacco, bananas, and bamboo flourish in the hot damp fields along the coast. And the sea still beckons in shades of turquoise, according to its depth. We made a wrong turn to reach the Byblos ruins and came upon a jewel of beach cove.

"Later today," said the Rev to his eager crew rummaging for swimsuits. "First Byblos and the Dog River."

The guide at Byblos had long curling fingernails on the little fingers of each hand. With an umbrella over his head he began eagerly, "Byblos is the oldest continually inhabited city in the world."

"Same thing they say for Damascus," whispered Nan.

"Sixteen cities is it on top the other," continued the guide, leading us to a high parapet of the Crusader castle from which we could look at the ruins between the castle and the sea. Some of these ruins date back to 3200 B.C.

"Pretty old." Clark.

"Pretty hot." Em.

"You will see this Crusader castle has five towers. Is in each corner of the castle one with a well for water in it."

"The fifth is a spare," added Dave in an aside.

Dicker tried to pry out a British cannon ball imbedded in the wall during more recent fighting in 1840. The parapet overlooked the foundations of seven city walls — two Phoenician from 3000 B.C., one Ammorite from 2400, a Hittite from 2000, an Egyptian from 1800, an Assyrian-Babylonian from 1000, and a Persian from 700. Near the sea stand six columns of a Roman temple to Jupiter. The temple granite came from Aswan. There is no granite native to Lebanon. Stones from ancient temples were used to build the Crusader castle. Today Byblos is called Jebail. Ezekiel called it Gebal in his book of prophecy.

The old history of Byblos came to light in 1922 when a landslide at the southeast corner of the Crusader castle uncovered part of a royal burial area. Excavations produced nine sarcophagi of early Byblos rulers from the days when it outranked Tyre and Sidon. A special fleet of ships carried cedar wood to Egypt in exchange for papyrus. On the sarcophagus of King Ahiram, first king of Phoenicia about the time of Moses, is the oldest Phoenician inscription known. It was the Phoenicians who gave the world the twenty-four letters from which came Greek and later alphabets of Europe.

"Was found here also heads of a boy and girl used in sacrifice," says the guide, giving his parasol a twirl for emphasis. "And the dye rooms where was made famous purple color from murex shells. And twenty-four hundred jars of human skeletons."

"Jars?" whispers Clark to the Rev.

"Yes, they used to bury people that way with their bodies curled up in big pottery jars."

"How'd they get 'em in?"

We paid the guide and took shelter from the sun in the restaurant-souvenir shop where the children admired many things and the proprietor was irritated that we did not translate all this enthusiasm into purchasing. We did buy coke, one thing we missed in Turkey, where the government will admit neither the finished product nor American enterprise to produce it.

"I'll tell you something about Byblos for nothing," says the Rev. "This is the place from which we think the word 'Bible' comes. The Greeks got their papyrus from Byblos and called it *biblion*. So *biblion* meant a papyrus roll, which was for them a book. Many rolls were *biblia*. The early Christians called the New Testament books *biblia*. And so we call the Book of all books the Bible. Isn't that interesting?"

"Could I puleeze have another coke?" Dicker.

Twenty miles to Beirut. The beach is whiter, more pebbly, more swimmers, more resorts. There are important rock inscriptions at the mouth of the Dog River which ancients called the Lycus after a sacred dog by that name. Nineteen inscriptions in eight languages mark the advance of conquerors dating from the Egyptian Ramses II in the thirteenth century before Christ to the evacuation of foreign troops from Lebanon in 1946. Nebuchadnezzar, Alexander, Marcus Aurelius, the Mamelukes, Napoleon III — these are some of the mighty men whose armies passed here. The older carvings are above, over the tunnel carved for the modern road. The more recent, like Napoleon's and that of the First World War, are at road level. Each inscription is identified with a Roman numeral. Like the Cilician Gates, this strategic pass has felt the surge and ebb of empires for thousands of years.

Beirut is the busy hub and jumping-off place of the Middle East. It is deceivingly Western in appearance, with big buildings and imposing signs on the offices of firms and airlines. The University Christian Center is across from the campus of the American University.

"You mean we can drink water right from the faucet?" said Nan when we were shown a fifth-floor suite of three rooms and bath. The rooms opened with sliding glass doors onto a balcony facing toward the Mediterranean.

We made Beirut our jumping-off place, too, and abandoned ourselves to shopping and swimming. At The New Oriental Store, a name mirroring the paradox of Beirut itself, we learned that a Lebanese pound is a hundred *piasters,* and a dollar is worth about 3.15 *piasters.* Silver filigree jewelry sets cost from two to three dollars. We bought some of the delicately spun pins and earrings for gifts. One set of silver cedar trees is my favorite for the Christmas season.

And there were camel bags, leather draw-string imitations of bags carried by camel drivers, with little pockets all around the outside. Imprinted with gold designs, these make ideal purses. For Dicker we bought a string of wooden camels, led by a donkey, of course. Nan went to look in the adjoining room and came back a bit dazed. Outside she explained that the teen-age boy who helped in the shop had tried to kiss her. In Arab lands the visitor learns to keep his daughters firmly in tow.

In another shop the boys bought water goggles made in Japan. We all bought paperbacks in a bookshop displaying the latest titles from the States. Harold Lamb's *The Crusades* seemed like good background for the Crusader castles we were seeing.

The public beach was opposite the airport, with a highway between. A steady procession of planes roared into the sky. The beach was filled with common families like ourselves, though less fair of skin and hair and with mothers in skirts covering their ankles. People watched us with friendly curiosity.

On this beach United States marines stormed ashore in 1958 by order of President Eisenhower. The sun sank flaming orange into navy blue water and we went on swimming in the crashing surf until dark. Dave lost his Athens ring and persistently sifted through yards of sand until, miraculously, he found it. Up and down the beach went the vendor of flat round rolls. He balanced a big tray on his head and carried a wooden frame like a high three-legged stool on which he set the tray while he made a sale.

That night on the balcony outside our rooms a good friend from the Near East Christian Council introduced us to some of the complications of Arab-Israeli-American relationships. We began to understand why the Arabs feel that the United States, though speaking of freedom for all, has reached out a long arm to intervene in the affairs belonging to the Middle East. First we supported the Arabs against the Turks. Then we supported the Israelis against the Arabs, backing the Zionist drive to found the state of Israel. The Arabs are understandably bitter about the creation of Israel. They are bitter toward the United Nations which did nothing when the Israelis rejected the 1947 U.N. partition plan and fought doggedly until they won a million and a half acres more than the plan awarded them.

A million Arabs displaced to dusty barren refugee camps watch their former fields grow green with water drained by the Israelis from the Jordan. They see the remarkable progress Israel has made, bolstered by Western support and the arrival of many talented aggressive Jews from advanced countries. Many observers say that there were the beginnings of Arab-Jewish cooperation in the Middle East before Israel was created.

Later, when we had returned to Michigan, we heard Kenneth Cragg, an English authority on Islam, describe these things in his quiet incisive way. Remember, he said, that Israel seeks "salvation through statehood." This is understandable to Europeans because of the cruel annihilation of Jews there. But it is utterly foreign to the mind of the Arabs in whose midst the Jews logically have chosen to have their new state. For the Arabs this is a recurrence of the Western invasion of the Crusades whose knight armies held almost the identical territory that Israel now holds. While a surging nationalism has put the British out of Egypt and India, the French out of Lebanon, and so on, it is this same nationalism which has created the state of Israel. And so Israel is not a departing imperialism in the Arab mind but a fresh incursion of the nationalism they desperately want for themselves even though they may not have the capacity to achieve it.

You can see, said our Beirut friend who had lived sixteen years among the Arabs, how these countries feel about the Americans, how they mistrust us, how they misinterpret our belated attempts at friendliness and help. The Lebanese did not even appreciate American marines on the beach here, though they may have needed them. And while the Arab chafes and longs for the prosperity of his Western-supported Jewish neighbors, he is ready to listen to the apostles of change and to the Communist propaganda. The undeclared truce between the Arabs and the Israelis is an uneasy one, a lull in hostilities punctuated by frequent border incidents and gunfire.

Understandably then, the Arabs are less eager to listen to the Christian gospel which comes via American missionaries. That's why they must hear it from their own people, explained our friend, who was then working under the ARAMCO agency of the World Council of Churches to set up a strong radio station on which Arab Christians would broadcast to their own people. What red tape there had been, what quiet resistance and Moslem competition in every phase, from securing permission to place the transmitter in Ethiopia to getting the station on the air!

What will this witness mean for the Arab Christians speaking to their own people? Will they feel more ostracism, more persecution? Will the gospel message be more acceptable to their people than when brought by "foreigners?"

We had evening prayers together long after midnight. It was not easy to know for what to pray. We had ceased being interested onlookers. A new concern lay upon us. What must an American Christian think and do and pray about the Middle East?

ANIMALS MAY BE THE DRIVING HAZARD in Turkey, but American cars with Lebanese drivers are the peril around Beirut. To qualify as an expert driver one does not merely pass on a hill. Pass double; pass the car already passing another. Never wait for oncoming traffic when emerging from a sideroad. It is quicker to turn left and ride on the left shoulder until you can cut across into the lane of your intention. Brakes or low gear on down grades are for the faint-hearted, especially if there are curves involved. Overturned cars and trucks are usual sights. From Beirut toward Damascus the road climbs and winds to cross the mountains and there are many opportunities to display one's driving prowess. Behind the wheel of a car an Arab loses all the lethargy he shows when standing on two feet.

To reach the impressive ruins of Baalbek one turns north off the Damascus highway toward Zahle, capital of the province. Baalbek lies on the Biqa Plateau between two mountain chains, the Lebanon over which one climbs coming from Beirut, and farther east, the Anti-Lebanon range whose southernmost peak, Mount Hermon, supplies water for the Sea of Galilee. A bountiful spring of water made Baalbek a favorite caravan stop. Rome made it a colossal outpost of empire. Today, in isolated grandeur, marble pillars rise above an oasis of green vineyards and fruit trees in red soil still watered by the spring.

Baalbek is an old worship center named for the sun god Baal, renamed Heliopolis by the Greeks, for whom *helios* meant "sun." The ruins left today predate Roman emperor Caracalla who died in A.D. 217. Constantine a hundred years later stopped all pagan worship in the temples and built a Christian basilica in the middle of Jupiter's altar court. This began the seesaw between Christian and pagan worship in Baalbek. Emperor Julian removed the basilica and restored the worship of Jupiter, Venus, and Mercury. Theodosius installed another basilica after thoroughly destroying the pagan altars. Much later the Arabs turned the six-sided outer court into a fortress. In spite of all this, the Baalbek temples are the most imposing Roman ruins we have seen. "These columns are the largest ever erected, these stones the largest ever used, this form of architecture the most massive ever conceived." The guidebook speaks honestly.

What is seen at Baalbek is not all Roman. The temple arrangement, with successive courts and altars, is Oriental or Eastern. Only after ritual and purification might one progress to the temple itself. Weren't Moses' tabernacle and Solomon's temple in this general pattern, too? They developed a ritual of holiness. And the gods of Baalbek are not even all Roman. Their Roman names represented Syro-Phoenician deities — Hadad or Baal became Jupiter, his wife Astarte was Venus, and their son the Romans called Mercury. So the Romans built the temples after the Oriental pattern with Roman ornamentation and gave Roman names to the gods already worshiped there.

Up the steps and behind the wide portico is the hexagonal outer court with statue niches and priests' rooms. It opens into the great court of altars, three hundred feet square. The main altar must have been about sixty feet square. Behind these courts rose the Jupiter Temple itself on a platform twenty-five feet high and three hundred feet long. Around the statue of Jupiter was a peristyle of fifty-four Corinthian columns, each sixty feet high with a diameter larger than the height of a man. Each pillar was made of only three granite sections. All the stone had to be brought in over the mountains. No wonder the legend grew that only giants could have built Baalbek. The pillars were topped with a connected twelve-foot-high cornice richly decorated with acanthus leaves, geometric patterns, and open-mouthed lions' heads. We stood beside one piece of fallen cornice. A man's shoulder fit easily into the lion's mouth. Of all these columns six remain standing, connecting cornice intact, dominating the temple area. Each year the Baalbek International Festival is staged on the Jupiter Temple steps and the audience sits in the court of altars. We were too early for the festival which begins late in July.

The second Baalbek temple, better preserved than Jupiter's and larger than the Athens Parthenon, is called the Bacchus Temple because the carvings are appropriate to the god of wine, though some say the temple belonged to Jupiter's wife, Venus-Astarte. This temple door alone is as tall as seven six-foot men standing on each other's heads! It is covered with symbols: ears of corn for life, locusts for famine, poppies for death, along with satyrs, bacchanals, and cupids holding grape clusters. The ceiling panels, some still in the roof and others lying in the courtyard, were divided to give each god a square. Here are Mars with his coat of arms, Diana taking an arrow from her quiver, Venus pressing a winged cupid to her heart, Tyche with an abundance cornucopia, Ceres with ears of corn, and Bacchus with a wreath of vine leaves around his head. In the most sacred part of the temple, up thirteen steps, once stood the statue of the temple deity. Two rooms beneath held worshipers' offerings.

As we left the temples, limousines arrived from Beirut, bringing tourists for a guided tour. The drivers lounging in the shade watched while we ate a watermelon next to the redbus. Then one came to point out a spring for washing sticky hands, another brought a cup for drinking, and a third offered his handkerchief to dry Dicker's washed hands. Dicker brought his new camel string to show the men and they bent down to his level, patting his head and chuckling, probably at the goggles, camera, and crew cut. When the Rev shook hands with them, they felt welcomed and came to inspect the redbus and its contents.

A boy ran out from a fenced refugee camp when we stopped to photograph Baalbek across the vineyards. "My name is Mohammed, please give me some money," he repeated in sing-song, like a record stuck in a groove. Girls who passed in bright skirts and black head coverings had silver stars pasted on each side of their nostrils. When we stopped again to photograph camels grazing, a Bedouin and his three children flew at us out of nowhere.

"Bak-sheesh bak-sheesh," they shouted — a gift, a gift. Who had said, Remember that every Arab considers you a direct blessing sent by Allah to enrich him? The Rev held off the four with a wave of his camera and they posed. The boy braced himself like a track runner to dash toward us at the click of the camera. Each child carried a stout stick and wore light-colored, long-sleeved clothing. The boy's hands were stained with red dye.

No more candy and gum. Only cigarettes left. The father, lean brown face swathed in a black and white headdress, insisted on a cigarette for each child. Clever man! As we drove away he collared the children and took their cigarettes for himself.

Where is Esh-sham, the Arab name for Damascus? Which way is the Syrian border? At a confusing fork in the road a man misdirected us and two barefoot women outshouted and outgestured each other trying to get us back on the right road.

The Lebanese customs check went smoothly. Boys selling cold drinks offered American quarters in exchange for Lebanese currency, at large profit to themselves, of course. Syrian customs consisted of two checkpoints, both confused. At the first, Arab sheiks were trying to bring into Syria bolts of cloth, washing machines, and other large items. No one seemed to know what he was doing. A crowd of men watched. At the second checkpoint we paid for the privilege of re-entering Syria — $11.50 in addition to normal passport and auto *carnet* costs. At least there was enough activity and confusion to keep officials from practicing names and inquiring after daughters.

SYRIA IS MORE PROSPEROUS in the Damascus area than near the Turkish border. About fifteen miles outside the capital city begins the shady valley of the Barada River. El-Barada, "the cool," the Abana of which Naaman boasted that it was better than all the waters of Israel. Many people sat along the banks, celebrating a Moslem holy day.

The Grand Hotel was filled with a group of Roman Catholics en route to Jerusalem. It had been recommended by the Mennonite travel agency in Beirut's University Christian Center. Mention of that name provided the magic touch. For this agency, said the manager, he would give us his own, his private room. Ah, the Oriental exaggeration!

Dicker knelt down before a little lighted shrine on the table between the double beds. He touched his forehead several times to the green rug. To my question he replied, "Guess I oughta pray the way they do around here, mom," and was unaware that he had done Moslem obeisance before a Syrian Orthodox shrine.

Certainly, the desk clerk assured us, there was time before the evening meal to see the bazaar and the Straight Street. An old man in the lobby guided us to the Souk Hamidye, the covered bazaar named for a sultan. Few merchants were selling because of the holy day. Some men and boys followed us, walking close to Nancy. At one corner two small girls with matted hair and filthy clothing sat in the dirt and wetness. One was retarded. Listlessly they watched the passersby. Behind me Em said softly, "Nan, what if that was you and me?"

"Ananias' house — where?" we said to the boy speaking scraps of English who attached himself to us. He brought us instead to the treasury house of the Omayyad Mosque, on one of whose minarets Jesus the Prophet is supposed to appear at the last judgment. How frequently the Koran and the Bible speak of the same characters and events! This must have made Islam more palatable to simple Christians forced at sword point to accept it centuries ago.

The Omayyad Mosque stands on twelve pillars taken from an old Jupiter-Hadad temple which Emperor Theodosius turned into a church named after John the Forerunner. When the Arabs attacked Damascus in 635, the church was made available to both Christians and Moslems. Entering by the same door, the Moslems prayed to Allah in the eastern part toward Mecca while in the western part the Christians called upon the Trinity and the saints. The head of John the Baptist supposedly rests in a marble sarcophagus in a little chapel at the center of the mosque. It occurred to us that we had been shown other reputed parts of this good man's body in the Topkapi Palace of Istanbul.

The boy led us through twisting streets and changing odors but he was uncertain what it was we were asking. Another boy joined us. In a sidewalk stand the Rev found a garish postcard of the Ananias house chapel. Yes, the second boy knew. Nimbly he led the way past merchants holding out their inlaid boxes, past a gnome-like character asleep in the middle of a large pile of baskets, past all kinds of people working, cooking, talking in the streets. At the locked entrance in a gray stone arch he stopped, only a block from the street called Straight.

An old lady in black (aren't they all?) unlocked the gate and led us through a courtyard to damp stone steps. Some men and boys descended with us into the room shown on the postcard. When the candles were lit, we saw a few benches, an altar, a dark opening purported to be Paul's escape tunnel. To where, for what? No one knew. The Bible, of course, does not say anything about Ananias' house. Ananias went to Paul who waited, blind, in the house of Judas on the Straight Street. A man tried to explain the three pictures over the altar — Paul on the Damascus road, recovering his sight, and being lowered in a basket. The Rev prompted him when necessary, which was most of the time. Explained by two in French, English, and pantomime, these stories take on considerable flavor.

In a shop nearby, the proprietor welcomed us with tiny cups of sweet thick coffee and laid out his exquisite inlaid boxes. Though his English was only fair, his flattery was irresistible. We bought four small jewelry boxes costing about a dollar each. Dave chose a pearl-inlaid chess board which pretty well depleted his souvenir allowance, and the Rev picked a beautiful large jewelry box for me. Glowing from the merchant's effusive display of Oriental courtesy, we turned into the Straight Street which still runs the length of the city from east to west. It is, more literally, the Long Street, and passes through the arch of the east gate by which Paul, blind and still called Saul, probably arrived in Damascus.

The city wall is still twenty feet high with little houses hanging over it, even though the street level of the city has risen about twenty feet since Paul's day. There is a modern insert in the wall, a sort of twin-towered gate with a window opening where Paul was let down in a basket, guides point out. The people of the Middle East have a passion for assigning exact locations for every story or legend associated with the Bible and the Koran.

The taxi ride back to the hotel was wild. Damascus taxi drivers have two horns in their old American cars. One is on the floor, the other on the wheel, and both are in constant use. Driving with one foot on a horn and the other on the gas makes the brake superfluous. Horns blaring, we careened through the narrow streets with inches to spare, scattering people, animals, and all movable objects like a vacuum cleaner in reverse. I cringed in a corner of the back seat. "Close your eyes and whistle," shouted the Rev above the horns. The boys loved every minute of it. Limp and laughing with relief, we entered the Grand Hotel just in time for dinner.

It was a good dinner from a French menu. Cream soup, cucumber-tomato salad, lamb and vegetables, sweet melon for dessert. That some guests cooked for themselves we discovered when we went onto our balcony after the children were asleep. Within arm's reach of us on the next balcony a couple was eating from a charcoal brazier. The woman covered her face with a veil when we appeared. The man, reclining on an elbow, ignored us. Across the square was a government building, brightly lit and guarded. In Syria another coup is always lurking in the shadows.

How many kings and caliphs has this old city seen? More than any other, it lays claim to being the oldest continually inhabited city in the world. It was originally called Dimashq. Abraham and three hundred servants pursued the four kings of Genesis 14 "to Hobah, north of Damascus" to rescue Lot. Paul came to Damascus after A.D. 30 during the fifty-year interlude when it was ruled by the Nabatean king, Aretas IV, whose capital was the rose-cliff citadel of Petra, south of the Dead Sea.

"The governor under King Aretas guarded the city of Damascus in order to seize me," writes Paul in II Corinthians 11:32-33, "but I was let down in a basket through a window in the wall, and escaped his hands." The Pharisee turned fugitive, the persecutor turned preacher. Having come to Damascus "breathing threats and murder against the disciples of the Lord," he departs "a chosen instrument" to carry Christ's name "before Gentiles and kings and the sons of Israel." That was a turning point!

Breakfast coffee at the hotel turned gray-green when it was made *au lait*, but the jam was good. When we carried out our luggage, boys were washing the redbus windows, eager for a tip. Dicker, wearing goggles and camera, stood on the sidewalk calling *"Bak-sheesh, bak-sheesh,"* without results. The morning crowds moved quickly, anticipating the sun. Black-veiled women, men in fez or burnoose, people in Western dress — the curious mingling of East and West which in Damascus, more than in Beirut, makes the Oriental mood dominant.

Leaving the redbus outside the wall, we walked through the east gate into Straight Street. "With that name they should be making tents," said Nan about a little inlaid box place called St. Paul's Shop. A man working in front of the shop showed how, by slicing off thin cross sections from the glued-together rods he held in his hand, intricate patterns were made and glued onto the wooden boxes. These inlaid boxes are a Damascus specialty.

The Straight Street was busy. A man sold yellow melons from a wooden cart. At a public water point boys were loading tin cans of water onto a flat cart, in the shafts of which stood a puny donkey wearing a head decoration of colored beads and tassels. A man in a burnoose whizzed by on a motorbike. Occasionally a bus managed to skin through the gate without scraping its sides. One boards a Damascus bus by leaping aboard the rear steps while the vehicle is in motion. An old couple in veil and fez tried unsuccessfully to swing aboard several busses and were still waiting when we returned to the crowd standing around the redbus.

A horse fell and lay still on the busy road outside the wall. Mud villages clung like shabby suburbs to the city. The cemetery, a dry mud area with oblong mounds for graves, had a few whitewashed mounds in it. We looked back for the last glimpse of Damascus, a green oasis lying in the desert plain. Was this how it looked to Saul as he neared the end of his hot two-hundred-mile trek from Jerusalem? He was almost there when the Lord confronted him.

S YRIA PASSED US ON SLOWLY to Jordan, which has a pleasant rest house at its customs office. We bought cold drink and hot dogs served cold, sliced lengthwise, on dry bread.

"Where's the catsup?" asked Dicker to the amusement of a stocky middle-aged American in khaki-colored clothes who was drumming his fingers on one of the tables.

"Seen a big well-drilling rig on the road from Damascus to the border?" the man asked.

"No, unfortunately not, sir."

"Where could that blankety-blank thing be? Been sittin' here two days waiting for it. Yup, been drillin' wells in this part of the world for fifteen years. Could tell ya a lot of stories. This Jordan country's so barren it wouldn't last a year without U.S. help. Got my wife — she's Arab — and son up in Beirut. The boy's in high school there. Sent for this rig a week ago. You woulda seen it if it was on the road. Couldn't o' missed it. Where you folks from?"

When we left him he went on drumming his fingers, waiting for his rig.

Along the road a shepherd was counting his sheep. "Wonder if he lost one, like in the Bible. He hasn't got as many as ninety-nine." Em.

We rode up and down the long dry hills until Jerash appeared on our right, pillared ruins blending into the dust-colored landscape, relieved by a cloudless blue sky. Jerash is the old Gerasa, one of ten independent Greek cities liberated by Pompey and called, literally, Decapolis. The Decapolis cities lay east of the Jordan and the Sea of Galilee. Damascus was one, and Amman, for a while called Philadelphia, and Pella, to which early Christians fled. It was in the Decapolis area that Jesus healed the raving man who lived among the tombs. Mark, in his Gospel, reports that the healed man, denied his request to accompany the Lord, "began to proclaim in the Decapolis how much Jesus had done for him." When Christ returned a second time to this region, he was welcomed by the people who previously had begged him to leave. Evangelism begins at home!

At the main entrance of Jerash's extensive ruins is a triple arch built to welcome traveling emperor Hadrian in A.D. 130. Two shepherd boys came walking down the Street of Columns which leads to the forum. They wore black and white headdresses held with black cord. One carried a reed flute; the other led his pet black goat.

Amman, Jordan's capital, lies in and up the steep sides of a narrow valley. Its name is a reminder that this was once the chief city of the Ammonites, descendants of Lot. Though busses wait for passengers in front of an old Roman amphitheater, Amman lacks the flavor of Damascus. We drank coke across from the police station, and the only tables in the shop were occupied by police officers absorbed in playing cards.

In mid-afternoon we began the twisting descent via the city named Salt to the Jordan Valley. After Salt the land is pitifully barren, humps of dry earth with deep parched cracks and crevasses. The road drops twelve hundred feet beyond the sign marking sea level to where the Jordan flows, a cloudy green stream on its way to the Dead Sea. It is heavily guarded and signs forbid photography. There seems little left of the Jordan here to guard, since much of the water has been diverted into Israeli irrigation projects farther north. We drove on to higher ground and then photographed back toward the thin line of green that marks the course of the Jordan in its curving bed.

"What's all this about flowing with milk and honey around here?" Dave.

"No more." Clark.

In Jericho busses came and went in clouds of dust. We did too, eager to reach Jerusalem. The ascent from Jericho to Jerusalem is an indelible memory. In twenty miles the road climbs 3500 feet. For centuries the faithful Jews climbed up this rugged way on foot or donkey to keep Passover or celebrate feast days in the city of David. Approaching the magnificent temples of Solomon or Herod, the travelers sang the psalms called Songs of Ascent:

> I lift up my eyes to the hills. . . . Who shall ascend into the hill of
> of the Lord? . . . Those who trust in the Lord are like Mount Zion,
> which cannot be moved. . . . As the mountains are round about
> Jerusalem, so the Lord is round about his people. Blessed be the
> Lord from Zion, he who dwells in Jerusalem! . . . I was glad when
> they said unto me, Let us go up to the house of the Lord. . . .
> Jerusalem, built as a city which is bound firmly together, to which

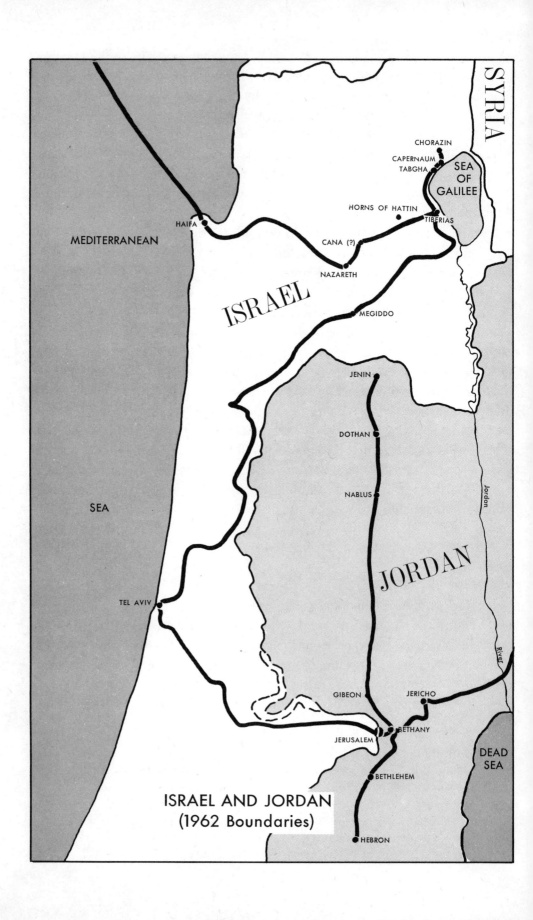

SYRIA

CHORAZIN

CAPERNAUM
TABGHA

SEA
OF
GALILEE

HORNS OF HATTIN

TIBERIAS

HAIFA

MEDITERRANEAN

CANA (?)

NAZARETH

ISRAEL

MEGIDDO

JENIN

DOTHAN

NABLUS

Jordan

SEA

JORDAN

TEL AVIV

GIBEON

JERICHO

BETHANY

JERUSALEM

River

DEAD
SEA

BETHLEHEM

ISRAEL AND JORDAN
(1962 Boundaries)

HEBRON

the tribes go up, the tribes of the Lord, as was decreed for Israel,
to give thanks to the name of the Lord (from Psalms 121 to 125).

Several times we climbed the road from the Jordan Valley to Jerusalem.
It is most memorable at day's end when sunset casts a halo of red and gold
behind Jerusalem, and the hills through which one climbs are already deep
in shadow. There, high on a distant peak, is the first spire of the city. Closer
and closer one comes. Cool breezes descend to encourage the traveler.
Cresting the Mount of Olives, he sees the old city snug within its walls and
gates, all its beiges turned to luminous gold, a vision suspended between
earth and heaven.

PRAY FOR THE PEACE of Jerusalem! . . . Peace be within your walls,
and security within your towers," wrote David in Psalm 122. His words are
ominously appropriate today when his city is divided by a new wall through
its heart.* On one side of the wall is Jerusalem-Jordan, the old city. On the
other side is Jerusalem-Israel, flourishing educational headquarters of the
modern Israeli state. The new wall is reinforced with barbed wire, no-
man's land, sandbags, walled-in gates, and tower sentries with guns poised.

"More shots fired here than in Berlin," said one Arab.

"Don't forget we are still at war," said another, grimly.

The Jericho Road, rising westward out of the Dead Sea depression, runs
along the Kidron Valley, which is between the old city wall and the Mount of
Olives. The road skirts the old walled city, inside which no cars ride, and
climbs up to end at the Damascus Gate on the north. It ends because
straight ahead, at right angles to the gate, is a no-man's land and a piece of
the new wall. From the Damascus Gate the Nablus Road runs north,
passing the American consulate, the YMCA, Saint George's Cathedral, and
the American Colony Hotel. At the American consulate another road
branches left, but few talk about it because this road leads to the Mandelbaum
Gate, only land entrance into Israel.

A stay in old Jerusalem is like a reunion. Streets and hotels are full of
English-speaking people. The Moslems may hold Mecca inviolate, but they
share Jerusalem, profitably, and in this Christian mecca the American pilgrim,
for better or for worse, far outnumbers and outspends all others.

Within an hour of our arrival we had seen or heard from more ac-
quaintances than it would be possible to find in any other foreign city. By
pre-arrangement, missionary friends were staying at the Y with us, stopping
over on their return to Korea, where John headed a large amputee center
for Church World Service. Our friend from Beirut had arrived with his

*This section was written before the Israeli-Arab war of June, 1967.

wife for a conference on Islam. The professor whom we had met in Corinth called from his school on the Mount of Olives. There was even a Philippine teacher who had been in graduate classes with the Rev in New York ten years earlier. Our experience was not unique. The American in Jerusalem finds people from his own state, town, denomination, or alma mater. He talks English, eats American-type food, and bumps into more Americans wherever he goes. Sometimes we had the feeling that all the natives of the area were acting their parts in a ceaseless pageant designed for visiting Americans. Not that we had any right to complain about this state of affairs, since we by our presence contributed to it. It was just that two weeks in Turkey had spoiled us. We had now to search for the authentic among tourist-conscious natives in a tourist-ridden locale. Akhisar was not like this, nor Pamukkale, nor even Ephesus and Istanbul.

The new YMCA was still on the drawing boards when we were in Jerusalem. The old one was a friendly family-like place with many potted plants, wide halls, and balconies. Mail covered half a bed in one of the two rooms assigned us. For the first time since Zandvoort I ironed and hung clothes on hangers. To the laundry went several cotton loads — towels, too, but no synthetics because friend Juli had sent some and rued it. The Rev applied at the American consulate for Israeli visas, which take three days to secure. One waits to do this in Jerusalem in order not to irritate the Arab countries through which he passes first.

There was also the problem of getting additional pages for the *carnet de passage,* the document needed to get the car into and out of non-European and Communist countries. We had trusted the ANWB, Netherlands tourist agency, to give us enough sheets for the itinerary we had listed in detail. This they had not done and now it appeared that we would use our last tear-out page for re-entry into Turkey — leaving us no sheets for Bulgaria, Yugoslavia, and Hungary, fussy borders to cross even with all proper papers. So we cabled The Hague for instructions, asking the ANWB to cable in return at our expense within five days.

There was no response. Two months after we returned home Oom Frans, whose name we had given as Dutch reference, wrote that he had been billed for twenty-eight *gulden,* about seven dollars, for some *carnet* sheets mailed — not airmailed — to us in Jerusalem. Two years, yes YEARS, after we returned home, Oom Frans wrote that he had been billed twelve *gulden* by the ANWB for some costs involved in our transit through Turkey. Apparently the Turks and the Dutch have more than tulips and blue ceramics in common. We trust this is the end of the matter and shall not trouble the ANWB on further expeditions.

While we attended to practical details, John and Juli's children and ours entertained themselves. With white towels they dressed like Arabs and gave plays in the wide upstairs hall. The girls made paper dolls, and the boys played pool or listened to Dirk's guitar on the balcony. They exchanged books and comics and celebrated Mary's birthday with a cake. We stored part of it on a high shelf for an evening treat but the ants got to it before we did.

Days we explored, often with fourteen of us wedged into the redbus — two families plus the professor as guide. Nights we talked in the cool breeze on the Y balcony or walked inside the old city walls. When we drove the professor back to his school on the Mount of Olives, we always stayed for a look westward across the Kidron Valley. Moonlight illumined our whole stay. Beyond the old city, quiet and with no lights showing, there was a string of fluorescent tubes marking the boundary between old Jerusalem and "Dixie," the nickname for modern Jerusalem beyond the dividing wall. Overhead the American Telstar satellite picked its way among the stars and disappeared behind a black pine tree silhouette. How the centuries meet in a place like this — the twentieth exploring the heavens, through which in the first Christ ascended from near where we were standing! And all the centuries between confronted with what happened here at the hub of history.

The spell of old Jerusalem at night is so great that we waited until we had seen neighboring cities and ruins before visiting it by day. Often after dark we went in through the Damascus Gate into tiny streets so silent that we spoke in whispers. Certainly no other large city withdraws from its streets as early and completely as this one. Long before ten everything is deserted and still. Chinks of light escape through shuttered windows. Moonlight breaks through in irregular patches between the roofs. A soldier on guard at a corner looks more like a statue than a person. Only the smells linger in the streets. One night the hooves of a donkey made sharp staccato sounds as he was led up the steps of a street. The hooded silhouette vanishing around a building could have been Judas, slinking away from the last supper to his rendezvous with the leaders of the Jews. Near the Stephen's Gate a man dozed while guarding a mountain of watermelons. At the Dung Gate a dozen men slept on the ground, rolled in blankets. The golden Dome of the Rock glowed in the moonlight. Its great courtyard was empty. No one walked the Via Dolorosa. We had the city to ourselves and were loath to leave it. When we did, it was under the watchful eye of the guard outlined in the opening high above the gate, where he held his gun ready and kept his eyes on the lights of "Dixie."

For the people attending the conference on Islam, the Archbishop of Jerusalem conducted the pilgrimage he usually leads on Palm Sunday. Archbishop Campbell Mac Innes is a distinguished citizen of David's city. While caring for the wounded in the fighting of 1948, he lost an eye and still carries an open leg wound under his purple vestments. To join the pilgrimage we rode a local bus through the Kidron Valley and around to the far side of the Mount of Olives where the group waited for the archbishop near Lazarus' tomb. One should say, certainly, near Lazarus' *supposed* tomb. Most places in the Holy Land must be supposed and only to the Arab guides are they certain.

A man in white headdress stood at the narrow entrance to Lazarus' tomb, handing out long lighted tapers for the descent inside. Two American teachers in gaudy straw hats were asking him loudly where they could buy shepherds' flutes for their rhythm bands back home.

Standing on a rock, wind ruffling his cassock, the archbishop began to read from his Bible and litany. It was the first of seven readings as we moved along the pilgrimage in silence. Even the small boys hawking their wares fell back and stopped shouting.

Six days before Passover Jesus came to Bethany where Lazarus was, whom Jesus had raised from the dead. While the archbishop read of this in John 12, we looked back toward Jericho from which Christ had come, climbing to Bethany where Mary anointed the Lord's feet with costly ointment during the last supper he ate in their home. Silently we walked up the back slope of the Mount of Olives from Bethany to Bethphage. How close together these villages are! In Bethphage, almost at the crest of the slope, was the tethered colt on which Jesus began his procession. Were the garments laid in the way also to suppress the fine dust that swirls around one's feet?

Two crowds met as Jesus began his descent into the Kidron Valley. One group came out from Jerusalem, carrying palms and crying hosannas, having heard that Jesus was coming. The other group came with the Lord from Bethany where many had gone to see the risen Lazarus and the One who had raised him. All together the people escorted Jesus into the city, passing near the Garden of Gethsemane where Christ's agony of blood would be stark contrast to the triumph of his Palm Sunday entry.

W E RAN TODAY WHERE Jesus walked" is a jibe applied to many tourists in the Holy Land. Not to us, we resolved. And yet we could have stayed much longer than the week allotted for Jerusalem and its environs.

Hebron is only eighteen miles southwest of Jerusalem, but the Hebron Road runs through Israel. So Jordan has built a by-pass which skirts the United Nations truce headquarters in a no-man's land. The new piece rejoins the Hebron Road before it passes the pink-domed shrine over the tomb where Jacob buried his beloved Rachel. Barren country is giving way to fruit orchards and vineyards in this area because of a new waterline coming down to Jerusalem.

Joshua gave Hebron to Caleb during the conquest of Canaan. Samson set down the city gates of Gaza on a hill overlooking Hebron. David had his first capital here for seven years and his son Absalom used the city as head-quarters when he challenged his father. Most of all, Hebron is Abraham's city. Its name today is el-Khalil — "the friend" — in honor of Abraham of whom the Koran says, "And the Almighty adopted Abraham for a friend."

Over the Cave of Machpelah is a most sacred mosque. Tourist folders warned that a special pass was necessary to enter it, but this was not true. We did need kerchiefs for our heads and bare arms, and we left our shoes at the entrance — fourteen pair of them, from Dicker's thongs to the professor's outsized loafers. No tourist walks unattended in the mosque al-Haram al-Ibrahimi. One speaks in low murmurs, if at all. There is more reverence here than in most of Jerusalem's holy places. Old men sat cross-legged on the carpets and eyed us as we passed.

The cave itself has been sealed for four hundred years beneath the floor of the mosque. Cenotaphs covered with richly embroidered tapestry stand in pairs over the supposed burial places of Abraham and Sarah, Isaac and Rebecca, Jacob and Leah. Next to Abraham's cenotaph there is a little grate through which one sees a few feet downward into the black cavern below.

The mosque windows are made of the glass for which Hebron is famous. In the shop adjoining the mosque we bought a small pitcher of clear blue glass and admired the fleece jackets for sale. Two men leaning against the redbus demanded to be paid for watching it. One spat indignantly when the Rev offered him ten *piasters*. He spat still harder when the offer was withdrawn and we all climbed in and drove away. In the last few years when Americans began excavating in Hebron, one of their first challenges was to overcome the natural suspicion and hostility of the people.

"House of bread" — *bet lehem* — birthplace of the One who called himself "the bread of life." City of David and of his grandparents Ruth and Boaz, Bethlehem lies a few miles south of Jerusalem. A short hawk-nosed man in a fez met the redbus as we parked in the square at the cream-colored Church of the Nativity. He would show us something special, he said. No, thank you. Later perhaps. First a cold drink and a look in the shops full of olive wood crèche figures and inexpensive pearl-like necklaces, typical of Bethlehem crafts. Let's buy the silver *lepeltje* with the star at the tip of its handle. Dicker laid aside his goggles at last in favor of a white Arab headdress with a royal blue band. It continues in annual use for Christmas pageants.

Hawk-nose-in-fez blocked the doorway of the shop. Not to the church first, no, but to something very special, he urged. So we all trooped up the street and were introduced to the Milk Grotto, a large cave-like room, heavily decorated. Here, precisely here, the virgin mother hid forty days and nights before fleeing to Egypt! Drops of "his" milk (this repeated mistake in gender colored the story considerably) fell, causing all the stone, especially on the ceiling of the grotto, to turn milk-white. There is a resplendent statue of Mary nursing her child. At its base are little packets of crushed stone intended to render supernatural assistance to the modern nursing mother. Just like the packets in the cave of Ignatius Loyola in Tarrasa near Barcelona, though his packets were perhaps designed more to encourage visions than milk. Juli sent a few Milk Grotto packets to an obstetrician friend in Michigan. Clark surveyed the glittering virgin. "Man, they sure fixed Mary up, didn't they?"

Perhaps a visit to the church would be more meaningful, we thought. Hawk-nose scurried ahead to lead us into the cluster of chapels, monasteries, and churches whose jurisdiction is shared, not always peaceably, by the Greek Orthodox, Roman Catholic, and Armenian churches. Television covers this site at Christmastime and the Bethlehem bells are heard all over the world.

The first church over the nativity grotto was built by Constantine after his mother Helena had verified the spot. Justin Martyr, the church father, is said to have identified this cave as early as A.D. 155, though other authorities claim that Hadrian devastated it in the second century and the site was lost for two centuries, probably until Helena "found" it. There are more caves and grottoes in this area, used by shepherds today for shelter from storms and possibly used by innkeepers of Jesus' day to quarter the animals of their guests.

The nativity grotto lies under the main altar of the cruciform church. It is lined with marble and hung with glowing crystal lamps on silver chains. In the floor is a many-pointed brass star centered with a polished black stone, and around the star in a circle are the words, *HIC DE VIRGINE MARIA JESUS CHRISTUS NATUS EST*. Down a dim passage in the grotto is the spring used by the holy family. The wise men's star fell into the spring and is still visible today to virgins looking into the dark water! There is the place where Joseph had his dream about fleeing into Egypt, and the place where Saint Jerome worked on his Latin translation of the Bible in company with his friendly lion and attended by the two women whose bodies are buried here. There is even the Place of the Innocents, where lies interred the body of an infant boy who did not escape the murder by Herod's soldiers.

"But where's the manger, dad?" asked Dicker, peering out from under his new headdress. We stooped to leave the church through the low door designed to encourage humility.

The glows of a pink sunset and the early full moon converged from opposite directions on the shepherds' fields east of Bethlehem. This is our favorite memory of the city of Christ's birth.

T HE MORNING we drove north to Gibeon, a native boy had fallen into one of the excavation trenches there. He was rushed to a Jerusalem hospital for treatment of cuts and a broken arm. Then we arrived, with nine children in tow — an archaeologist's nightmare. Dr. Pritchard of the University of Pennsylvania was working in the city now called el-Jib. Under a shade tree the pottery crew washed and sorted pieces found in the dig. Please be careful and hold onto your children — over and over we heard it.

Nowhere was the warning more apropos than at the pool of Gibeon, a remarkable discovery of Dr. Pritchard's in 1956. In a book, *Gibeon, Where the Sun Stood Still,* he tells about identification of the site through pottery handles marked *gb'n.* This is the pool of I Samuel 2, where about 1200 B.C. the men of generals Abner and Joab fought a duel in pairs, twelve against twelve, each seizing his partner by the beard and attempting to run him through with a sword. The round shaft to the pool is a stairwell eighty-five feet deep and twenty feet across, open at the top with no protection around the rim and plenty of loose stone to slide on. I held Dicker's wrist in a vise-like grip.

The older children descended the spiral steps carved into the side of the shaft. There is no water in the pool now. Is there water anywhere in Jordan, where over the past thirty years rainfall has decreased from thirty-nine to thirteen inches a year?

Through rocky prickly fields with figs and cactus in them we returned to the redbus and the villagers gathered around it. From the yellow plastic jug the Rev poured some water over my feet before I changed from thongs to the protection of sneakers. Such service no Arab woman expects. Behind me, as I bent to tie the shoes, a pair of hands stretched out above a pair of bare feet. The owner of these limbs was motioning for me to give her my thongs. Of course. Did I need the extra shoes when she had none?

From Gibeon one looks out across the plain at the end of which begins the Valley of Ajalon. What was it like on the day when Joshua commanded the sun and moon to stand still so that Israel could complete its slaughter of the Amorites and their five kings? "There has been no day like it before or since, when the Lord hearkened to the voice of a man; for the Lord fought for Israel."

Fighting has not stopped on the plains beyond Gibeon. Facing the valley stood a seventy-five millimeter gun, pointed west toward the Israeli border. There is no through traffic on the road in the valley.

The professor offered to take us to Jericho and the Dead Sea at noon one day. Heat did not affect his planning. Grown thinner and a bit gaunt under his sun helmet, he was impervious to the weather.

"Absolutely crazy," said friends at the Islam conference. "No one goes to Jericho this time of year until after four o'clock. You'll be scorched."

We went anyway, carrying cold water and sack lunches the Y prepared. Halfway along the descent to Jericho is the ruin of an old *caravan-*

serai. "Here the Good Samaritan left the wounded man he helped," said the professor, tongue in cheek, waiting to see who would remember that this was not fact but parable told by the Lord.

The temperature was far above a hundred when we parked at the foot of the high mound into which excavators have cut deep trenches to discover Jericho's secrets. The whole tell is about six acres with stone wall remnants. The latest trench was cut by Kathleen Kenyon, who followed up the work of Dr. Garstang in the 1930's. Unfortunately, nothing very conclusive has been discovered, even though the cut went down as far as bedrock and revealed a pre-Abrahamic round defense tower. "From 7000 B.C.," boasts a guidebook. Miss Kenyon lost a photographer here when he stepped back to focus his camera and fell to his death. We were glad the children were down in the redbus, stretched out, panting, too hot to move.

Juli and I led the descent from the mound. We did not even pause for a decent look at the Mount of Temptation which looms behind the ruins. After a flock of sheep passed, we crossed the road to stand in the flowing water of the stream which Elisha sweetened with salt. A cow stood in it with us and women came with pottery jugs to get water. Modern Jericho has green in it, date palms standing tall above the flat roofs. My notes say Mark Antony gave Cleopatra "this" — meaning, perhaps, the whole city, and no doubt in the wintertime.

All we could think of was to escape the furnace. The Rev drove straight to the Dead Sea Hotel where there were cold drinks served luke-warm and for five times the proper price. The men decided to look at the Qumran caves and the ruins of the Essene community made famous by the discovery of the Dead Sea scrolls. Juli and I and the children were finished. At four o'clock in the shade the thermometer registered 61 de-grees centigrade, which we translated into 110 degrees Fahrenheit. What had it been in the sun in Jericho at two?

The children rushed into the water and those with any bites or scratches rushed out as fast as they went in, leaping grotesquely to get rid of the stinging salt in the open skin. Some got salty water into their eyes and had to be led, blinded, to the fresh water showers for relief. The heat took the thrill out of being at the lowest spot on earth, thirteen hundred feet below sea level. Even the water was hot until it became deep, and then its buoyancy kept swimmers from reaching the cool water beneath.

"Don't tell me Lot's wife caused this much salt when she turned into a pillar," said Dave, bringing back twigs crusted with salt crystals from a small island near shore. Somewhere at the bottom of the southern part of the Dead Sea may lie what is left of Sodom and Gomorrah, destroyed around 1900 B.C. by earthquake and fire heaven-sent but helped by the presence of many natural gases in this plains area. The Arabs call the Dead Sea Bahr-Lút, "Sea of Lot." Today it is forty-six by ten miles in size.

The men came back from the Qumran caves, and while we all bobbed around like corks in the water, they told stories of the caves where Bedouins discovered the scrolls stored in clay pots, wrapped in linen sealed with pitch. They also told about the Essene community, dating from 150 B.C., where frequent bathing in fresh water pools was part of the ritual. Now that sounds like adapting one's ritual to the environment!

What luxury to shiver in the cool air of Jerusalem. Sometimes we still say to each other, "Remember Jericho," and immediately the sizzling heat of that day is conjured up. Remember Jericho. How could we forget it?

To ANYONE who views the map with Arab sympathies, the eastern border of Israel appears like wide open jaws from which a tongue protrudes to take in half of Jerusalem. We traveled one day from the tip of the tongue to the roof of the mouth at Jenin where one looks across the plain of Jezreel in the direction of Megiddo and Nazareth. Megiddo is at the pass opening onto the plain where Deborah and Barak fought against Sisera's chariots of iron. Saul fought the Philistines on the plain of Jezreel in the battle that killed his three sons with him. And Ahab came fleeing this way from Mount Carmel to reach his Samaria palace before the rain with which the Lord ended the three-year drought.

The following week we hoped to be on the Israeli side of the border within sight of where we stood at Jenin. But to get there we would have to cross at the Mandelbaum Gate in Jerusalem. There is no other way.

How small the Holy Land is! From Dan to Beersheba, cities the Israelites counted their northern and southern limits, the distance is only a hundred fifty miles. From Nazareth to Bethlehem as the crow flies is not more than seventy miles though the road made it closer to a hundred. From the Sea of Galilee to the Mediterranean coast is only thirty miles. And the length of the Jordan, flowing from the Sea of Galilee to the Dead Sea, is just sixty. Though the settings for Biblical narrative range from Persia to Italy, and from the Black Sea to the Red one, yet the heart of history is in that small rectangle between the Mediterranean and the Jordan. Ancient kings and empires were in orbit around the focal happenings in that little spot. And who can say that modern powers are any less so?

Let's go back now from the roof of the mouth to the tip of the tongue. First stop: the tell of Dothan, a flat-topped mound standing in a wide plain. The professor patiently explained the Hellenistic-Roman excavations in which he was especially interested. He showed us the tomb in which he had found more objects than had been uncovered in any other tomb in Jordan. From the top of the tell it is a surprising distance to the plain. Sheep gathered at a well were like those of Joseph's brothers. How easy it had been for them to spot the approach of a solitary figure in a many-colored coat and to plot what they would do with the brother they hated.

Beyond the fertile plain is a line of mountains. For Elisha's protection the Lord made them "full of horses and chariots of fire," ringing Dothan to protect the prophet from the Syrian army arrayed in the valley to take him. This great army God struck with blindness, and Elisha led the might of Syria down the plain and delivered them to Ahab's palace in Samaria.

The redbus rides south on the direct route from Galilee to Jerusalem, a three-day journey on foot in Jesus' day. The road passes between mounts Ebal and Gerizim where the Israelites stood massed on the lower slopes, the ark resting on Levite shoulders in the valley between, while Joshua read the words of the law given Moses on Mount Sinai.

Christ passed through Samaritan country when he went from Galilee to Jerusalem. The remnants of the Samaritans are still here, about 250 of them, and they still celebrate their own form of Passover on Mount Gerizim, joined by 150 more Samaritans allowed to cross from Israel for this yearly observance. Here, at a crossroads close to Mount Gerizim, is Jacob's Well, the place where Jesus spoke to the Samaritan prostitute about living water. Today's Jacob's Well is within a half-finished, roofless church, and the steps descending to the well are covered by two small wooden structures, padlocked. All around are one-room houses whose flat roofs are secured by stones, of which this area has an abundance.

Nearby, at Balata, an American team is excavating for ancient Shechem, the city Albrecht Alt calls "the uncrowned queen of Palestine." Its temple, dating from about 1600 B.C., is the largest found in Jordan. Ahab and Herod the Great had splendid palaces a little farther north where there has been an excavation at Sebaste.

The living city in this area is Nablus, a mile or two west of the Shechem excavation. It is the Samaritan center today. Women in colorful costume walked erect down the main street, balancing lumpy bundles on their heads. One man pushed a wooden cart of watermelons. Another, in flowing brown robe, with a large key and dagger attached to his belt, was leading a blind man. On the sidewalk was an elaborate brass brazier from which a man in a white apron was selling wedges of warm sweets served on thin paper. Though served like American pizza, the taste was sweet with orange and spices in the cheese. There were other Nablus sweets, strange to our taste, made of seeds and nuts held together with thick syrup and coated with something like crumbled shredded wheat.

The last two days in Jordan we explored Jerusalem by sunlight. This way one learns more and loves it less than by moonlight. The men found a barber just inside the Damascus Gate. Juli, the girls, and I stopped in the pottery-making place on the Nablus Road. Expertly the potter spun his wheel and formed his pieces. In another of the rooms around a courtyard young women painted patterns in predominant shades of blue and green before the glaze was applied. They let our girls paint with the delicate brushes until the shadow of the overseer fell across the doorway. One could buy a houseful of lovely pottery here — mugs, tiles, vases, bowls of every size.

When we found the men inside the gate, they were the center of a crowd. John, a double amputee, had been observed by an Arab who also had lost his arms up to the elbows. The Arab's prosthetic devices were not as new and dexterous as those of John, who is superbly skillful and very candid about using them. The two men stood outside the barbershop demonstrating to each other. Clark sat in the barber's chair, half shorn, waiting for the barber to return from watching the demonstration.

The twin pools of Bethesda are in the northern part of the old city near the Stephen's Gate. They lie within the compound of the White Fathers who are still digging to reach remnants of porch pillars around the pools which measured three hundred by one hundred fifty feet. Down a worn flight of stone steps one can reach the water level. Did Christ walk on these steps when he visited the pools on a Sabbath and healed the lame man lying on one of the five porticoes?

Most of the streets on which Jesus walked lie from thirty to sixty-five feet beneath the level of Jerusalem today. The rubble from pillaging and destruction has raised the valleys between the city's seven hills. Over the centuries in numerous rebuildings the city has crept northward so that the Dome of the Rock, site of Solomon's Temple, is now in the southeast corner of the city while it used to be in the northeast. Archaeologists and scholars have been working to ascertain the location of the three successive walls around the holy city. On their location depends also the site of the crucifixion hill and Joseph's tomb, both outside the city in Christ's day, though today the Church of the Holy Sepulchre lies well within the city walls.

One place along the well-known Via Dolorosa impressed us. Underneath the convent of the Dame de Sion has been discovered a Roman pavement which was probably the courtyard of the Antonia Fortress built by Herod to guard his temple and named for Mark Antony. If Pilate was in residence here during the turbulent days of the Passover feast, then this pavement may well be the place of which John wrote in his Gospel, "When Pilate heard these words, he brought Jesus out and sat down on the judgment seat at a place called The Pavement, and in Hebrew, Gabbatha." Later Paul was taken into the Antonia Fortress for safekeeping after he had been rescued from a mob beating him for taking Greeks into the temple area.

The nuns in the convent over the Gabbatha are excellent guides. Ours, speaking fluent English, geared her commentary to the children. She explained the fortress and the pavement of yard-square, foot-thick blocks of limestone. She pointed out the grooves for water to run off, the places marked by horses' hooves, and at the foot of the stairs she lifted the scatter rugs which protect the ancient markings carved into the pavement for the soldiers' games of chance. There were no garish trappings, no distracting ornaments. A simple reverence prevailed.

Dicker reluctantly left a stout walking stick outside the convent door when we entered. He propped it carefully beside the entrance and was crestfallen to find it gone when we came out. From across the street an old bearded man in a straight long brown skirt got up and solemnly handed Dicker his stick. They shook hands.

"*Shook-ran,*" said Dicker with prompting and went clumping off triumphantly over the cobblestones.

The afternoon ended with a different experience in human nature. After searching for something to stave off Dicker's hunger, we found a place to buy a big sucker. We were walking along in a busy street when a little boy darted up from the opposite direction. He yanked the sucker out of Dicker's mouth, wormed his way through the crowd, and vanished.

T HE CHURCH OF THE HOLY SEPULCHRE is a mass of grey stone, none too sturdy, supported at points by steel girders angled against the walls. Finegan says this is indeed the site of Christ's crucifixion and burial, and explains that there was a pagan temple built here two hundred years before Constantine built a basilica over the site in 335. An official Jordan guidebook says that the emperor Hadrian built a Venus temple over this spot to stop the Christian worship and thereby ironically marked the spot "forevermore." The Crusaders erected a massive church in 1149 and the latest in the succession of buildings dates from after the fire of 1808.

The interior reminded us of a passage in Muller's *The Loom of History* (page 265 and footnote). Speaking of Constantine's mother, the empress Helena, he wrote,

> She went to Jerusalem to find the site of Calvary, and not only found it — helped by the usual dream — but dug up, with a speed and sureness that archaeologists must envy, the True Cross and the attendant relics of the Passion, including the Lance, the Sponge, and the Crown of Thorns. Thrilled by this blessed discovery, Constantine proceeded to build a monument worthy of it — the Church of the Holy Sepulchre. It was to remain a shrine for pilgrims through the ages, and an incentive for the Crusaders. . . . Some bases of its columns still show in front of the present church, built by the Crusaders. Unfortunately, the holiest spot in Christendom is an architectural horror and a religious scandal: a murky maze of altars, chapels, and grottoes on different levels, owned by different sects, alike chiefly in the gaudiness of their ornamentation,

the phoniness of their legends, and the attendance of panhandling clerics. Only a Christian of exceptionally firm and simple faith could visit this shrine — and others in the Holy Land, such as the site of the Nativity and the Virgin's Milk Grotto in Bethlehem — without having his faith shaken.

The site assigned to the crucifixion is viewed through glass surrounded by gold and lamps. One can hardly see the rock for the trimmings. The sepulchre is joint property of two branches of Christendom, with a priest at either end of the tomb. Each tries to persuade the visitor to look in on his side. One sprinkles scented holy water on the head, but the other gives a lighted taper and allows the pilgrim to stoop into the tomb to see the short smooth stone shelf. On both sides the air is heavy with incense.

Everything has been meticulously assigned a place in the church with a chapel or shrine to cover it: the place where the nails were driven in, the stone on which Nicodemus anointed Christ's body, and even the cave where somehow Adam had been buried and shared in the resurrections which accompanied the earthquake at Christ's death. The Holy Sepulchre is a gloomy church, confusing, smothered with man-made trappings, difficult to explain to children, let alone to appreciate as adults. The words of Jesus to the Samaritan woman took on new meaning. "Woman, believe me, the hour is coming when neither on this mountain nor in Jerusalem will you worship the Father. . . . the true worshipers will worship the Father in spirit and truth, for such the Father seeks to worship him. God is spirit, and those who worship him must worship in spirit and truth."

There is a quiet place in which to remember Christ's death and resurrection. It is very likely not the place of Christ's burial, despite the claims advanced for it by General Charles Gordon late in the nineteenth century. In 1842 a German pastor found the features of a skull in the side of a rocky hill which is now next to the main bus station. You can see it today when busses are not parked in the way — the two deep-set eye sockets, the mouth opening. Behind this hill General Gordon discovered a rock-hewn tomb. Scholars say it is neither old enough nor properly located to be Christ's tomb. But it stands in a peaceful walled-in garden, a simple unadorned tomb built into the rock with a single finished grave shelf inside. At its low entrance is a groove in which a stone could be rolled.

This Garden Tomb is on the Nablus Road, not far from the Damascus Gate. We came to it after a second visit to the pottery-making shop. Each child carried a moist lump of clay. There were no other visitors and we sat under a few trees, looking at the tomb, thinking, the children molding their clay. Here one could imagine soldiers fleeing in terror, angels arriving, and Mary Magdalene confronted by her Master in the cool silence of an early morning. The caretaker came to tell us how this tomb was discovered. It was interesting, but not essential. We were more intent on history earlier and holier.

The last day in Jerusalem was the Rev's fortieth birthday. At 6 A.M. the children, in procession, were at our door with cards they had made. In the YMCA gift shop Nan had bought a handkerchief with a Crusader's cross embroidered in one corner. The Crusader cross in silver or embroidery is one of the most typical souvenirs of Jerusalem.

John and Juli and their children flew to Beirut and on to points east toward Seoul. We set out to see the Mount of Olives, the Dome of the Rock, and the water places in the Kidron Valley outside the city wall.

On top the Mount of Olives is the Ascension Chapel, the round one with a wall full of tourists' names and a big footprint in a rock which is ascribed to Christ or Mohammed, depending on the faith of the visitor. Gethsemane has two churches. The upper one, the Russian Church of Mary Magdalene with its onion-shaped towers, has a fine terrace from which to look down on the old olive trees and across the valley to the landmarks of the city. The other Gethsemane church, the Church of All Nations, stands with its twelve domes and colorful mosaic façade in the garden of eight ancient olive trees. Their gnarled furrowed trunks give forth fresh shoots and blue-green leaves. Inside the church one is offered THE rock of agony.

When David's men went to capture Jerusalem from the Jebusites, he advised them, "Whoever would smite the Jebusites, let him get up the water shaft to attack." He was talking about the sloping passageway built from within the city walls to the cave in which the Gihon spring flowed. Today the Gihon spring is still in the Kidron Valley at the base of the high wall around the Dome of the Rock.

Even more interesting was the discovery in 1909 of another rock tunnel which extended almost eighteen hundred feet from the Gihon spring to the Pool of Siloam in which Christ told the blind man to wash the clay from his eyes. This tunnel, dug in solid rock, was completed under King Hezekiah in order to bring the water supply completely within the city wall. At a mid-point in the tunnel was found a carved inscription describing how the men tunneling toward each other met at that point. In hip boots one can still wade the length of the tunnel.

Pride of the Moslems and tragedy to the Jews is the magnificent mosque, the Dome of the Rock, on the site of Solomon's temple. The name, in Arabic Haram Esh Sharif, comes from a huge rock inside on which Mohammedans believe Abraham was ready to offer Isaac in sacrifice. The rock is large, fifty-eight by fifty-one feet, four to six feet high. This is also supposedly the rock on Araunah's threshing floor purchased by David for sacrifice. Last but not least, it is from this rock that Mohammed rode into heaven astride his horse Burak, leaving the promise that a prayer prayed here is a thousand times more valuable than one prayed elsewhere! The beautiful redecoration of the Dome of the Rock was in process when we were there. The great round dome is painted gold on the outside. It glitters in the sunlight. It glows in the moonlight. It dominates the old city.

To the Jews this is tragic. Here stood the glorious temple of Solomon. Here Herod was building his magnificent temple from 20 B.C. to A.D. 64 during the time that Jesus walked in its courts. Josephus says that Herod's temple was twice as large as Solomon's. Fourteen courses of stone in the retaining walls around its outer court can still be seen, some stones as large as sixteen by thirteen feet, distinguished as Herodian by their recessed edges. The mountain was not large enough for Herod's temple, so he built a stone platform out over the Kidron Valley. From the top of the wall around this extension there was a two-hundred-foot sheer drop to the floor of the valley. Some say that this was the pinnacle of the temple from which Satan tempted Jesus to throw himself.

Underneath the stone platform, supported by pillars and arches, is an endless subterranean area. It is called Solomon's stables, though Herod built it and the Crusaders rebuilt it and kept their horses here.

There were eight gates opening into the great court of Herod's temple. The one on the east, the Golden Gate, has been cemented shut since the partition of Jerusalem. Through this gate Orthodox Jews believe the true Messiah will one day ride to establish his kingdom. The southwest part of Herod's wall became the "wailing wall" to which the Jews came annually for centuries to anoint the wall and to wail and groan over the destruction of the temple. The wailing wall has been unused since the new wall split Jerusalem. Our Arab guide insisted that no one even stand against the wall while the Rev made photographs of it.

In late afternoon we walked the streets that were becoming familiar to us. The same row of men in fezzes sat on low square stools smoking their water pipes. Slim rubber tubes connected the mouthpiece with the knee-high silver apparatus of water to filter the smoke. We found some finely-worked, Crusader-cross cuff links in the silver shops near the Church of the Holy Sepulchre, and haggled the price down from fifty to forty *piasters*. They were a good birthday gift.

Bertha Spafford Vester, Jerusalem's most distinguished citizen, was sitting on a low wall at the gift shop of the American Colony Hotel, north of the YMCA on Nablus Road. Mrs. Vester is gracious about speaking to strangers who have read her book, *Our Jerusalem,* and who admire her lifelong contributions to the city, especially through the children's hospital. She has lived through more than seventy years of turbulent history in Jerusalem.

Supper was marred only by the fact that Clark told Hassan, the waiter, that we were crossing into Israel the next day. Hassan's face fell and it was necessary to mollify him with a promise of American stamps. A group of us had birthday cake and ice cream in a place with a big mosque-shaped cake in its window. Someone added a Crusader-cross letter opener to the Rev's collection of these. And we all stood a while on the Mount of Olives for a last view of the city below. It was a good place to turn forty, here at the heart of history.

From behind the YMCA came the sound of guards' feet pacing at the Mandelbaum Gate. With mixed emotions we would be there ourselves the next morning. The Y doors were locked at ten each night, in keeping with the mood of old Jerusalem. It was Ahmed who usually slept on the couch in the lower hall to admit late-comers. This last night we had to ring three times to rouse him.

"Tomorrow we are leaving, so we will not disturb you again," said the Rev, and Ahmed answered groggily, "Thank you very much."

OFTEN WE HAD PASSED the fork in the road at the American consulate, always bearing right onto the Nablus Road. Now it was time to take the left fork after we had packed, tipped, thanked, mailed, and done some final shopping and photographing. We bought gas at a Shell station where the attendant said, "All over Jordan is super." Nothing but the best in Jordan!

Several Arabs near the fork gestured for us to turn back. The yellow sign said, "DANGER — NO MAN'S LAND — KEEP OUT." There was the sound of dynamite blasting and the sight of barbed wire and sandbags. The sandbags at the gate had been there so long that ivy was climbing over them.

At breakfast a man in the Y had said, "Arabs are hopelessly disunited, weak, unaggressive. They fight in the desert, but they haven't the guts to carry a thing through. They can't even agree on where to hold a meeting to discuss Arab unity."

Well, we had loved that hopeless part of the world that we were leaving. On the other side of the gate flew the blue and white Israeli flag. A sign said in Hebrew, Arabic, and English, "Welcome to Israel." We emerged from customs onto Shemuel Hanavi Street. A group of tourists stood at the barricade, looking and laughing. Was there something to laugh about in the barricades and barbed wire?

THE TRANSITION from Orient to Occident was swift and obvious. Though we had anticipated the change, it caught us unprepared. So far from home we were not expecting to see a piece of Spring Valley, New York, where we lived seven years among good Jewish neighbors, both Orthodox and Reform. We had come looking for scenes of ancient history and for a populace to fit those scenes. And, admittedly, we had acquired new concern for the Arab plight and had identified strongly with them.

Now, in fairness, we had to look at Israel sympathetically, trying to understand this young nation of two and a half million Jews surrounded by forty million Arabs. Hitler had wiped out six thousand Jewish communities. We remembered the golden flower bed over the ashes of nameless Jews at Dachau and the gas chamber and red brick ovens of the crematorium.

White-maned David Ben-Gurion, Israel's contemporary patriarch, has said, "We are the people of the Book. . . . Everyone who wants to understand Israel must read the Bible — it is all there."

Is it? "And I will give to you, and to your descendants after you, the land of your sojournings, all the land of Canaan for an everlasting possession; and I will be their God." Was this promise to Abraham a literal one? We count ourselves among the spiritual children of Abraham, with whom God established his covenant of grace. Like Abraham, we receive God's promises by faith and believe these promises have been extended beyond Abraham and the nation he sired to the faithful of all nations. We too are people of the Book, the whole Book.

Yet we wanted to "feel" ourselves into the situation of the Jew for whom statehood was a return to the promised land, a modern Canaan conquest carving out explosive borders secured by an uneasy truce. How much of the reason for the new state is a passionate nationalism embodied in the Zionist movement and how much is religious, based on Old Testament promises and Judaism? Can the two reasons be separated? Probably not. What then is the tension between the laws of the Book and the pressures of modern Jewish thought? Is Israel a culture and a blood brotherhood more than a theocracy Biblically ruled?

For these questions we had no answers. It was difficult enough to achieve minds open to learn objectively from the people into whose land we had come. Taking time for this transition, we did not stop in Israeli Jerusalem to see Mount Zion and David's tomb. On we drove through streets lined with orange-white-green flags to honor the Ivory Coast's Houphouët-Boigny, a state guest who caught up with us in Tiberias two days later.

Along the Jaffa-Tel Aviv highway lined with woods there were abandoned armored cars, smashed, tipped, bullet-ridden, rusted to a dull red, some hung with wreaths. They lay where they were abandoned in the battles of 1948, grim memorials of the fight to wrest land from the Arabs. For lunch we bought bread and kosher pickles to eat with Spam beside the road.

The Automobile Club in Tel Aviv was closed for the approach to Sabbath, and could not advise us about the auto *carnet*. Boys with phylacteries walked the streets. Girls in uniform and felt berets hitchhiked on the open road. The city streets were broad, the buildings new, the bare-armed people speaking and gesturing with animation.

On smooth roads through fertile country the redbus rolled along to reach Tiberias before Sabbath. Past the Plain of Jezreel, which we had seen earlier from Jordan's side. Past the turnoff to Megiddo where there are remnants of stone stables, thought to be part of Solomon's fortress. Past Mount Tabor, rising high, round, and solitary from the plain. On to the bright blue Sea of Galilee, held in a cup of green hills.

Across the Galilee, on the Syrian side, the hills are cliffs and the terrain is rugged. This is part of the old Decapolis area where the herd of pigs rushed off the cliffs into the sea, propelled by evil spirits Jesus had cast out of the man living among the tombs. We also could see from the hilltop road how the Jordan leaves the lake and how its waters are diverted into many man-made ponds to water the Israeli landscape. Jordan and Israel have had a bitter feud over the Jordan waters, and this quarrel is intensified by Israeli plans to irrigate the Negev desert area. We drove down to photograph the river where its swift blue-green water leaves the lake between banks of lush vegetation.

The Sea of Galilee lies 682 feet below sea level and the Jordan runs downhill from it to the Dead Sea which is 1,297 feet below sea level. Low-lying as it is, the Galilee is a favorite winter area. In summer it boasts none of Jerusalem's mountain-top breezes.

A few people were swimming in an open beach area as we drove along the lakeshore to Tiberias, the city Herod Antipas built in A.D. 21 during Christ's life on earth. He built it on the site of an ancient graveyard, which made the city unclean to the Jews, so Herod had to import foreigners to people his luxurious Galilean capital.

We had made reservations in the Scotch Center, a sprawling grey-stone complex in the town, a block from the lake. In 1890 a Scotch Presbyterian doctor built it as a mission hospital for the area. His wife died there from cholera. The state of Israel has built its own hospital now, reducing Christian medical care to a clinic serving Arabs remaining in the area. The buildings now are used mainly for tourists — pilgrims, the Center likes to call them. The Dutch, who cooperated in staffing the hospital and its mission outreach, retain a minister in residence and two nurses in the clinic.

About forty elderly pilgrims from England were already in residence when we arrived. Some appeared too decrepit to do more than walk around the complex. We and our livelier pilgrims were assigned alone to the second floor of a separate building. We had two rooms, a large white-tiled one like an operating room, and a small one with two more hospital beds. The stairs and corridors were spooky at night. We were also informed that we could eat either before or after the older pilgrims and we chose to eat before, with the employees and one or two members of the UN armistice control. This early group set their own places and served themselves.

After supper we walked to the lakeshore where there was a colorful outdoor café. A long string of lights across the dark water marked the top of the Syrian mountains. We left the ceiling fan in our operating room whirring all night to stir the sticky air.

Pre-pilgrim breakfast on Saturday consisted of cold cereal, a little tough, and boiled eggs, very soft, eaten in the uneasy silence that seemed to hang over the staff. Zwart, the Dutch minister, arrived in his Volkswagen as we were ready to leave the Center. He suggested a few things that we should see, but he seemed preoccupied. The pilgrims were coming up the street from morning chapel a block away. One was being carried because she had fainted.

Over the lake a cloudbank turned the water slate-blue and the Syrian mountains a somber grey-black. The air hung as still as the dining room atmosphere. Because of *Shabbat* there was no public transportation, so we had the road to ourselves as we drove north along the lakeshore until we reached the yellow sign at Magdala, home of Mary Magdalene, who was among the women ministering to Jesus.

The Greek name for Magdala was Taricheae, "place where fish are salted." The city reached its peak in the latter years of the second temple and was heavily fortified by the Jews in their revolt against the Romans. In the field beyond the yellow sign there are crumbled remnants of a wall of black basalt stone which is common to this area.

The road climbs near the head of the lake. A crossroads sign in three languages announced that it was three miles to En Sheva-Kefar Nahum (Capernaum).

At the walled ruin the road ends. Not far beyond is the Syrian border. The ruin was not closed for *Shabbat* because Franciscans are the keepers of Capernaum. Through the gate we saw one monk instructing two workmen where to place a stone. Does the monk live alone in the big stone building topped by a flag and a cross? We blew the car horn after the gate bell had not attracted his attention. The monk allowed us to enter, one at a time, and he touched each forehead while he intoned individual Latin blessings. Leaving us a small descriptive folder about the ruin, he hurried back on sandaled feet to his workmen. We sat to read on the steps of the limestone second-century synagogue which faces toward the lake and toward Jerusalem.

Capernaum, said the folder, was the city of Jesus, the place where Matthew worked at customs, the home of Peter and Andrew, the city where Christ began his ministry, calling his first disciples and teaching in the synagogue. John says about his "living bread" discourse, "This he said in the synagogue as he taught at Capernaum." In Capernaum Christ brought back to life the daughter of Jairus, and cured a leper, a palsied man let down through the roof, a man with an unclean spirit, one with a withered hand who was healed on the Sabbath, and others like Peter's mother-in-law and the servant of the centurion who had given the Jews their synagogue. Here we were in the heart of the country where Christ conducted his three-year ministry. In the arc of towns and hills on this northeast coast of the Sea of Galilee he spent most of his time, making the three-day trip to Jerusalem only occasionally.

Yet this favored city was the one of which he had to say, "And you Capernaum, will you be exalted to heaven? You shall be brought down to Hades. For if the mighty works done in you had been done in Sodom, it would have remained until this day. But I tell you that it shall be more tolerable on the day of judgment for the land of Sodom than for you."

Probably the synagogue in which Christ taught stood on the site of the one whose ruin remains today. It is an attractive ruin, with four standing pillars and many decorative carvings of flowers, leaves, geometric patterns, and even birds and animals not found on earlier synagogues.

Inside an octagonal fence is a mosaic from the shrine Helena built over the supposed house of Peter and Andrew. Excavations have not progressed below this level, except for one stubby pillar in a square hole. "Maybe the storeroom of Peter's house," said the barefoot German who had been arguing with the Franciscan about where the workmen should place a stone. They were interrupted by the clang of the gate bell. Two couples entered. For the girls who were wearing shorts the Franciscan provided wrap-around gabardine skirts before he gave his blessings.

Dicker ferreted out lizards, almost as many as at Pompeii. The rest of us inspected and photographed black stones, old stone vats, millstones, and bowls arranged along the paths.

A boisterous group of young hikers poured through the gate, evidence of Israel's emphasis on physical fitness. The poor Franciscan was overwhelmed dispensing skirts and blessings. His supply of the former ran out before all the sturdy female legs were covered.

Outside the gate the road was so deserted that, had it not been asphalt, one might have expected to meet the disciples, arguing which would be the greatest in Christ's kingdom. And somewhere along this road near Capernaum Jesus himself had been sitting, with a child in his arms, telling his ambitious disciples, "Whosoever causes one of these little ones who believe in me to sin, it would be better for him if a great millstone were hung around his neck and he were thrown into the sea." We had seen the millstones. The sea lay at arm's length. Part of Capernaum is still buried beneath it.

A cluster of creamy-white sheep stood close together at the water's edge. Silky black goats, less gregarious, with floppy ears long enough to tie under their chins, picked their way along the stony ground. A clump of pink flowers lent color against the blue of the water. In the distance, across the upper end of the lake, were the white roofs of Tiberias and above them the road climbing up the plateau toward Cana and Nazareth.

We stopped at Tabgha, whose chapels stand between the road and the water. Pilgrims since the fourth century have worshiped here where seven springs feed the lake. Inside the Multiplication Chapel is a beautiful floor mosaic of plants, birds, and even a snake. The mosaic is highlighted by the loaves and fishes behind the altar. Did the thousands sit here, near the springs, shaded by the trees, listening to Christ as the sun fell into the water behind him?

At the water's edge is the Church of the Primacy, built anew in 1934, partly covering the mass of rock where legend says Christ broiled fish to eat with his disciples after his resurrection. Here white-trunked willows lean over the water and because of the springs, fishing has always been at its best. We were content to stay outside, on the old stone steps that descend into the water. Visitors of the Roman church prefer the inside of the Primacy sanctuary, which they honor as the site of Peter's elevation after Christ's triple questions and answers to him.

Above the road rises the hill of the Beatitudes, a thousand feet high, commanding a view of the whole lake. On a hill like this Christ retreated to pray and his disciples came searching for him, calling him back to the crowds waiting to be taught and healed. From such a hill he descended to walk on the stormy sea, appearing as a ghost to his frightened disciples. Legend calls this the hill where he gave the Beatitudes.

A breeze stirred the trees in the garden of the Italian hospice on top the Beatitudes mountain. Far below the lake lay still within its frame.

"Blessed are the poor in spirit," the Rev was reading, "for theirs is the kingdom of heaven."

"Blessed are those who mourn, for they shall be comforted."

"Blessed are the meek, for they shall inherit the earth."

"Blessed are those who hunger and thirst for righteousness, for they shall be satisfied."

"Blessed are the merciful, for they shall see God."

"Blessed are the peacemakers, for they shall be called sons of God."

Someday we are coming back to stay in the hospice and to sit on the hill, to walk the slopes, to watch the sea moods and the changing sky, to think, to write, and most of all to feel the presence of Christ which for us was more real here than anywhere else in the Holy Land.

Behind the hospice the road climbs a little and then a bumpy road branches right and drops to the ruins of Chorazin, in a hollow out of sight of the lake.

The ruins of native black stone are as desolate as the prophecy of Jesus. "Woe to you, Chorazin! Woe to you, Bethsaida! for if the mighty works done in you had been done in Tyre and Sidon, they would have repented long ago in sackcloth and ashes." This was the paradox of Christ's intensive ministry here in Galilee. The crowds allowed him no rest. Yet after two years of teaching and healing in this little lakeshore area, he had still to utter curses on Capernaum and Chorazin. And in Nazareth, where he lived most of his earthly life, the people tried to push him off a cliff.

In the desolate fields east of Chorazin are the mines and barbed wire of the Syrian-Israeli border. I thought, leaving the ruin, that I would not have liked living in Chorazin. It was set too deeply in a hollow, shutting out a view of the lake. And in this area, the lake is the heart of living.

Back on the road along the shore we met several hiking groups. Singing and shouting, with ruddy faces and black hair and short shorts, they covered far more than the Biblical Sabbath day's journey!

Midday was hot, the sprinkler on the dining room roof made little difference, and even coffee did not attract after a meal of soup, meat, potato, and vegetable, unrelieved by fruit or salad. We changed into swimsuits and found the open spot along the lake which we had noticed upon arrival. This was our first swim in fresh water since Verona. We stayed all after-noon, content.

"Does it really get stormy on this lake?" Em wanted to know, drying off on a flat rock. "It's not a big lake and it looks so quiet now."

"Try walking on it," said Clark, chuckling. "I guess I would have been scared too if I was Peter."

"I'm thinkin' about all those pigs," said Dicker, quiet for a rare moment, inspecting the sheer cliffs across the lake.

David contributed his kernel of wisdom: "I guess we could say that we swam today where Jesus walked."

At first there were a few other families with us. By four o'clock we had the beach to ourselves. Gold filtered out of the air onto the water, making the air luminous between the blues of the sky and the lake. The sun abandoned crevices and sheltered places to the shadows. Little waves washed the pebbles at our feet. The uneasy air of the morning cloud had given way to a glowing peace. Such times no camera can record and one can only hope to fasten them in memory, feeling the impact of history and faith and beauty and family all converge in one place at one time, filling the heart and soul to bursting.

While we lingered an old man and two women came down from the hills. Perhaps they had expected to find their bathing place deserted. The older of the women waded in to wash her legs, lifting one onto a stone and splashing water up to her knee. The old man ignored us, walked a short ways along the shore, peeled off his clothes which included long under-wear, and with cheerful unconcern walked a little farther before entering the water to wash himself.

When we returned to Tiberias we found that Houphouët-Boigny had arrived in our absence. His flag flew everywhere and limousines were lined up at the big hotel on the lakeshore.

Supper was redeemed by dessert of apple-in-pastry topped with cream sauce. There was even a breeze while the two Dicks sat in the garden, telling Sea of Galilee stories to the accompaniment of a brass band marching through the streets. The whole town seemed to be making as much noise as possible. *Shabbat* was over.

After dark the Rev and I investigated the heart of the noise and found Houphouët-Boigny and his wife being entertained at the waterfront café. They sat at a horseshoe-shaped table, she looking bored but beautiful in white, he slouched and wearing a felt hat while he ate. On a raised platform girls entertained with folk dances. Colored lights illumined decorated floats on the water and a large crowd jostled outside the roped-off area. The African guest was presented a painting and the Rev fell into a hole and spilled a paper cup of lemonade trying to see.

S UNDAY MORNING BREAKFAST, pre-pilgrim, was at the unearthly hour of 6:30. Afterward we wrote letters in our rooms and Em was approached by a strange man in the garden so we reinstated the rule about never being anywhere alone. A Church of England vicar preached at the 9:30 service in the chapel and afterwards we talked with some of the elderly pilgrims and invited ourselves to tea with them, the management notwithstanding. An Australian woman poured out her woes to us and Zwart, the Dutch minister, appeared to invite us to his home that evening. Things were thawing out a little.

In the afternoon we went back to our spot on the lakeshore. It was too hot for anything more ambitious. I was reading in Harold Lamb's book about the decisive Crusades battle at the Horns of Hattin on the plateau above Tiberias. That was in July, too, when men in heavy armor could be felled as successfully by dust and thirst as by enemy swords. In 1187 the Moslem hosts under Saladin met the Crusader armies advancing under Guy de Lusignan, King of Jerusalem. The twenty thousand Crusaders in heavy armor, most of them on foot, unwisely marched to meet the twenty-five thousand horsemen of Saladin who waited for them along the "brow of the great descent to Galilee. . . . If the Moslems could be broken and thrown back, they would be hurled down the descent upon the walls of Tiberias" and halted in their approach to Jerusalem and the Holy Sepulchre. But Saladin controlled the lake and it was water that made all the difference. The Crusaders, fighting bitterly, could not break through the Moslem ranks the first day of battle and at night they sat among their dusty dead, racked with thirst, while Saladin's horsemen ringed them in. The next day the battle was finished, and the King of Jerusalem with his lords surrendered when the brush in which they made their last stand was set afire.

So began the Crusader defeats which were finished with the fall of the great fortress at Acre on the Mediterranean. And so the cross disappeared from the Holy Land and was replaced for centuries by the flame and crescent of Islam. Seven hundred years later, after a modern crusade of armored cars instead of armored men, the seven-branch menorah and the six-pointed star of David were the symbols of new conquerors. "I came not to bring peace but a sword," Jesus said. Is it anywhere more true than in the history of the land in which his cross was reared?

Late in the afternoon we drove fifteen miles to Mount Tabor which lies only eight miles east of Nazareth. It is a surprising mountain, rising in perfect roundness a thousand feet above the long plain. A sign on the highway announces that the road to Tabor was built in cooperation with the United States. Busses carry visitors to the bottom of the mountain and there taxis take over, climbing up seventeen sharp switchbacks to the Franciscan church and monastery at the summit. Beside the iron gate to the church is a sign in three languages: "If you believe in God, you are welcome to pray. If you do not believe in God, you are welcome to visit. If you are vain and callous about the rights and property and feelings of others, write your name on our walls."

Historians say that there was a Roman stronghold on Tabor from the time of Antiochus Magnus in 218 B.C. to that of Vespasian's defeat of the Jewish rebellion in A.D. 66. None the less, this is the mountain celebrated for the transfiguration of Christ. It was a superb setting for this dazzling encounter.

The Hebrew word *Galil* means "circle" and the view from Mount Tabor encompasses a circle which includes most of Galilee. On a clear day, snowy Mount Hermon is visible in the north. Turning castward, one sees the small blue pool which is the Sea of Galilee and the Jordan which is the eastern boundary of Galilee. In the south is an endless checkerboard of fertile greens and tans covering the valley where Barak fought with Sisera while Deborah watched from Tabor. And on the west, vaguely, beyond Nazareth climbing up its private mountainside, is Mount Carmel facing the Mediterranean. It is a magnificent circle.

We returned over part of the Haifa-Nazareth-Tiberias road, passing the Horns of Hattin where two rocky prominences rise with a few level thorny acres between them. A roadside sign identifies the place but there is no marker or word about the battle of fifty thousand men. We approached the Sea of Galilee as Jesus must have done, coming from Nazareth and Cana to the edge of the plateau that drops steeply to Tiberias. The side of the plateau was already in shadow. Sun clung to the white roofs of the city. Tiberias is mentioned only once in the Bible, by John, who says that after the day when the five thousand were fed and the night when Jesus came down from the hills to walk on the stormy water, "boats from Tiberias came near the place where they ate the bread after the Lord had given thanks."

At supper we asked the two Dutch-speaking nurses to sit with us. Since we were leaving the next morning, there was not much to be lost by aligning ourselves with whatever side they were on. We limited our conversation to discussing the area. Yes, said the nurses who had been with the clinic many years, there were indeed fierce storms on the lake in November and December. The storms could arise quickly, the spray sometimes was felt a block inland, and the white ferry that plied from Tiberias to a *kibbutz* at the south end of the lake never set out if there was a hint of unrest on the water.

Once, years ago, they said, a sunken ship was found near Capernaum, its cargo of pottery almost intact. Archaeologists lined up the pottery on the clinic's shelves and spent some time exploring for streets that lay underwater.

Cautiously the nurses volunteered information about their work. The clinic helps about three hundred people a month. Dominee Zwart runs a bookstore and has increasing contact with the Jewish people because he has shown interest in them and sends his children to their Hebrew schools. He has been invited to take part in *kibbutzim* discussions. The nurses said they would be at Zwart's home with us that night. We wondered why they had avoided us before. Our conversation was cut short when an agitated Arab rushed into the courtyard, carrying a small child who had had some sort of seizure.

On Dominee Zwart's porch the atmosphere was relaxed, open, in contrast to the uneasiness in the Center. Gradually we deduced that there were differences between the *dominee* and "Miss Malevolent" who was in charge of housing pilgrims and running the Center. This nickname which we applied matched her personality and was similar to her real name. Miss Malevolent wished to run the Center as an impersonal profitable hotel. The *dominee* disagreed, holding that this church-supported place should continue to provide spiritual atmosphere and service in keeping with the Christian purpose for which the buildings had been erected and were known in the area. The impasse, to be settled by the Dutch and Scotch home churches, was not helped by the fact that the *dominee* and the nurses were Dutch, while Miss Malevolent was Scottish. Other Scottish staff members tried not to take sides. Eventually Miss Malevolent was recalled to her homeland.

An Englishman named Lindsay was on the porch, too. He was staying in Israel to make a new Hebrew translation of the Bible. Mrs. Zwart told me, when we were looking at her sleeping children, that Lindsay had lost half a leg in a mine explosion when he crossed the border to bring back a boy whose mother was in Israel and whose father, in Arab country, refused to return the boy to her. For this the Israelis considered Lindsay a hero, and the newspapers carried long accounts of the rescue.

Is it possible to present the Christian religion to the Jewish people in Israel? Not directly, said Zwart, explaining how long it had taken him to win their confidence and to be invited to discussions in the *kibbutzim*. A Polish Jewish doctor had been coming to see him at night, like Nicodemus of Jesus' day. But the doctor could not become a Christian openly and remain in Israel. He needed an invitation and a sponsor from another land who would help him find employment, even as a hospital orderly until he could pass medical exams in the new country. For some months after our visit we corresponded with Zwart about his "brother," having been warned not to mention names in our letters. Finally the "brother" was able to go to Montreal where he is happily settled and accepted as a member of a Christian church. Non-Jewish Christians in Israel concentrate especially on scholarly work, discussions of the Old Testament, and publishing literature with Old Testament emphasis. Christian businessmen have set up a factory for producing citrus juices in dry concentrate. The factory hires Israelis to bring them into closer contact with Christians.

Theodor Herzl, Zionism's founder, buried beneath a black marble stone on a hill near Jerusalem, said, "So build your state that the stranger shall feel contented among you." The stranger may bring his religion with him. But for the Jew Judaism must remain inviolate.

By virtue of his blood, he is not only citizen of Israel but adherent of Judaism, and the two belong together. The non-Jew cannot become a citizen even if he embraces the faith of Judaism and lives in Israel. The Jew in Israel is not free to leave his faith while retaining his citizenship.

We talked about practical things, too. Lindsay thought we ought to get photostats made of our last *carnet* sheet and try to get through the remaining countries with these. Zwart warned that Nazareth is full of bold children and haggling shopkeepers. The nurses offered us medicine and first aid supplies. We had found friends by the Sea of Galilee.

Even Tiberias was quiet when we walked back to the Center at midnight. The moon shone on the white jeep of the UN men who had rooms across the street. It shone on the water, riding the ripples in streaks of silver. Sometime during that night someone broke a window catch on the redbus in the courtyard and stole Em's Beirut camel bag containing Dutch sunglasses and a Jerusalem necklace. This was the only theft or loss of the trip.

The pilgrims climbed onto a big bus and departed before we did the next morning, because Miss Malevolent would not accept our traveler's check and we had to wait for the bank to open. In the final reckoning the

Rev had a little discussion with her about charging for seven beds and providing only six. His firmness surpassed hers and reduced her profits by seven and a half pounds.

Halfway up the plateau behind Tiberias we took a final picture of the lake in its bowl of hills with the rocky point of the fishermen steps jutting out and beyond it the trees shading Capernaum's ruin. Busses passed us on the twisting asphalt road. After the Horns of Hattin we came into Kafr Kannah, one of two sites suggested for Cana, where Jesus was a wedding guest and turned water into wine.

The Greek church in Kafr Kannah has a coral-colored dome, two coral-tipped towers, and stone vats said to be from Jesus' time — the very ones he used! The cacti and pomegranate trees are green, the flat-topped buildings cream-colored. The courtyard walls and donkeys are grey. An old man in white sat watching barefoot children playing. A woman in black balanced a large bowl on her head with ease, but a little boy in baggy pants looked like a figure eight holding a package on his head with both hands. Kafr Kannah and Nazareth are in an area which the U.N. armistice commission of 1947 wanted to neutralize or give to Jordan because its inhabitants are mainly Arabs.

One comes upon Nazareth from behind. A Franciscan hospital shows above the top of the broad cliff and the rest of the city sprawls down the cliff, unseen from the east. Perhaps it is better to say the town climbs up the cliff, rising from the valley. On the "brow of the hill on which their city was built," the townspeople of Jesus' day tried to push him to his death. West of today's Nazareth is the place which the monks of the Middle Ages called the Mount of Precipitation and here they built a slender little church called the Tremore for the trembling of Mary. Legend says she fell exhausted as she rushed to save her son from being pushed to his death.

"Can any good come out of Nazareth?" may have referred to the despised status of upper Galilee, but it did not imply that Nazareth was remote from the traffic of its day. Nearby was the main caravan route from Damascus to Egypt. Armed horsemen and royal messengers rode three miles north to Sepphoris, the largest city in Galilee until the Romans destroyed it in A.D. 6, forcing Herod to build a new capital at Tiberias. Jesus spent most of his earthly life in a village close to the traffic and culture of his day and close to some of Palestine's most varied and impressive landscape.

From the west the square ivory-colored buildings of Nazareth form a random pattern of steps all the way up the hill. They have many Moorish arches, and are linked by winding streets, separated by low stone walls, and interspersed with a surprising number of green trees. Another painter's landscape — green, cream, beige, coral, topped by an azure sky, cloud-flecked.

In the cramped streets and at the "holy places," this idyll turns to bedlam.

Barefoot boys besieged the redbus, tugging on the door handles while we were still in motion. One boy, failing to convince us where to park, tried to shove the redbus into a position advantageous to him.

We stopped first at the Greek Orthodox Church of St. Gabriel where Mary's well is found. Of all the spots identified in Nazareth, this is the most likely because for centuries there has been only one well in the town. It is little used today because Israel has supplied a pipeline of water, but probably Mary did come here, and also Jesus himself as a boy. The Gospels do not say it was here that Gabriel appeared to Mary, though a second-century writing, the *Protoevangelion,* added this detail.

The spring still bubbles in a small tiled room under the main floor of the church. A metal pail on a clanking chain brings up water. In the church there is a profusion of lamps, lights, icons, and oleographs. "Flat pictures instead of images," our children say, to distinguish the Orthodox from the Roman churches. The barefoot boys following us ran noisily in and out of the church.

Over the supposed cave house of Mary and Joseph the Franciscans have a big church. It is cold in the cave, which is down a long flight of dim damp steps. The steps allow only one-way traffic, and busloads of people driven from Haifa or Tel Aviv were trying to get in and out of the holy spot. In the cave itself, beneath a naked electric bulb, a guide was intoning about the wall niches and the stone in the middle of the floor. Did Jesus grow up in such a dark damp hole, even if his father's carpentry shop was above it on street level, open to air and sun and talk and people? We climbed back up as fast as the one-way traffic would allow and avoided the overcrowded gift shop attached to the church. Farther down the street we spent the equivalent of thirty-five cents for a graceful vase-shaped thing of olive wood, its light wood veined with curving lines of darker wood. It catches the morning sun in our kitchen window and we love the feel of the smooth wood.

Away from the bedlam we bought two luscious orange-skinned melons to eat for lunch in the shade of a Plant-a-Tree-for-Israel grove. Oom Bee had told us, shaking his finger emphatically, to look for the tree with Tante Fenna's name on it, because she had taken part in reviving the promised land.

And so we came to Haifa, as obviously Jewish as Nazareth is Arab, with stout ungirdled bare-armed women and slim assured teenagers without make-up. Except for the palms and an occasional Arab outfit, it might have been a summer scene in Monticello, New York. At the AAA we were directed to Photo Brenner for *carnet* photostats and on the way we noticed Bahai Temple's golden dome halfway up Mount Carmel. The newer part of the city is spreading out above it and will soon be at the summit, site of Elijah's contest with the prophets of Baal.

Photo Brenner turned out three clear copies of the remaining *carnet* sheet. The copies were on heavier paper and unperforated but the Rev pushed them into the *carnet* binding and we determined not to worry until necessary. Before we reported to the shipping agent we stopped at Steimatzky's, one of Haifa's many bookstores, and bought paperbacks to read on the ship. All the latest publications from the States were there, so inexpensive that we came out with an armful.

Poseidon Shipping Ltd. and I. Shubinsky had offices on the main street along the docks. Poseidon, I explained to the children, was the Greek god of the sea who carried a trident and a dolphin in his hands and kept his golden-maned horses in a palace at the bottom of the sea. The children were more interested in guessing which ship would be ours for the trip to Istanbul. "Nothing like the *Rotterdam,*" the Rev cautioned.

The gentleman in the shipping office insisted that our cabins had been given to others because we had not made contact earlier. So the Rev produced the letter telling us that we did not need to make down payment or appear to claim tickets before sailing time. Then we received, according to the gentleman, even better cabins than we had been assigned in the first place, and for the same price.

There was, however, one more unfortunate matter. The charge for loading and unloading the redbus was eighty dollars. But why was this never mentioned in the correspondence which had quoted the cost for shipping the redbus? Ah, this the good man did not know. He was helpless to explain. He was at the mercy of the dock hands whose fee this was, and he was as deeply grieved as we over this inexplicable charge.

What does one do in a situation like this? One pays. The Rev insisted on doing it with a personal check in order to preserve the dwindling balance we were carrying in cash and traveler's checks. After this we all went down toward the dock and the Rev, without due regard for intake and output, agreed to buy king-size bottles of Pepsi. We sat on benches at an intersection looking up at the Bahai dome, trying to finish the soda. The people who passed were curious.

"That your car?" asked a man. "Is a good car?"

Another said, pointing to the children, "All these from you? My, my, vunderful."

The tickets for the ship were in Turkish and French, and we were listed as Class I-C passengers, whatever that meant. We parked the redbus on the pier, took out luggage for the voyage, and sat on it while the Rev joined the slow-moving line of passengers waiting to have their tickets processed. The processing took two hours, during which the other passengers had ample opportunity to inspect us and the redbus. It was almost like being in backwoods Turkey except that the attention we received was more subtle. People gestured with their eyes to each other about the foam rubber, the brass tray, and the ends of maroon towels which could be seen through the dusty redbus windows. They discussed the license plate and the row of stickers in the back window. After that they discussed us. We, in turn, watched with interest the demonstrative farewells, the big arguments at the desks, and the screaming about luggage which porters were piling haphazardly on the main deck of the ship.

Finally, near six, we boarded, having stood and leaned the last hour after our luggage was removed from under us. For a pack of cigarettes each, two burly porters unearthed our luggage from the jumbled mountain on the deck and showed us to our cabins. Each had three beds and a bathroom. One bathroom was ankle deep in putrid water which the raised tile molding at the door kept from flooding the bedroom. The steward assured us that this would subside and it did when we put out to sea and it recurred every time we lay in port.

Eight o'clock was dinner hour for first-class passengers. By that time Dicker was ravenous and in a miserable mood. He devoured at sight all the rolls and bread sticks waiting to be used with the soup course, which followed the hors d'oeuvres. By the fish course he was satisfied. By the main course he was stuffed and half asleep. While we lingered over fruit and Turkish coffee, a crewman called the Rev to drive the redbus onto the loading nets. It rose shakily, copper tray gleaming in the docklights, and was set down on the center deck to be driven into position, locked, and shrouded in canvas against damage by salt air and spray. At 10 P.M. the S.S. *Istanbul*, with crossed red anchors painted on its white funnel, eased out of Haifa harbor.

West

A SHIP SEVERED from its dock is a world alone, a community of people inescapably thrown together until the next gangplank is attached. Some water-borne communities are more successful than others. Ours from Monday evening to Friday noon was a curious mixture, seldom relaxed, not always pleasant, a challenge in human relationships.

The ship itself, American-built around 1930, moved with deliberate dignity as if to mask her age. Ahead of the cargo deck rose a small section for captain and crew. Behind this deck was a large passenger section with open and closed decks and a café-game room. From the hall leading to the first-class dining room an iron ladder descended into the "other class" section, which appeared from above like a bottomless pit.

Dinner in the first-class dining room included six courses, waiters in tuxedos, and a grand array of silverware on the linen tablecloths. The only table large enough for our family was a round one in the center of the dining room which exposed us to continual scrutiny. One of our waiters, the singing one, rode platters through the air on his fingertips like a ship in heavy seas. The other, more inhibited, had a smile which turned off and on like a flickering bulb. It was simply a baring of the teeth, unrelated to inner feeling. We began again to say *Teşekkür ederim* and *Merhaba* and whatever other Turkish phrases we could remember. Dicker was practicing "beer, icky, ouch" all over again. A trio of violin, accordion, and piano provided dinner music. The first night's selections began with "Old Black Joe." Every night the wizened violinist bowed low at our table before leaving the dining room, encouraged, probably, by the enthusiastic applause of the children and by the hope that their father would be equally enthusiastic in his tipping at the end of the voyage.

The food was unusual, if not always appealing. One night for hors d'oeuvres we had a whole fish, and Dicker poked the eyes and exercised the jaws with energy. Boiled eggs arrived in a liquid state for one breakfast, reminding us of the first ones Nancy boiled at home when she timed them four minutes from cold water instead of from boiling. We asked for harder ones with the result that three came harder and four were still liquid. There was a noon meal of omelet and lamb chops, offset by a mediocre evening repast of cold cuts and cold fish, though this ended with tiny cream puffs in hot fudge sauce, as many as one could eat. On our last full day at sea the noon meal featured *pilaff necdet,* a yellow rice mixture covered with pastry, topped with a skewer holding the crescent and star of the Turkish flag in raw potato dyed red. Undulating toward our table on the fingertips of the singing waiter, this was a sight to see. And if one were hungry, he could look forward to tea at five, which was served with an abundance of cake and cookies. Better still, the fresh fruit bowl after dessert was a pleasure, especially because it never included watermelon. We had eaten plenty of that between Athens and Jerusalem.

The crew members outdid themselves to be helpful, expecting in return what is expected of every American traveling abroad — substantial tips and a few other favors. The first evening our room steward asked in broken English whether he could store a big doll in a box and a toy rifle under one of our beds. The next day the hostess interpreted for an old Turkish woman who wondered whether we would take some things through customs for her and let her pick them up at our hotel in Istanbul. We explained that we would not be stopping in Istanbul but would go directly on toward Bulgaria. As we eased ourselves out of that dilemma, it began to dawn on us that perhaps this was also the intent of the steward who had "stored" the doll and gun under our bed.

Most of the hundred passengers in first class were Jewish. We were the outnumbered ones, yet their attitude toward us was wary, defensive, and generally uncommunicative. They watched us carefully but avoided any direct confrontation. Though they squabbled loudly and on the last morning even fought among themselves, yet, had occasion demanded, they would no doubt have stood solidly together against us. It was a strange situation. Was this the instinctive reaction of Jewish people removed temporarily from the security of their homeland?

There were exceptions in both extremes. One woman, who seemed to be traveling alone, took an empty cigarette pack away from Dicker in an effort to get him to talk with her. He thought she was stealing his treasure and when I went back to explain to her, she was very communicative and we talked in German. That same day a man rushed up to the deck chair where I was reading about the Maccabean revolt.

"You shildren," he shouted, pointing wildly toward the bow of the ship. I leaped up, deciding as I ran which clothes to shed before plunging overboard for rescue. The man's wife sat in a deck chair facing the bow, clutching her heart. Below on the cargo deck Clark and Dave were threading their way back between the shrouded cars. Two other boys, black-haired, were still standing on the crew deck of the foresection. Pieced together from the by-sitters, the story was that our boys and the two dark ones had gone to the foresection deck where they climbed on a bench to see better. The woman had shrieked at them, in Hebrew, gesturing for them to return. The blondes had returned, the blacks had remained, but the husband had been sent to find us — not because of danger to the boys but because of danger to the woman's heart. Obviously the husband had not been dispatched to the parents of the dark boys still standing on the forward deck. I apologized profusely for causing the woman concern, and though she did not understand my words, some of her companions did. When I returned to my deck chair with Dave and Clark in tow, the chair was gone, despite the fact my book had been left on it and Nan had tried to save it for me.

We had one unexpected supporter, a heavy blonde whose first-class cabin opened onto the main deck. She kept a deck chair, of which there were too few, inside her cabin and always sat just outside her door, munching, usually on grapes. One day when I left my chair, she laid a heavy leg protectively over it and said, mouth full, "Keep it for you. Gotta hold onto your rights around here," this with a rolling of her eyes toward the "other class" who "aren't allowed up here in the first place." She was very talkative. Having moved to Israel from New York, she was beginning an extended vacation with a stay at the Istanbul Hilton where I assured her she would be well taken care of.

The last night the Rev had a long talk with three Jewish journalists who were guests of the shipping line so that they could write about it in the Israeli papers. For three days he went out of his way to speak to them and had changed money for one who wanted to go ashore at Izmir. It was a good talk. The men were eager to discuss the prosperity of Israel, to explain the absence of formal Jewish worship, to assess the future of their new state. They were lean, intelligent men with keen eyes. Disarmed, they talked freely and incisively. The last morning they stopped at our table to wish us a good trip. Our good-will campaign had not been a total failure after all.

W E DID NOT GO ASHORE at Cyprus where the ship lay anchored off the coast and small launches removed passengers to visit Larnaca. Famagusta and Nicosia, the Biblical Salamis and Paphos, were too far away to be reached by rented car. Besides, our dwindling finances were not due for replenishing until Salzburg. It was peaceful on the ship, reading, typing, sunning. Dave read from a folder that Larnaca had its own claim to fame — Noah built the city and Lazarus was buried here when he died the second time. Little boats bobbed between us and the shore, where a thin string of dusty-coral roofs lined the shore, broken by a minaret and a square steeple. Behind this was a wider ribbon of green and behind it rounded mountains in a hot haze. Dicker had so many cookies at tea that we put him to bed after the first course of dinner for which all the passengers had returned. At night there was an old pirate movie, shown on a screen hanging from the mast, and we corralled the children for bed before the second feature, a still older Western. The two of us sat on deck awhile watching shooting stars plummet into the water while the last lights of Cyprus disappeared behind us.

Wednesday all day we steamed where Paul sailed, going the reverse of the route by which he went from Ephesus to Caesarea. It seemed we had been making his journeys in reverse whenever we made them. The ship passed between the island of Rhodes and the rugged uninhabited Turkish coast. At the level east end of the island is a harbor astride which the Colossus statue stood, a wonder of the ancient world. We passed east of Patmos in a sunset glow appropriate to John's heavenly vision. That evening the adult passengers flocked to the ship's salon for "horse races."

Thursday morning we awoke in the harbor of Izmir, third city of Turkey. A tug pulled barges alongside for removing freight. Our steward brought a vase of red gladioli. This kindness, we suspected, was related to the doll and gun under the bed but no further word about these had been given. We left the ship to explore on foot the city in which we had slept some weeks earlier.

Izmir, the old Smyrna, is the only one of the seven cities of Revelation 2 and 3 which survives prosperously today. Despite wars and earthquakes and sackings, it is alive and thriving, thanks first to its indomitable Greek citizens, and later to its harbor which remained while the more famous ones of Miletus and Ephesus became silted and useless. Ships leave Izmir daily with raisins, figs, olives, cotton, tobacco, licorice, anise.

But the city is a conglomeration of the prosperous and the miserable, the Western and the Oriental, and most of it is haphazard and uninspiring. Chief of the few noteworthy places is the archaeological museum in Culture Park. An international fair is held annually in the park, and many crates on shipboard were marked for the Israeli exhibit there. The park is the city's beautiful face — trees, fountains, walks, benches — a worthy setting for the museum whose courtyard is filled with elaborate sarcophagi. They are covered with voluptuous carvings, naked nymphs holding clusters of figs and pomegranates larger than they, a plump winged cherub asleep above a Greek inscription, garlands of fruit tied together with giant bows.

The interior is dim, designed perhaps to implement the No-Photography signs. There are many pieces from ancient cities of this area — Ephesus, Pergamum, Sardis, Miletus, Laodicea. We were intrigued by the head and arm of a Domitian statue, first-century A.D. from Ephesus. The arm from wrist to elbow alone was five feet long.

The great treasure is the statue of the Ephesian fertility goddess, Diana-Artemis. Four guards circle her to prevent sneak photos. She stands about five and a half feet tall. Traces of gold are in the crevices of the elaborate carvings on every inch of her. Across her bosom are three rows of breasts, from her waist to her ankles are six rows of three animals each, and below them are two rows of lotus flowers. There are five animals on either side of her headdress and down the sides of her slim skirt are beetles, more lotus flowers, and a male angel. Even in her neck there are carvings. Her forearms are missing. So is the nose on her face, which stares out in placid assurance of her role. Such a statue, if not this one, stood in gleaming gold behind the altar in the great temple of Ephesus and was reproduced in smaller silver form for the worshipers who came from afar to revel in the orgies surrounding her fertility worship.

A student on a bench near the statue pretended to inspect his camera in the hope that he might get a picture. One guard casually rested directly in front of the goddess and another walked ominously close to the student. Diana may be purchased in postcard form at the information desk.

The beauty of Culture Park ended abruptly at its gates. Through shabby cobblestone streets we picked our way to the *agora* ruins, stepping from stone to stone to avoid trickles of something running between.

The *agora* is in the Namazgah district, not far from the bazaar. Protected by a wall, it looks like a piece of another world, sleeping in the middle of the noisy city. The admission charge relieved us of curious escorts and we walked alone beneath an imposing row of thirteen pillars. Marcus Aurelius was responsible for these in the rebuilding he authorized after the devastating earthquake of A.D. 178. Here it was easier to imagine the old Smyrna for whose church Christ had words of unmixed commendation when he wrote by the pen of John. Some say this is why Smyrna still prospers, but they forget that Philadelphia, whose letter was twice as long and even more commendatory, has vanished except for a remnant of old foundation.

The Rev was humming the tenor aria from Mendelssohn's *Saint Paul*. "Be thou faithful unto death and I will give to thee a crown of life." He pulled out his pocket testament to read more of the letter. "Do not fear what you are about to suffer. Behold, the devil is about to throw some of you into prison, that you may be tested, and for ten days you will have tribulation. Be faithful unto death, and I will give you the crown of life. . . . He who conquers shall not be hurt by the second death." Interestingly, early writings talk about the "crown of Smyrna" as garlands worn in worship rites for the goddess Cybele. Christ promises to the faithful his own crown, a crown of life.

Polycarp, the old bishop and disciple of John, deserved that crown. "Eighty and six years have I served him," said the old church father to the Roman proconsul who arraigned him, "and he has done me naught but good. How then could I revile my Lord and Savior!" Polycarp was burned at the stake in the Smyrna amphitheater, and he became the most famous martyr in the fierce persecutions of Marcus Aurelius' twenty-year reign.

At the far end of the *agora* we found Poseidon, the bearded sea god, and Demeter, the earth goddess, lips turned downward. Perhaps these large patched-together statues were once part of the altar ornament in the center of the *agora*. Over the heads of the marble deities men on lunch hour shouted greetings from a factory window. And above their heads rose Mount Pagus where one can still see remants of a wall built by Lysimachus, Alexander's general, who concealed a fortune in gold at Pergamum.

The bazaar was as much an experience of smell as of sight. Leather, yogurt, fish, cheap perfume, dung, garbage, a dead cat, tea leaves, sawdust — these odors swam in the air of the crowded alleyways. Green vines arched from side to side, making shade patterns on the wares beneath. Merchants without a shop or stall spread their goods where people walked. Women carrying string bags were busy striking bargains, watching shrewdly while their purchases were weighed on hand-held scales. A fortune teller sat behind a blue box on which were four cages with a dilapidated chicken chained on top. Business there was poor.

We bought a spool of white thread and some paper-covered caramels, and we tried to buy bottled cold drink. It was bottled, to be sure, but something hovered in the bottom of the orangish liquid. "Looks like spit," said Clark with indelicate accuracy. We did not complete that purchase.

Descending to the wide street along the harbor, we hired a horse-drawn taxi to return to the ship. It had red wheels, cushions, and tassels, and a laconic driver who drove in stockinged feet and yawned when we took his picture.

This was the noon of the *pilaff necdet* meal. David, dubiously surveying the concoction topped by a skewered Turkish crescent, said, "Wish we could travel with home food like mom's chicken and mashed potatoes." This was also the meal at which I went over to talk about Turkish money with the blonde grape-eater (how effective she would have been, installed beside the plump cherubs and grape clusters of the museum sarcophagi!). Slowly the dining room grew still and everyone looked at us as if we were plotting espionage, so we lowered our voices, and the stillness grew more intense until it was unbearable and I returned to our own table.

At supper, along with chocolate cake dessert, we received word about the doll and gun under the bed. The English-speaking hostess gave us a map of Istanbul marked with the place where we should deliver the toys. She thanked us with a dazzling smile and disappeared before we could question her. Apparently we were saving some crewman the heavy duty levied on Turks bringing things into their own country. We debated whether to leave the doll and gun under the bed but finally decided to take them ashore.

Friday morning we looked out on the Sea of Marmara and soon the scramble began for docking at 10:30. Crewmen unveiled the cars on deck and we put our luggage, doll and gun included, into the redbus. Before we could find the old violinist, he sent word via the children that he needed our tip to buy himself some comforting spirits ashore.

Now came the finest scenes of the voyage. Ashore the minarets of Istanbul appeared, the six of the Blue Mosque and the four of Hagia Sophia. Around us the water was teeming with boats of all sizes. Below, on the open cargo deck, the cabin baggage had been piled in a mountain. There were other doll boxes, we noticed. As we neared the dock on the Galata side of the Golden Horn, passengers began to jostle for position near their luggage. When the boat had been secured, the fight began in earnest to see who could get a porter and be off the ship most quickly. Porters boarding ship and passengers leaving it all had to go by way of a steep steel staircase from the baggage deck up to the gangplank. At the top of the staircase stood a customs official who allowed no porter off unless the passenger whose bags he carried was with him.

Sweating and disheveled, the passengers shouted, pushed, elbowed, clawed, and tugged at porters to get one for themselves. Those weatherbeaten men loaded suitcases on their backs with rope and staggered up the one-way steps, bent double. The sun beat down relentlessly on the battle which lasted almost an hour. With our luggage safely in the redbus, we withdrew to ringside seats on an upper deck. At the end one grandmother remained, sitting atop her conglomeration of bags and baskets, flatly refusing to be moved from the iron lid over the forward hold.

Meanwhile, cranes had been lifting cars over the embattled passengers. The redbus had its turn last, after the crane operator scratched his head and shouted to the men attaching cables to it. It rose uncertainly and dangled in mid-air.

Why were we back in Turkey for the second time within a month? The customs official could not understand. A man from Cyprus, whose car had been lifted off ahead of ours, helped to interpret. He had a doll box, too, and the customs official asked him about it. For once our ignorance of the language was an advantage.

The children petted the mangy harbor cats and Dicker hunted burnt match stubs to sail down a rivulet of dirty liquid running in the gutter. Ah, if our well-heeled friends could see us now!

With many guilt feelings we delivered the doll and gun to a dingy hotel on a dead-end street near the dock and sped from the scene, crossed the

Galata bridge, stopped for mail at the YMCA, and departed through the city walls, leaving the minarets and palaces of Istanbul behind. By 4:30 we were in Edirne, main crossing point from Turkey into Greece and Bulgaria.

Edirne is the old Hadrianopolis, one more of Hadrian's building achievements, a city fought through by Goths, Avars, Crusaders, Turks, and Bulgars. Until Constantinople was subdued in 1453 it was the Ottoman capital. Here was born Sultan Ahmet I who built the Blue Mosque in Istanbul. Today Edirne is a nondescript town of thirty thousand which boasts only of mosques and white cheese. It is hospitable to tourists entering and leaving Turkey, and there is an interpreter for their benefit in a booth at the main intersection. We needed him.

Instead of a shadeless field behind a gas station, we chose a campground called Sögütlük, which is through the city and across the Meriç River on the road to Karagac. It is a shady park on the river's edge and if one pitches tent far enough from the S.Q. facilities, the atmosphere is pleasant. How our standards for camp sites had sagged! Sögütlük we called good, despite the S.Q. and the water unfit for drinking. It even had picnic tables and benches of split logs.

Here we cooked Em's birthday dinner in anticipation of the next day, July 28. The boys ferreted out frogs around the waterspout. "Mine's huge," said Dicker, holding his hand triumphantly over the top of a can the Rev had given him.

While the sun threw a flaming road across the river, we sat at a picnic table eating canned ham, instant mashed potatoes, canned corn, sliced tomatoes, and a round pumpkin-colored melon. Later a Swiss car arrived from Bulgaria and we exchanged information about the areas from which we had come. There is a fine camping spot in Sofia, they said. Then came a little trailer from France and after it a beat-up car with Dutch license plates and two pup tents. Early the next morning a British car arrived, having driven all night through Bulgaria. So we were quite an international group — Swiss, French, Dutch, British, American. The Britishers warned that the Bulgarians were friendlier than the Yugoslavs and that the road from the Bulgarian border into Yugoslavia was impossible.

EMILY LIKES TO TELL PEOPLE that she celebrated her tenth birthday in three countries. This is true, and it is certain she will never celebrate another like it. In the morning we returned to Edirne, singing birthday songs in Dutch and English. As we approached the main intersection, a runaway horse with wooden wagon was in full flight down the street. Men chasing him caught up when he crashed through potted plants into a light pole and curb. The wagon, wrecked, lay with one wheel off and the other spinning crazily in the air. Goods were strewn about, a crowd converged, and a man loosened the frightened horse from the wreckage and delivered him a smart crack of the whip so that the animal reeled sideways toward our bumper. Em, whose passion is dogs and horses, wept.

And then everything returned to normal. The streets were being sprayed to keep the dust down, women in black scurried about, horse-drawn taxis waited for business, waiters rushed around carrying coffee or tea on brass trays suspended on chains. The Rev had fun spending his Turkish money buying birthday treats in little shops — one treat every hour, he promised, little dreaming how long the day would be. Caramels and nuts and salted seeds, in little hand-pasted sacks, and big luscious peaches. In another shop he found Jerusalem-made colored pencils and squared paper for making designs. Dave bought Em a silver ring with a boy and girl on it for eighty cents American. Nan gave Em Korean paper dolls from friends in Jerusalem and a magnifying glass from a Dutch uncle. Dicker gave her some smooth little sticks wrapped in the cardboard of Clark's camera box, and Clark parted with a ballpoint pen. In high spirits we left for the Bulgarian border, where we were processed through Turkish customs in twenty minutes.

Cars entering Bulgaria pass through a flat bed of straw treated with disinfectant. The driver is also instructed to walk through the straw on his way to the customs building. The rest of us stayed inside, waiting to contaminate the Bulgarians later. Guards walked curiously around the car. Half a dozen other cars arrived, and after a delay of fifteen or twenty minutes, each driver reappeared and drove on. After half an hour the Rev appeared on the porch of the customs building, gestured to indicate that he had no idea what was holding us up, and threw us into a state of anxiety about the *carnet*. What else could be causing the delay? If Bulgaria would not let us through, we would have to return to Turkey — if they would take us for the third time within a month — and find a ship to Italy where *carnets* are unnecessary. This would mean missing Hungary and Sandor's family after all our work to get a Hungarian transit visa. Our hostility toward the Dutch ANWB agency was intense.

We waited an hour for the Rev to return. He was smiling and shaking his head. It was not the *carnet* at all. They had not even looked at it. After fifty minutes of studying our passports behind closed doors they had determined that one seal was lacking on them, a seal which should have been stamped on at the Bulgarian consulate in Washington, an omission which should have been noted by the Detroit travel agency designated to handle Balkan passports. We could either pay four dollars per person there at the border or return to the Bulgarian consulate in Edirne to get the stamp there. The Rev elected to save twenty-eight dollars, though it took considerable explaining at Turkish customs to get them to take us back when they were scarcely rid of us, and they kept our *carnet* for security.

It was 11:45, Saturday, when we re-entered Edirne. The interpreter at the main intersection told us where the Bulgarian consulate was and added that it closed at noon. At five to twelve the heavy doors swung open. Soon the Rev emerged with two men and they walked back to the interpreter to make the situation plain. Once they understood, the consular officials were very kind. They even discovered a second error on the passports. We were listed as traveling from Yugoslavia via Bulgaria to Turkey instead of vice versa. Pity poor Turkey, getting us back a fourth time! While one man changed and stamped the passports, the other brought out a bottle of vodka as a gesture of cordiality.

Visas in order, the Rev negotiated the seventeen twisting miles back to the border, picked up the *carnet* from the Turks, crossed the decontaminating bed of straw, wiped his feet in it, and re-presented the documents. In minutes he was back, carrying the *carnet* book from which the first of the photostats had been used. The official had trouble ripping off the first part of the sheet because it was unperforated but he never questioned it. We even paid the Bulgarian road tax in Turkish *lira*. Things were looking up again. We got out another bag of birthday treats. For lunch we ate the peaches which were as *gezul gezul GEZUL* as the merchant had promised they would be.

The road was good two-lane pavement, with little traffic except cars we had seen at the border. Native wagons were pulled by oxen or donkeys. People worked in the fields and sat in groups stringing tobacco leaves to be hung under shade trees for drying. It grew hotter as we drove into the interior and there was no breeze. The highway was lined with propaganda signs, all in Bulgarian, about consumer goods and sports. There was one about Africa, picturing a Negro waking and breaking his chains. After Plovdiv, hardly recognizable from the tourist literature about it, we poured in our two gallons of reserve gasoline, hoping to reach the Yugoslav border without buying gas and getting Bulgarian money. A woman in a bikini looked up at us from a river where she was washing clothes.

Three miles east of Sofia we passed a fenced-in camping area next to a public swimming pool. Dave was discussing the country with his father.

"Doesn't look bad, dad, not as poor as I thought. Much better than East Germany."

"Maybe it's not so much in the things you see," his father answered, "like the swimming pool and the people's clothes. Maybe it's more a matter of freedom in the heart and being able to speak honestly and worship openly and vote with true choice."

Certainly Sofia was an attractive city. Fine buildings, tree-lined streets, large parks, ponds, statues — and long bread lines at the bakeries. In the heart of the city we had a near collision with a trolley whose tracks turned into a side street. The Rev expected, as we came toward the trolley, that we had the right of way. We will never know whether we did or not. The trolley swung across our path, we ground to a screeching halt, the conductor rose from his seat and stood at the open door shaking his fist and berating us soundly in Bulgarian while the passengers inspected us with interest. There was nothing to do but wait it out. By the time the first trolley had gone on its way, a second was coming close behind it. Dutifully we waited, but this conductor laughed, stopped his trolley, motioned us through, and waved a cheerful greeting as we passed. Just like the taxi drivers in New York. There are all kinds.

In the suburbs children swam in canals and in public pools. Old women were spinning wool. The countryside became rolling and wooded, and some cultivated fields were irrigated. In the late afternoon, as the day's heat abated, we arrived at the border along with two French cars traveling together. With the piece of Bulgarian paper money we had received as change from the road tax, I bought a wooden miniature of a peasant girl who comes apart at the middle to hold needles. It was the most confusing purchase of the trip because the girl in the booth answered my pantomime with nothing but expressionless Bulgarian and a deadpan face. At the Yugoslav customs we had a few anxious moments when officials asked for additional cards which we had been given in the States but had forgotten about. They were tucked away in the documents folder. It did seem that one border refusal was enough for the day.

Now began the ninety-mile obstacle course to Nis. Had the Britishers at Edirne not warned us, we never would have believed that this was an international road leading somewhere. Not even in back country Turkey was there anything to compare with this. Top speed was twelve miles an hour and this only because the redbus had a high carriage so that in missing one and hitting two holes every wheel rotation we could travel more easily than regular cars. First we braced ourselves against the bumps and pitch holes. Then we tried bouncing with them. Neither worked. We crossed a ditch to ride on a wagon trail along the edge of a pasture and this was fine for a mile until it ended in a drainage ditch and we had to turn around in the pasture and retrace our way to the place where we had crossed over.

We were still bumping when it became dark. How is it possible for one road to have so many holes? Each car we met, and they were few, saluted us and we them with great shouts and blowing of horns and blinking of lights, glad to take courage from the other's progress. Nancy caught the yellow dishpan of melons in her neck a few times before she put it between her feet. Em flung herself against the stack of sleeping bags which kept bouncing loose from their pile. Dicker fell asleep in my lap and to keep him from bouncing like a rag doll, I braced him until my legs and arms ached. It was even too bumpy to pass out treats. No one could get a hand into a bag. The only vehicles immune to the road were huge Belgian trucks, emerging like roaring monsters out of the night.

The French cars stopped at dark to set up their tents in a field. They waved for us to join them but we decided to try for Nis where there was a listed campground. Why get up early to fight the road again?

At eleven o'clock we saw the lights of Nis in the valley and found the campground in a big fenced grove of trees. Water, toilets, showers, groceries, even an iron we found in the morning. At night we only pitched the tent, unrolled the foam rubber and sleeping bags, and flopped into bed. Em murmured sleepily, when I kissed her unwashed face, "It was a good birthday anyway, mom."

Church bells woke us in the morning. We washed the dirt of three countries from our skin, took out clean clothes, stools, and folding chair, and ate an unhurried breakfast of melon, bacon, hot chocolate, and bread with strawberry jam. A wind blew in the trees and the sky was overcast. For morning worship we read and discussed Psalms 101 and 102 which had new meaning since we had seen Jerusalem. Em basked in the reflected glow of her birthday. "Bulgaria birthday," we decided to call it, and the Rev promised hourly treats for any child who would have a birthday on Saturday or Sunday.

"Only it won't be like mine," said Em. How could it be?

WE ABSORBED little of Yugoslavia. It was transit for us, both in time spent and attention paid. This was the lull before Hungary for which all our senses were keyed to acute perception. We know that Yugoslav currency is the *dinar,* that its middle-aged people can understand German because of the Nazi occupation, that Beograd is a big modern city, and we can tell in detail about one place we visited accidentally. Our route was through the northeast corner of Yugoslavia, Nis-Beograd-Novi Sad-Subotica, the last of which is the town at the only southern border-crossing into Hungary. Sometime we want to meander down the Adriatic coast where Dutch cousins have camped. Until then, our memories of Yugoslavia are of bumps, mosaics, and mud.

The mosaics were at Oplenac which we visited because we saw a sign on the main road and had time to explore without plan. We were driving on the main road from Nis to Beograd, a distance of four or five hours on excellent road with little traffic. The sign said Topola and Oplenac, but the names and the history they represented were strange to us. Topola was the home town of Karadorde, leader of the First Serbian Insurrection in 1804 when the Serbs launched their successful attacks against the Turks who had ruled them four hundred years. At Topola Karadorde built houses and a fort with four towers and a church with a separate crypt for his burial. But when he was killed in 1817, his head, stuffed with cotton, was sent to the sultan in Constantinople as proof that a great enemy was dead.

It was Karadorde's grandson, King Petar I, who began building the church-mausoleum on Mount Oplenac above Topola. This was to be a mausoleum for the Karadordevic dynasty. But the church, begun auspiciously in 1910, was dismantled by the enemy during the First World War and was not completed until 1930. Today it stands in gleaming Vencac marble at the top of the green slopes in a park setting, with golden crosses and orbs on each of its five domes. Over the main entrance the Karadordevic coat of arms surmounts a gold-and-color mosaic of Saint George destroying the dragon. The inside is a glittering example of medieval Serbian art with mosaics completely covering the walls and ceilings. The mosaic in the curve of the large dome at Oplenac shows the head and shoulders of Christ Pantokrator surrounded by angels. In the crypt below, also covered with mosaics, we saw the graves of the Karadordevic family except for Karadorde himself (head included?) and King Petar I who are honored by burial in the church itself.

One should sit and study a week amid such glory, learning why in Eastern Orthodox churches there are certain places for the four evangelists, for Mary's death scene, for scenes from Christ's life and suffering, for the bishops' procession and the apostles' communion, and the holy warriors of the fourteenth century. Perhaps the most unusual mosaic sequence in the Oplenac church is the procession of sovereigns beneath a long sequence of Christ's sufferings. Crowned, haloed, and each carrying a model of the monastery or church he built or supported, the monarchs stand in brilliant colors, from Stevan Nemanja, whose dynasty ruled Serbia two centuries, to Durde Brankovic. Who are all these kings? What is the proud history of Serbia? And where was King Petar I when the assassin killed the archduke at Sarajevo?

Travel produces a consuming passion to learn history, to evoke the past in all its blood and glory, to keep filling in great blanks in one's understanding of what God has been doing in his world.

Many Yugoslavs were coming and going at Oplenac. Is this to them what places like Mount Vernon are to us? The Rev photographed the legs of a peasant in dark brown knee breeches, feet encased in a kind of moccasin with long curling points at the toes and leather straps and buckles around his ankles.

Rain began as we arrived at the Beograd campsite, Camp Kosutnjak, on a hill overlooking the city. We surrendered our passports at the office, a common procedure in European campgrounds and hotels, and pitched tent on high ground. The rain became a steady downpour. Two Dutch boys in

Sunday suits, stranded by the weather, watched us from the doorway of their pup tent opposite us.

The way to the washrooms was a sea of mud and clay. Not only did one sink in up to his ankles but upon trying to extricate a foot to take the next step, he lost his shoe unless he could dig his toes into the sole to maintain leverage. If the shoe did come out of the mud, it was enlarged to twice its size by the clay that came with it. Where the mud and clay did not suck one in, it was as slippery as ice. Sinking and slipping, the girls and Dicker and I arrived at the washrooms' cement steps. We used them, as had others, to scrape off what mud we could from the bottom of what shoes we had left. I washed Dicker's legs to his hips and carried him back to the tent on my shoulders, a perilous journey.

The muddy shoes we lined up under the redbus out of the rain. With water from the five-gallon can we washed our feet in the yellow pail at the tent door and crawled inside to wait while the Rev cooked a hot meal, sitting cross-legged in the opening with the camp stove under the overhang. It was the cosiest meal of the trip. Rain which we had not heard for weeks pattered on the tent roof and we sat snugly inside, eating from our plastic bowls beef stew mixed with string beans. Miraculously, no one spilled.

The Rev carried each of three children to their redbus bed. While late-comers shouted and pounded to get settled in the darkness and rain, we sat at the open tent door, drinking coffee, listening to talk in many languages and to tinny train whistles in the distance, watching the lights of Beograd through the drizzle. That night I dreamed about the perils of visiting Sandor's house in Hungary and wakened with relief when some loud-talking Frenchmen drove their stakes so close that it seemed they would pierce our tent wall.

In the morning it was cool and grey, weather for sweaters and long pants. Except for nights in Jerusalem, this was the first cool weather we had had since Switzerland. Oh yes, and Les Cèdres! The Dutch boys shared our breakfast and then hiked off with tent and gear compactly stored in their knapsacks. We took time to type letters, clean shoes, and "neaten" the redbus inside, as Em used to say.

At the American embassy in Beograd we converted money into *dinars,* and asked directions to the post office and the apartment of a Reformed bishop's widow we had been asked to see. But the widow was not at home. An old woman with frowsy grey hair and a crutch explained in German that the lady was away at a health bath until August 15. Yugoslav tourist literature has a long list of these health spas, listing which ailments are relieved at each. The list ranges from "chronic disease of the liver" to "increased blood pressure, gravel in the urinary passage, diabetes," and just plain "women's diseases."

The Rev asked where the church of the widow was and the old woman, hoisted with difficulty into the front seat, took us to the Roman Catholic instead of Reformed church. There the Rev had a good talk with a young English-speaking priest born to Hungarian parents in Novi Sad. The old lady and I talked in German. She had lived in Beograd sixty-three years, since she was born. Beograd has about one and a half million people now, many foreigners. She was happy there. Living was good. When I commented that she spoke excellent German, she answered candidly that she did not like to do it because of memories associated with the German occupation. "I know," I said, "it was the same in the Netherlands." Where did we live in the Netherlands? Ah, Americans! *Wunderbar.* Her questions about the children and the way we lived poured out. The Rev came back too soon to answer them all.

The young priest, hearing that we were going through Hungary, pleaded, "You, a Christian and a pastor, when you are in Hungary, you will know why I beg of you to pray every night for that country."

For a while that afternoon we wondered whether we would ever reach the country in need of prayers. We left Beograd, full of big grey buildings under a grey sky and new apartment complexes under construction across the grey Danube. At noon we were in Novi Sad, bells chiming, shops closing, no bakery in sight. Quick arithmetic showed that a woman's raincoat in a store window would cost thirty-two dollars. Maybe my arithmetic was wrong. It is one of my weak points. The Rev was busy looking for a bakery. Finally he called to a young woman walking on the street. She had us wait while she ran around a corner and returned with a warm fresh loaf for which she would take no more than its price in payment. She was also the kind one who pointed out the wrong road to Subotica and the Hungarian border.

Later, too late, we discovered that two roads lead north from Novi Sad. One, the international highway, is smooth and paved all the way to Subotica, with rest stops, a small zoo, and a lake along the way. The other, paved a few miles out of Novi Sad, deteriorates into an unkept muddy trail which passes desolate villages and creaking wagons and flocks of scraggly chickens and ducks. There is only one road marked on the map. Perhaps the young lady in Novi Sad had never gone far enough down either road to know the difference. Ironically, while we were eating the fresh bread along the roadside, we saw a few cars whizzing along a highway half a mile across the fields. At that point we were still on good road and surmised that the other road led somewhere else than to Subotica.

We were not the only travelers to make this error. In one bleak ramshackle village a black Mercedes with German license stood with a gaping hole in its windshield and a crumpled bicycle next to its wheels. The boy on the bicycle seemed to have only an aching arm, but where would one repair a Mercedes windshield unless he returned to Beograd to wait there? A carload of Dutchmen and a plucky Englishwoman coming from the north had also missed the good road. A man we asked along the way gestured on north. Rain fell steadily.

The road was marked with a detour sign though no one was working on it. The detour arrow took us down into a wide ditch beside the road, an alternate route for wagons in dry weather. We slithered along in the ditch, hubcap-deep in mud, mud, mud, expecting any moment that the sucking sounds around our wheels would stop us altogether. And then who would haul us out?

Finally a sign at an intersection pointed north to the Hungarian border, yards away, and in the other direction, south to Subotica, down a lovely highway. Then we knew.

We circled back to Subotica down the road we should have taken. A man on a bicycle, after stopping for consultation in the town, led us to a grassy area next to Lake Palic which was the name of the campground on the camping map. The campground was listed as having water, electricity, restaurant, sanitary installations, bathing, and parking. Even without these things, after the mud it looked attractive enough. We were the only campers and we used a nice stone table and the box toilets behind a building that looked like a community hall. The boys went down to the dock and made friends with a fisherman while they watched the sailboats on the lake. The fisherman, whom they called Bub, understood neither English nor German but he understood when they said Chicago-America, and after he brought his poles away, he returned on his bike to inspect what we were doing. Gravely he watched Dave put up the tent and he stood close while the Rev made a casserole of Spam and pork and beans. The camping stove intrigued him. "Gas?" he said, pointing to his cigarette lighter. He declined to stay for supper, but he did sample the Spam. When we were ready to eat, he formally shook hands with the Rev and me, waved to Dave, and pedaled off.

We were a little jittery about our entry into Hungary the next morning. In a neat bonfire we burned the letters, names, and instructions from Sandor except for a master sheet which went into the zipper compartment of my purse. A Dutch friend had told us how his luggage was searched in a hotel. Others talked of hotel rooms being bugged.

Dave broke the tension by practicing from the military section of the U.S. government's Hungarian language book, as he had done at home. "I'll ask the border guards, *Vannak errefelé csapatok*? That means, Are there any troops around here? Then I'll say, *Mutassa meg hol vannak*. Show us where they are. Or how about, *Van a csapatoknak tankelhárito agyújuk*? That's, Do the troops have any antitank guns? *Fene bele,* what a language," Dave exploded, using the Hungarian expletive Sandor had given him to vent his anger unintelligibly.

We laughed around the little fire, but our minds were full of other

things. At Edirne the Swiss had told us they were not allowed to stay overnight in Hungary on their transit visa, even though it was good for forty-eight
hours. Tourists at that time were allowed little freedom in Hungary and a
tour group was the acceptable way to visit. We could only guess why our
request for regular visas had been denied. Sandor himself told us how conspicuous we would be in the town where his sisters lived. Take a thermos and
go to the door as if you need water, he advised, and then play it by ear.
All these thoughts tumbled through our heads when we tried to sleep, and
the dogs of the area howled all night until the roosters took over before dawn.

BRACED BY MORNING PRAYERS, we reached the border at nine, left
the Yugoslav officials chuckling about how many children we had, and came
to a halt before the remote-controlled barrier into Hungary. Soldiers with
guns in hand were patroling the barbed wire fence through the fields. Ours
was the only car in sight.

The men at the border station spoke Russian and Hungarian, which was
to our advantage. They pantomimed for cameras and such to be declared,
they motioned for the brass tray to be loosened so that they could look behind it, and they poked each other in amusement when the Rev signed the
declaration sheet with his left hand. Without question they accepted a
photostat *carnet* sheet. In fifteen minutes we were driving down the asphalt
road past harvesting groups and fertile fields. Or did it look doubly fertile
after the parched soil of Arab lands? Soldiers on the road stopped us once
but waved us on without question. In the distance we saw the twin spires
of Szeged. All the names we had heard from Sandor began to fall into place.

In Szeged we asked for IBUSZ. IBUSZ is the official Hungarian tourist
agency which controls visas, hotel reservations, gas coupons, and every other
aspect of a tourist's visit. We wanted to clarify our rights as transit tourists,
having been unable to do this at the border. Flags were flying as for a
holiday, umbrellas shaded sidewalk tea tables, and people on the street
watched us though they did not return our waves. A woman carrying fresh
flowers stopped at the car to look in and smile. The IBUSZ people told us
in broken German to ask our questions in Budapest when we got there.
They did not seem accustomed to counseling individual travelers.

We followed the main road to Budapest as far as Kecskemet and then
turned off for Nagykörös. No Vopo motorcycle roared out to protest our
change in route. It was all smooth and easy. We approached Nagykörös
past two cemeteries. The Communist charge had been five hundred dollars
to allow Sandor's father to be buried with his family in one of them. Sandor
had sent the money, grimly. There was also a large army barracks on the
edge of the town — Russian, the sisters told us later, one of many troop

concentrations in the towns around Budapest, ready on a moment's notice, but not visible to visitors who seldom got beyond the capital or the Lake Balaton resort area.

In whispered excitement we looked for number 57 in the row of houses and walled courtyards that stood in unbroken line at the street's edge. It was near noon and we would have preferred arriving after lunch, but time was valuable in case we would not be allowed to stay overnight in Hungary. Armed with the quart thermos, the Rev pulled the clapper on the bell beside a weatherbeaten door in an ochre-colored wall. The street was silent and deserted. How many eyes watched from behind curtains? Sandor had written his sisters that a friend Dick with his family might be driving through Hungary about August 1. More than this he dared not write. We were a day early.

And then the door opened and out came Olga, the schoolteacher, followed by short plump Klarike, the oldest sister. Olga answered the Rev's German in a burst of joy, apologizing for the paint brush in her hand. "It is too wonderful! But why did you not telephone us to say what day you would come?"

Telephone? *"Ist es nicht gefährlich für Ihnen?"* the Rev answered in amazement. Of course it was not dangerous, Olga said, laughing, but we noticed that she urged us quickly through the doorway into the protection of the courtyard. As long as we were inside, she said, no one would know to whose visitors the car belonged. It stood conspicuously alone on the silent street.

The courtyard was surrounded by living quarters, all of which once had been part of the family's town house. Here they had lived since the Communists in 1946 had confiscated their country estates and the serfs had pillaged the country mansion, stealing its treasures by night. Now the sisters used only part of the town house. The rest of it, taken over by the government, was rented to others. Into a few rooms with broken plumbing and a wood cook stove were crammed what treasures remained of a proud family whose christenings had been attended by royalty.

Olga, at fifty-three the youngest sister, was exactly like Sandor — keen, warm, dynamic, independent. Emmike, the middle sister, had gone on her bicycle to the doctor to see how well her broken ankle was mending. Emmike had wanted to be a nun when she was eighteen, but Sandor, upholding the tradition of his grandfather who was a Reformed church bishop, stole into the cloister at night with a friend and carried Emmike out in a sack. For this she bore her brother no lasting malice and she practised her Catholicism peacefully at home, since no one practised any religion very publicly anymore. Klarike was the oldest, the sturdy Martha type who cooked, cleaned, and cared for the others. Beneath a severe center-part-and-bun hairdo her eyes twinkled, her smile was wide, and her face guileless like an open book.

Almost fifteen years had passed since Sandor's escape from Communist prison into the free world. His was the first Balkan spy trial after World War II. While Stalin and Roosevelt were still carving up the Hitler-Mussolini empire at Potsdam and Yalta, Sandor was convicted of betraying the people's republic to the American underground! He had been a history professor in Kolozsvar, Transylvania, now Cluj, Rumania. At the request of the Hungarian prime minister, he was collecting photos and data on unbelievable Russian atrocities as they "freed" the Balkans. The day before his arrest he had hidden his files with a friend in a little village. The story of his torture, trial, imprisonment, and escape is worthy of a book by itself. For almost a year the sisters had hidden him in a false ceiling while placards promised large rewards for his recapture. Even from America he had used an assumed name to correspond with his family. We were the first direct contact with Sandor that the sisters had had since his escape in 1947.

For days after our visit we were sifting and evaluating what happened in Nagykörös. We had been fearful that our visit might bring some retaliation on the sisters. They assured us profusely that this would not happen, yet they were careful to keep us inside the house and courtyard, they would not ride with us into the center of the town or to the cemetery, and they posed for pictures on the outside steps as briefly as possible. We had brought small gifts including photos and canned goods, and stockings from Sandor's dear wife Els, a Dutch social work professor he met in New York when both of them were studying there. But the sisters were more intent on giving us gifts, on creating the impression that they were not in need, though we knew differently. Olga even offered us money when we left. It was a display worthy of them and we accepted graciously, except the money, sensing what it meant to them to have us convey this brave picture to Sandor.

To compress fifteen years into an afternoon visit was demanding the impossible, even in English. How could we do it in German, the only common language we had? Olga spoke German fluently. Emmike seemed to understand it somewhat, answering *egan* and *nem* appropriately as we talked. Or did she only reply to our inflections? Klarike understood nothing, but she was busy in the kitchen, Clark helping her, devising out of their meager stores such delicacies as one would not have thought possible.

The sisters would not hear of our bringing in our own bread. They felt badly that they had not known exactly what day we would come so that they could have stood in the meat line at 4 a.m. to get chicken for *csirke paprikás*, the Hungarian specialty. That they had expected us soon was obvious. Platters heaped with cookies stood around the living-eating room, along with bowls of fruit — the apricots of which Sandor raved, and plums. The bell at the courtyard entrance clanged several times, startling us at first. Were friends bringing things for the meal? We surmised that Emmike came and went several times before she appeared to be introduced. The children came in anxiously from the courtyard where they were watching the rabbits kept for meat. "Dad, there's a helicopter going slow over the house. Is it looking for us?"

And then we were all sitting around the table with its white cloth and china from a bygone age, and the Rev prayed in English and we drank a toast in German to the freedom of Hungary, and Klarike ladled apple soup out of a large tureen, and Olga got up and went around the table, kissing each of us and bidding each a formal welcome. We sat, with tears falling into the apple soup, while the old clock filled the silence with its ticking and the grandfather of the family looked down on us all from within a wide gold frame, a black-bearded man in the prime of life, well capable of ruling estates and a family of renown.

After the apple soup came bean soup, also expertly seasoned, and then hard-boiled eggs in sour cream sauce, fit for a feast, and bread, and fruit and cookies and even coffee. All the while we talked in German with Olga. The air throbbed with the intensity of sharing for Sandor's sake and theirs, and even the children were impressed and ate quietly.

Could we see the large estate house? Ah, it had burned down, and they had not told Sandor who still dreamed of it as it stood. Olga told of her two vacation weeks with other teachers at Lake Balaton. It was hard living closely together because no one could trust the other. In the school where she taught there were several informers in the faculty of thirty. No one was certain who they were and so no one spoke honestly or openly. Pressure, tension, fear — always. Church attendance brings reprisals, too. For this, one teacher was transferred to a school seventeen miles away. There was no housing there, officials told her, so she would have to bicycle each day to reach her classroom. "Only when I am in another city I go to church," said Olga. Parents do not send their children to religious instruction at the churches. For this a father can lose his job. In the Nagykörös Reformed Church, once full with two thousand people, there are two pastors, one a *Frieden Pfarrer,* a peace pastor, patently loyal to the Communist line.

Ten per cent of the people, that is, the party personnel and the informers, can buy whatever they want. The others do without or stand in long lines, hoping. "Yes, since the 1956 revolution the method is more permissive in order to keep the people quiet, but the goal is the same as before. And yet" — Olga spread her strong hands on the table and spoke in an intense whisper — "do not think youth believes all this indoctrination. I know my students. They listen, but in their hearts they do not accept it. *Nein, nein, Sie glauben es nicht."*

Only once did Olga say wistfully that she wondered what would have happened had they left Hungary when the way was open in 1956. Quickly and firmly, as one bolts a door and leans against it, she added that this had been impossible because father had been too feeble to go. Katy came then, godchild of the sisters, daughter of their best friends, a sober thoughtful teenager. She brought us a fresh-cast plaster plaque of Arany János, great Nagykörös poet. With it she brought a little tin of vaseline to rub into the surface of the plaster when it had cooled. We sat on the sofa under the gold-framed grandfather, telling everything we could remember about Sandor and Els.

At five o'clock we tried to suggest leaving. For pictures of Sandor's school and church we needed sunlight, and we also had to decide whether to drive out of Hungary or try to stay in Budapest overnight. It was hard to leave. There was too much finality about it. Klarike was putting cookies into bags, Emmike packed apricots and plums, Olga showed us the false ceiling behind which Sandor had hidden and she impulsively picked up an embroidered pillow from the couch in that room. "Choose," she said, holding up one and then another of several with peacock pattern in intricate red cross-stitch. Oh yes, do not forget the little gifts for Sandor and Els, figurines and Hungarian paprika and some books that could not be mailed across the border. And two big jars of apricot jam, one for Sandor and one for us.

When we came out of the courtyard door, Katy's parents were hurrying down the street to see us. Josef kissed my hand, his mustache tickling it, and he greeted the Rev cheek to cheek. Barbara had fresh flowers for us. We stood together briefly, lacking the security behind the wall or in the house. The sisters did not even walk to the redbus with us. But Katy rode her old bicycle to the center of town where we photographed the church and school and she said a last *"Auf wiedersehen."* Fortunately the church faced west, the sun was full on it, and we made an extra jumbo slide of the tall dark spire rising from the ivory-colored stucco building. A little funeral procession, people in black walking behind a horse-drawn cart, turned the corner. An old man sat motionless on a red bench in the park.

I T WAS NEARLY SEVEN when we entered Budapest, limp and emotionally drained empty from the effort of the afternoon. We had neither gas coupons nor hotel reservations, so whether we drove to the Austrian border or attempted to stay in Budapest overnight, we needed official help. The first IBUSZ office to which we were directed was closed. In the second one a woman was working overtime. She explained very casually to the Rev that gas coupons could be purchased at the main post office three blocks away, and that we were welcome to stay overnight in Budapest if we could find hotel rooms available.

While the Rev made these IBUSZ inquiries, a woman rose from a table at a sidewalk café and came to the front window of the redbus. She seemed sixtyish, petite, dark, well dressed, with nail polish and lipstick. Her male companion disappeared into the twilight. The woman began to talk to Dicker who was on my lap. She crooned in German as though rocking a baby. And where was the dear little boy going to lay his tired head, she was saying, and all his brothers and sisters too in this big, big, strange city of Budapest? She would help, yes, she would help, and these sweet children would be taken care of. They could come to sleep in her nice house, yes, they could, the dear sweet children.

The woman was cold sober. There was not a whiff of anything about her. I wondered momentarily whether I was having delusions after the strenuous afternoon. Then the Rev returned and I explained to him in English while the woman explained to him in German what was going on, and he answered us both by saying that we would purchase gas coupons at the post office and then drive on to the Austrian border. He thanked her while she protested that the children should not drive so late, and we left her standing on the curb. (Wave, children, wave.) We had had enough for the day. Just across the Austrian border was a campground we could reach by midnight.

But when the Rev came out of the post office with the gas coupons, here was the woman again, hurrying along the sidewalk to catch up to us. She said, breathlessly, that she could understand our reluctance to sleep in her home, but at least would we let her ride with us to some of the hotels she knew, and she would inquire for space for us? So up she climbed beside us in the front seat and the moment I spoke a word in English she interrupted to say firmly that if I would speak in German, then we *all* could share in the conversation. None the less I added, grimly and in English, that we were not going to sleep in her house, no matter what.

The first hotel, where we parked at the entrance, was full despite the woman's Hungarian pleading with the reservation clerk. To reach the second hotel, she had the Rev park the redbus on a street with no hotel in sight. The two of them disappeared around a corner into the darkness. They were gone twenty-five minutes, each of which seemed like an hour. In this interminable time I became convinced that we soon would be sharing the American embassy's hospitality with Cardinal Mindszenty and I debated whether to fly the children home to grandparents while I stayed to search for a missing husband caught in some web of intrigue. It was a nightmare. Nan suggested that we ought to pray, a suggestion I already had put into action.

Then the two vanished ones reappeared, the woman began to talk again about lodging us in her own home, and we decided in German that we would try once more, and failing, we would drop off our benefactor at a convenient spot and proceed to the free world.

This time she directed us to a kind of travel bureau. The Rev gathered from her inflections that she told the girl to produce space or she would house us herself, to which the girl replied that this was not allowed (which it wasn't and some tourists had been asked at the border for proof of the hotel in which they had stayed) and so the girl telephoned and then handed us a confirmed reservation for the Grand Hotel Royal at VII Lenin körut. Best hotel in the city, said our woman, adding that it had been reopened recently after damage in the short revolution of 1956.

Large foreign cars lined the curbs at the hotel and Hungarians walked up and down looking into them enviously. No, our benefactor did not wish a ride to her home. Neither did she want any payment for her services. But did I have any American lipstick? I had only one tube and offered her a bottle of 4711 cologne instead. She seemed pleased and said, as she slid down out of the redbus, that she thought she would go home and get some gifts for us, too. What next?

Clutching our duffel bags and looking bedraggled, we entered the grand lobby of the Grand Hotel Royal and were assigned a suite of two rooms and a third room with twin beds for the boys. In the hall, before entering, Dave instructed Clark not to talk about Nagykörös or the names of people because the room might be bugged.

The suite was beautiful, thick carpet on the floor and thick towels in the bath. Luxurious lamps, chairs, and sofas filled the convertible sitting room. Dicker and Em were bathed and in pajamas when the knock came. Don't tell me, said the Rev.

But yes, here she was again, smiling and eager. She sat down on a sofa and began to take out her gifts. Where were the boys? Get them, she said. Meanwhile she observed to me that Nan's dress was too long. By European standards she was correct. She looked fondly at the Rev and explained that her only son had died when he was nine years old. Had he lived, he would have been about the Rev's age — how old was he? — and she might have had grandchildren the age of our children. She hoped we would remember her as our Budapest *Grossmutter*.

There was a gift for every child. For Dicker a plump gold-covered chocolate, for Em a locket from East Berlin, for Clark a Moscow-made model of the Russian sputnik. Nan received a little Hungarian peasant doll which swung for months from the mirror of the redbus. Dave was pleased with a big packet of Hungarian stamps which the post office would not let our benefactor send to relatives in South America. Each child kissed the Budapest *Grossmutter* and said *Danke schön* with enthusiasm. Dicker's kiss was smeary with chocolate. In my keeping she placed two little cans of Cuban pineapple juice — good for the children's health — and two jars of home-canned pears — vintage pre-World War II — which we left behind in the bathroom wastebasket. The children bade her good-night and she settled back to have a talk with her adopted American son.

Thirteen years she had lived in Budapest. Before that, Berlin. No wall yet when she was there. Her husband was an importer. He was on a trip and she was home alone. It was lonely alone. But she liked Budapest. Fine city in which to live if one had lots of money. How was it in America? She had a brother-in-law in New York. Was New York like Budapest? Nicer? She wondered sometimes what the world was coming to. How could people be happy? What was there to live for? On such questions the Rev had some thoughts to share. The talk ranged from governments to God and how one could be happy. If the room was bugged, it was an interesting conversation to monitor. The woman neither asked nor gave any direct criticism of the current Hungarian government. She had more need to unburden herself than to be curious about us. Or was it easier to indulge her *Grossmutter* fantasy if she knew little about the real world from which we came?

It was near eleven when she left. Her son-for-the-evening kissed her good-bye and so did I. On a card she wrote her husband's name — Laszlo Baum on Sziv. Utca 95 — and she offered to show us the next morning where to take the children swimming. We sent her a card from Vienna and another when we returned home. These she answered and we exchanged greetings at Christmas. Without her help we would not have stayed in Budapest and so would have missed the unusual events of the next day, though when we fell asleep in the Grand Hotel Royal we wondered how any day could be more unusual than the day just ended.

D AVE REPORTED IN THE MORNING that Clark had said Nagy-körös only twice. The hotel bill was 467 *forints,* about twenty dollars, and listed us as Van Halsema *család* — tossed, probably. In the lobby and on the wide stairs were clusters of diplomats and businessmen, a group of Red Chinese, others less identifiable, moving, sitting, talking, in pairs or groups. It seemed to us that no man walked or sat alone and that the usual banter and laughter of an American hotel lobby were conspicuously absent. There were a few women, but not a child in sight. The maids who came into the suite before we left exclaimed and put their arms around our children.

Outside, women were driving taxis, busses, and street cleaners. A man asked about the Istanbul sticker on the redbus window. "My daughter, she is living there. What kind of city is it?" he asked in German. The curious were still inspecting the foreign cars. I was curious about the elegant shops along the wide streets in the center of the city.

We drove to find the church of Bishop Ravasz on Calvin Square. Ravasz, the venerable retired Reformed bishop, preached to thousands gathered in the church and in the square during the brief days of freedom in 1956. On one inside wall of the church is the text, *"Isten Lélek Akik Öt Imádják Szükséges Hogy Lélekben És Igazságban Imádják."* Hopeless Hungarian —

one cannot guess at a word of it. Who would decipher that this is, "Those who worship him must worship in spirit and truth"?

A lace cloth lay over the central pulpit and a canopy topped it. There were fresh flowers for sale in the square and beds of them planted in the green grass. The church dome was gold-edged.

While the Rev visited the church offices, I returned to the children in the redbus. They were excited because a man had stopped at the window, pointed to the Bible lying on the map shelf under the dashboard, and asked something in German. Dicker, remembering Arab curiosity, had seized the Bible to protect it. The man returned to the redbus window to talk with me.

"Sie glauben auch im Christus?" he asked. Yes, we do believe in Jesus Christ. Where did we come from — the Netherlands? America? Ah, what is life in America, that wonderful place? We talked at length in German, and the man had many questions.

"What do you think of Budapest?"

"It is a beautiful city," I answered honestly. "Can you buy the things in the shops?"

"Not we," said the man. "None of us can. This is only to impress the *Ausländer* who come from all over the world. How old are you?" he asked next.

"Sieben und dreissig," I answered. Thirty-seven.

"Sieben-und-zwanzig?" he said. Twenty-seven?

"Nein, sieben-und-dreissig," I corrected him.

"Impossible," he said, shaking his head, and then he added, as if the explanation had just occurred to him, "But of course, you don't work."

I knew what he meant, even though I had my own ideas about whether I work or not. He was thinking of all the women working in the streets and factories of Hungary while their children are kept in nurseries.

"Living looks good on the surface," he said, "but here," pointing to his heart, "it is poor and sad. We do not hear the Bible preached any more. Religion is a secret thing. Freedom is gone." He turned his head to mask the tears in his eyes. What would it be like if his sons, aged fourteen and twenty-four, could grow up in America? He also wished, though he said it kindly, that the Americans had kept their promise of aid when the Hungarians fought to throw off Russian rule in the 1956 revolution. "But now, what is there to hope for? We know better than to try again."

The Rev came back and stood on the sidewalk talking until the man's wife came out of a little basement store. Though the man looked around occasionally as he talked, he did not seem to be afraid to be seen with us. We wished him God's peace. He thanked us. "We need it," he said.

Only the gatekeeper was at the Reformed seminary where we wanted to buy a few books for Sandor. The seventeen students were on vacation.

Seventeen? There used to be over 150. The bookstore was not there; it was in the church headquarters across the city.

"Wait," said the gatekeeper, "a student is here who speaks some English and he will ride with you."

"Thank you but it is not necessary," we said, but the gatekeeper insisted, doing us more favor than he knew.

Laszlo, the student, introduced himself.

"My father was part of the seminary faculty here, and he was in Evanston, Illinois, for a World Council of Churches meeting, too."

"What is your father doing now?"

"Since 1956 he is a village pastor." Now an abrupt change of topic.

"Budapest is a big city," said Laszlo. "It has one million, eight hundred thousand *inhibitions*." One would have thought he chose the word advisedly. "Look, here is the heroes' monument with Arpad in the center. Arpad united seven Magyar clans and conquered Hungary about nine hundred years after Christ. Now the square around the monument is used for May Day parades."

The Rev returned to the subject of the church. "We have Hungarian friends in America who talked about your bishops. There are four of them?"

Laszlo named three, those we knew were loyal to the party line. He omitted the name of the fourth whom the regime had not yet eased out of the way. "The Budapest bishop will assign me a church when I graduate — if I graduate. I hope he will be kind and not put me far out in a little country church."

While the Rev was in the bookstore I pursued matters more directly. "Does your father know A or S or O, Hungarians now in the United States who formerly taught in Reformed seminaries here?"

Amazement. Laszlo remained guarded.

"We have been interested in the Hungarian Reformed church a long time. My father has an honorary degree from Sárospatok seminary for writing and working in behalf of the Hungarian Reformed churches."

More amazement. Now Laszlo remembered the name of the fourth bishop who lived in Sárospatok. "I wish you could talk with my father," he said, "but he has gone to visit someone today."

"Let me show you the Fisher Bastion and the Saint Matthew Church if you have time," offered Laszlo. Up we drove to the heights of Buda above the Danube, past the Horthy governor's house, still in process of repair, past a large group of Polish tourists alighting from a tour bus. Buda is the old city, dating from Arpad's dynasty, a splendid city until the Turks toppled it, ruled it 150 years, and surrendered it after a devastating siege by the Hapsburgs who incorporated Hungary into their holdings until their empire was dismembered in 1918. The city of Pest grew rapidly late in the eighteenth century and the famous Chain Bridge was built across the Danube to link old Buda with newer Pest.

Through the stone arches of the Fisher Bastion we saw the parliament buildings across the river, where they lie like London's do along the Thames. Laszlo pointed out landmarks from this vantage point. We admired the statue of Saint Stephan, sitting on his horse on top a white marble base guarded by stone lions. "He was first king of Hungary in 997-1038, and he is called Holy Stephan because he Christianized Hungary. Hungary was a very Christian country. And here is the church of Saint Matthew. It is from the thirteenth century."

The Rev was sorting out statistics in his mind. In 1937 Christian Hungary was 63% Catholic and 22% Reformed, making its Reformed Church the largest in all Europe. When the Communists took over, there were more than two thousand Reformed congregations, some with ten thousand members, and thirteen hundred parochial schools and four Reformed seminaries and several Reformed universities. In name, three schools remain: the seminaries in Budapest, Debrecen, and Sárospatok.

"Shall we see whether my father has come home? Do you have time?" asked Laszlo eagerly. "On the way I can show you some other things."

So we passed the National Gallery, famed like Madrid's Prado for the treasures it contains. And the Communist Party Headquarters in front of which the 1956 revolution began.

"The new statue is in memory of the Communists killed there," said Laszlo in an emotionless tone. A nude giant with heavy arms and legs stands, knees flexed, reaching one monstrous arm into the air, like an ugly contemporary Atlas holding up an imaginary world.

"We tried," said Laszlo simply.

"And we did not help you," I added quietly as the sense of guilt descended on us again. It engulfed us often those two days. People were gracious, considering. The sisters did not even mention it. The man on the street spoke of it with a sad smile. Others said, with limp resignation, that they would never try to rise again because they knew that their friends would not support them if they did. And we could only suffer with them, wondering why the country that sent Marines ashore on Lebanon beaches and sends troops in increasing numbers into the jungles of Vietnam remained silent and immobile when the Hungarians, achieving ten days of freedom unassisted, cried to us for the help we had promised.

A man was walking on the street, holding his coat over his shoulder by a finger through the loop inside the collar. "My father," said Laszlo, but when we stopped, the man looked at us without response. Laszlo called to him and the man motioned for us to ride on. We waited for him at the family home three blocks away.

In a second-floor apartment on an unpaved dead-end street we talked for several hours behind a locked door. We talked in English, with interpolations for the Professor X's wife and daughter. How much we had in common!

Professor X's wife had gone to school with Sandor and she knew the sisters. The professor had read my father's religious magazine for years. He had studied in Utrecht, the Netherlands. He had just come from a visit with Bishop Ravasz, so he could give us late information on the bishop's health and would bring Sandor's greetings to the bishop when he saw him again. He knew the people in Sárospatok, the medieval walled city of treasures in the far northeast of Hungary, and would send them the photographs entrusted to us for them.

He talked evenly about what had happened to him. "I returned from a visit to Geneva the week before the revolution broke out and was accused afterward of bringing back instructions and assurances from Visser 't Hooft and John Foster Dulles. This I did not do, though my sympathies were plainly with the cause of regaining independence. A lifelong colleague denounced me publicly to assure his own ascendancy in the new regime, and I was removed from the seminary after twenty years and assigned to be assistant pastor in a small village to which I go weekends by bus. In these years the Reformed Church as an independent organization has disappeared. It is dead. A few living congregations fight against the stream. Somehow we have a surprising number of promising young pastors. But how effective can they be when they are reassigned every few years to prevent their gaining the confidence of their congregations? No one trusts his brother, even in the church. There are always informers. Pastors who do not parrot the party line at monthly meetings to discuss their sermons are emeritated at any age, pensioned at ten dollars a month and offered a job in a factory. The regime has not overthrown the church. It has infiltrated it so that from within the old shell the regime wields complete control. And every pastor must decide with his own conscience how much or how little to concede and what his loyalty will be. He will have to struggle with himself to see how much of his integrity he can sacrifice to secure a college education for his children or a continuing ministry for himself."

Professor X had made his choice. He did not boast of it or even mention it directly. But it was implied in what he said. He made no concessions to the regime. He asked from them no favors. He was at peace with himself and with his God. At least one prominent European university had asked to have him on their faculty, but the government would not allow him to leave the country. "You see," he said quietly, "in Hungary we no longer know the word 'why'. Yes and no, yes or no or maybe, but never why. Here there is no why." This from the man called the most profound and faithful contemporary theologian in Hungary.

Professor X autographed a book for Sandor and one for us. His wife brought tiny china animals for the children — a dog, a lion, a squirrel, a cat. I found nylons, a slip, and a string of pearls for the wife and daughter. But the best sharing we did was intangible. We sang a Dutch psalm together, one they remembered and one we knew, and we prayed together. In what other unity can men continue when they are separated by iron curtains?

"What can we send you or do for you?" we asked.

"Pray for us," Professor X said, "and keep in contact with us. We need to know that you care, and it is good for the regime to know that we are not forgotten."

Laszlo rode a few blocks with us to direct us to the highway. In a restaurant adjoining a gas station we ordered *dobos torte,* savoring for Sandor each bite of this seven-layer delicacy.

Guards in camouflage suits were coming on duty in the twilight at the border. More guards, with guns and binoculars, and four electrified fences protect Hungary from the free world! Inside the building an official pounded his desk and roared in German at the Rev.

"This is no *carnet,*" he shouted, waving the loose photostat sheets. "It is not valid. You cannot come into this country with these." But we had come in and the first half of a *carnet* sheet had been accepted at the southern border. So the official could only rant a while and let us out. One more providence for which to give thanks. The list of them was long for our thirty-four-hour stay in Hungary.

Two guards inspected the car casually. The books for Sandor were on the front seat, slightly shielded by a large map I happened to be reading. The men asked that the tailgate be opened but they touched nothing. From inside the building a man released the electric gates and we rode through them, pausing to survey from the other side the gates and fences that stretch from north to south, from the Baltic to the Black Sea, shutting in a captive people.

A quarter mile farther one man leaned casually against a post at the Austrian entry point. *"Guten Abend,"* he said pleasantly, flipped through the passports, and wished us a pleasant journey.

"You run a different sort of border here," said the Rev.

The man answered simply, "This, *mein Herr,* is the free world."

EVEN THE INSECTS seem to know where the air is free. We swatted oversized mosquitoes while we ate a late stew supper in the campground at Podersdorf on the lake. Next morning we observed oversized adults lolling and walking about. Unquestionably we were back in Europe, continents removed from Arab modesty. Why bulging oldsters should choose to go around in bikinis and high heels or in the most minimal of men's trunks is a riddle. In comparison, the American of this age and size is modest. While pulling out tent stakes, Dave and Clark convulsed as certain specimens wobbled by. It was good tonic to drain away the tensions of the previous two days.

One of Vienna's six campgrounds was listed as having a swimming pool. There, at Rodaun Campingplatz, we set up camp and spent a lazy day swimming, writing, meeting neighbors. US Army Verona was next to us. Army Heidelberg was across the way. A Wayne University professor returning with his family from the Greek islands was amazed that we had been given transit through Hungary. "I asked at the Paris consulate," he said, "and they turned me down flat. 'Go around Hungary,' they said."

A little sedan drove into the campground, top and insides exploding with dolls, plastic bath tub, playpen, stroller, and camping gear. Is it worth the effort? we said, but we got out our limited conveniences, too — stools, the chair, a single air mattress to rest on, and we ate supper at leisure.

"Did we just get off the boat in Istanbul last Friday?" asked Nan. "Seems like years."

"Seems like another world." Dave.

"Will we ever see the sisters again?" Clark. "Ever, d'you think? Or Baki Banar Bas?"

"Beer icky ouch," began Dicker and then, "Think that boy in Jerusalem got any more suckers?"

"I'm thinking of those girls in the bazaar in Damascus." Em.

"Sounds like we're talking about a trip that's over," commented Dave. "Maybe the best part of it is."

Dave spoke for all of us. It was true that the big challenge was past, the major goals accomplished. From now on it would be easy, and still interesting, but the peaks were behind us. We were descending gradually, reluctantly, toward home. Peaks would not be peaks if they were not exhausting and rare.

W E SPENT FOUR cloudy days in Vienna, but even without sunshine on the grey-stone buildings and statuary, it was a romantic city.

Two Hungarian pastors were our guides. Pastor Soos pointed out on Stock-in-Eisenstrasse the place where apprentices of the Middle Ages drove nails into the wood before leaving home. We walked along the Augustinerstrasse to the Josefplatz where the National Library is. Hercules in life size guards the baroque inner staircase of Prince Eugen's town house. In his country palace, Belvedere, Austria's state treaty of freedom was signed.

A whole row of marble composers lean out of upper story windows in the Mozart death house. Schubert has a birthplace in Vienna and Beethoven has many houses because in his lifetime he kept moving from one to another, leaving unpaid rent bills behind him. In a *Konditorei* on the Opernring we sampled Vienna coffee and *Sacher Torte* and watched tour groups arrive at the famous State Opera built by Franz Josef in 1868.

Great composers did not only live in Vienna. They are also buried there. Hopping over puddles and darting from tree to tree to escape the rain, we came to the musicians' corner in the enormous Central Friedhof. Mozart has the central monument in the composers' circle though his grave is unknown. Next are the graves of Brahms and Johann Strauss and his wife. Beethoven's monument has gold carvings from which green streaks have made stains on the white stone. The upper carving is of a bee within a circle made by a snake with its tail in its mouth. Next to Beethoven, as he wished it, lies the body of Frans Schubert under a stone with swans on either side of a lute. These two stones have been redone after the originals and the bodies moved here together. Gluck and Hugo Wolf lie in the outer circle with two more Strausses, Eduard and Josef. A live couple, standing in the rain with newspapers over their heads, told the children stories — the one about Schubert's wish to be buried beside Beethoven, and about Brahms autographing Strauss's book with the opening line of the Blue Danube Waltz and the words in German, "Unfortunately not mine."

Schönbrunn Palace, says the tourist folder, is "the only royal and imperial residence in Europe that remains completely equipped with its original furniture." That is quite a feat for a palace of fourteen hundred rooms. The formal gardens were ablaze with azaleas and geraniums. Here another chapter of history calls to be studied — the Maries and Louise, the beautiful Empress Elizabeth and Frans Josef.

Off one of the grand halls the Rev found a dark closet in which to see why his camera film seemed endless. Disaster! The film changed hastily before Nagykörös had not been inserted properly and no film had been winding through during all the slides taken since then. We sat on the steps of Marie Antoinette's childhood home, assessing our losses. All the Hungary pictures, too? You mean we have nothing? What will Sandor say? Well, Nan photographed the sisters in color. Dave took many black-and-whites. The Rev made a jumbo slide of Sandor's church. How many worse things could have happened to us!

The woods and hills around Vienna are beautiful and the Danube has a bay arm for swimming and boating. Pastor Soos showed us the way up the Kahlenberg through the Vienna woods to a lookout over the city and the river. Then he came along to the campsite where he approved the Nagykörös cookies and apricot jam, and denounced the current Hungarian regime. Soos had come out of Hungary a short time before. Our other guide had been gone from there ten years and was inclined to be more conciliatory about the situation in his homeland.

"Schwein," said Soos bitterly, describing as a pig the colleague who had denounced Professor X after a lifelong friendship. At the campsite while the children splashed and shouted in the pool, the whole conversation seemed unreal. It was more real when Soos took the Rev to visit a Hungarian refugee housing area.

The evening that we visited at Pastor Nemeth's home there was a girl there from Beograd. She was on her way to attend a Student Christian Movement conference in Graz and laughed heartily to hear about the wrong road we had taken from Novi Sad to Subotica. Marta was the daughter of a Reformed pastor in Yugoslavia and she promised to bring greetings to the pastor we had missed. "In our country," she said, "there are about a hundred Reformed churches, all in the northern part of the country which was formerly part of the Austro-Hungarian empire. Only thirty of these churches have ministers, and no young pastors are being trained. The government tolerates the churches but gives them no support."

Nemeth added that it is worse in Rumania than in Hungary. In Rumania a pastor may not travel in his own country without a special pass, and no tourist may enter without a visa for a specific city. Nemeth's wife served pudding with berries while we filled in the picture about Reformed churches in several countries. It was a good evening — Hungarians, Americans, and a Yugoslav talking German in Austria.

Saturday night we heard the Vienna Symphony play in the Arkadenhof of the Rathaus, the courtyard of the city hall. There were hundreds of people on folding chairs set up in the immense enclosed courtyard. The Rathaus tower loomed like a dark silhouette against a navy sky and there was a black herald at its tip. Pillars on the sides of the Arkadenhof were wrapped in flag colors of many nations. Those at the front, behind the brilliantly lit orchestra in full dress, were in the red and white of Austria. A formally dressed matron motioned for Dave and Nan to sit with her near the front.

Dicker fell asleep halfway through Schubert's *Fifth Symphony*. On the end of our row a man leaned out into the main aisle to see and burst into solitary applause after the first movement. Everyone around him glared, and he glared back as if to shame them into showing their appreciation. The man smoked despite the *"das Rauchen verboten"* line on the program and he beat the tempo with his free hand to assist the conductor. He allowed the *andante* movement to pass without benefit of his response but the *menuetto* stirred him to applaud again, hands held high, cigarette dangling in his mouth. More glares. When the storm of applause greeted the end of the last movement, the man leaned back motionless, puffing on his cigarette.

Dave and Nan were enraptured. "Why didn't I bring my violin along to practice on the trip?" Dave.

"I can't stand to wait so long to play my cello. If I could only play in an orchestra like that someday."

Under a spell we left the courtyard, mingling with students in flat heels and ladies in glittering gowns. Top-hatted drivers waited outside in horse-drawn carriages. We walked past the Grecian-style parliament building, bathed in light, with pillars and a cluster of statues surmounted by a goddess with golden helmet and gold-tipped spear. Here at night old world charm was spread lavishly and the days of carriages and courtiers, of powdered wigs and parties seemed just through the next arch in the Ring that circles the heart of Vienna.

Army Verona next to us had pancakes, bacon, and eggs for Sunday breakfast. "Those luckies," groaned Clark who had to admit that his own breakfast had been filling though the menu was less American. Riding down to church inside the Ring, we had a family talk about different ways of living, about being satisfied with fewer luxuries, about the difference between living as bountifully as we could or saving to share with others or to make ourselves more useful through travel and study. But the bacon smelled good.

In the empty Sunday streets Walt Disney technicians were filming a sequence with the Spanish Riding Academy's famous horses. We almost missed church watching them. We would not have missed much, because the sermon was a poor lecture, though the American Community Church met in an elegant little church on the Dorotheagasse. In 1784 the emperor gave land and materials for two non-Roman Catholic churches to be built in the city. One was Lutheran, and this one was Reformed. There was coffee in the courtyard afterward and we met a family from Osaka who knew our missionary friends there. Together we walked to see the Holy Trinity statue, a three-sided, intricately sculptured, thirty-foot grouping erected in 1679 after deliverance from the pest. We also saw the Stephansdom, most venerable building in Vienna, a Gothic cathedral with its coat of arms on the roof.

Monday the sun appeared shamelessly when we ate lunch off the *Autobahn* on the way toward Salzburg. We used our last can of food, some sliced pineapple, with bread and apricot jam, Hungarian cookies, and milk. The Salzburg festival program appealed, but with the retreat schedule of meetings in Berchtesgaden, it was unlikely we could include any of it even if we did get tickets. "Next time," said the Rev, thinking of Florence and Mount Sinai and Petra and other things we are saving to do on a trip together.

"Do you know our trip is almost over?" said Nan as we sat in the grass. "Two weeks and we'll be in London and then the boat home."

"Terrible." Clark, bacon and eggs notwithstanding.

"Who wants to go home?" Em.

"Not me for sure," finished Dicker, biting into a chocolate bar with hazelnuts in it.

Salzburg's castle sat high above the city's church spires. All around is Austrian beauty — jagged grey mountains, deep green forests, streams and jewel lakes and waterfalls, chalets perched in unexpected clearings of lighter green high in the hills. And, of course, in the city there were floods of tourists attending the festival. At the German border we converted our last ten-dollar traveler's check and bought gas.

BERCHTESGADEN, lying in a little part of Germany that bulges into Austria, is the US Army headquarters for retreat and recreation of troops in Europe. We had been here before for a retreat. The streets were choked with people. We checked in at headquarters for billeting authorization and then drove to the Alpine Inn, one of the army centers, a little complex of rustic buildings arranged on a green slope on the outskirts of the city. It was as we remembered it, and the brown onion-shaped chapel spire rose against a background of snow-streaked mountain peaks. We were even assigned the same room with bath and patio, and the children were in two rooms across the hall. Clean luxury, American style. Time to get out the clothes we had been saving in the bottom of our suitcases for this encounter with the American way of life.

We had enthusiastic reunion with well-dressed friends from Verona, Dreux near Paris, Orleans, Wurzburg, and scores of servicemen, teachers, nurses, gathered for the Reformed Faith Retreat. All evening the reunion atmosphere continued. Boys identified themselves by their home churches, most of which the Rev had visited in his traveling work for the domestic missions board. Someone remembered to tell us that Marilyn Monroe was dead. Someone else led the singing of "Happy Birthday" for President Kennedy. An abundance of mail informed us that the four hundred dollars we had requested from home was at the Salzburg American Express, that Oom Johan was nearby at Wolfgang-am-Zee and would contact us, and that Tante Fenna would be arriving on the *sneltrein* from Amsterdam the next day. Dicker and Barry from Verona were walking the grounds with their arms around each other. "This is living," said Clark at the first breakfast, reaching for his fifth slice of French toast with butter and syrup.

For many those days were a retreat. But for us they were more of a return. We were at home again after a foray into many strange places. Familiar food, money, language, friends, and news. And cleanliness.

And though we were an isolated bit of America gathered in the German Alps, this identity reminded us of the problem every perceptive American faces when he returns to his own abundance after viewing other people in their corners of the world. It is the problem of evaluating his responsibility for those he has seen, and of deciding how he must discharge this responsibility. For it is his, simply because of what he has seen. There seem to be those who travel and do not feel this way. They go to see the places tourist folders show, to buy souvenirs and specialty items, and to regale their friends at home with humorous and insensitive stories. This kind of American is conspicuous, demanding, and his noisy reactions account for a poor American image abroad.

But on those — and there must be many — for whom travel creates a burden of responsibility toward others, there is a gamut of action possible: interpreting faithfully what one has seen, sending CARE packages or contributions, working at home with agencies of help, volunteering for work in relief or education or missions abroad. We struggle with this each time we return to the comfort and complacency of home. Perhaps a man whose work is bound up with men's souls feels such responsibility doubly because his is a spiritual as well as physical concern. It is not easy then to be at peace serving a comfortable complacent people who can be stirred upon occasion to give generously, but whose more consuming concern is to perpetuate their own luxurious security. All of which sounds very like a sermon and quite abstract when one is changing a tire in Turkish dust or spitting watermelon pits beside a Roman temple ruin. But it is there, underneath, all the time. In Berchtesgaden, fresh-showered, over-fed, and drowsy between smooth sheets, we glimpsed these questions waiting for an answer.

It was a good retreat, rewarding in fellowship, study, prayer, climaxed by Holy Communion at an early service on the final morning. In free time we toured the salt mines, wearing absurd black uniforms with leather aprons on the back for sliding down long wooden chutes in the darkness. This was terrifying for adults, exciting for children, and did Oom Bee at seventy-four and father at seventy-three honestly slide down these when they were here?

We rode the Jennerbahn ten and a half thousand feet up a mountain to a view obscured by mist, visited wood-carving shops, and paid Oom Johan a birthday call across the border at his summer place in the Austrian Salzkammergut. The first two days of the retreat the Austrian border was almost closed because of a strike. This could have been catastrophic for us because we had a dollar and six cents in our pockets when we arrived in Berchtesgaden and did not know until opening the mail that our money was not there but in Salzburg. The border officials finally let us through after hearing our story and inspecting the copper tray.

Tante Fenna is a woman who has spent her life directing hospitals, sometimes with a thousand employees under her jurisdiction. Fortunately, she has a boundless sense of humor. "If only your staff could see you now," we said to her the first night out of Berchtesgaden when she sat on a folding stool in the dark peeling cucumbers more by feel than by flashlight which was needed at the camp stove. We had ridden through a sunny Austrian countryside, browsed in Innsbruck, lunched in a meadow, coffeed in an out-door café, and climbed a pass. With difficulty we found a campground with a room nearby for Tante. It was in Dalaas and the farmhouse room was made fragrant by the nearness of many cows. Supper was a dim affair, served beside the tent. After weeks of German we tried to talk in Dutch, but the conversation was a garble of these two languages and our own, punctuated by peals of laughter.

When we rode during the day, Tante sat in the second seat with a string bag of fruit hanging on the coat hook over her window. With a little knife from her purse she peeled and quartered and handed out fruit all day. When we stopped she replenished the supply and bought little souvenirs for every-one.

We came through Fürstentum Liechtenstein, the postage-stamp-sized principality with lovely shops, hotels, and a castle in Vaduz, the capital. There was not even a border official to stop us at the covered bridge that leads from Liechtenstein into Switzerland.

In Schwanden, where the clock has a bright blue face, we bought bread and cheese and more fruit to eat in a field of wild flowers before the Klausen Pass. Who can describe this country? No matter how often one sees it, it is as breath-taking as before. Red flags and red geraniums, green shades in grass and forest, blue-green mountain streams filled by waterfalls crashing down from snow fields higher up, deep purple gentians and pink-red Alpine roses, cow bell music, and valley floors of orange-red rooftops with a white spire at the heart of them. A village nestles beside a turquoise lake whose smooth surface stirs to let a ferry pass and leave its wake. Snow-covered peaks wait around each hairpin turn. Low stone and dark wood houses cling to the sheltered sides of hills. And over all warm sun shines from unbroken blue sky.

After the Klausen Pass we descended through Altdorf with the William Tell statue and turned off toward the Süsten Pass, shifting gears for the steep climb, higher, higher, more snow around us, and then the descent through twenty tunnels, one with a waterfall over the top. Broc, Brulle now, and then the valley after a last big climb in the late sun through the Jaunpass. Down into Lausanne, a fine city, and the first glimpse of Lac Leman, Lake Geneva.

To avoid the congestion of a festival in Geneva, we camped short of it in Nyon. Tante had a floodlit castle view from her hotel in town and we had a walled campground with streetlights to illumine our soup, spaghetti, and oranges supper. The noise of fireworks in Geneva punctuated the evening. In Jerusalem that same sound would have meant gunfire.

JOHN CALVIN would not have been pleased with the atmosphere in his city on the Sunday we were there. Confetti lay in the streets, water skiers performed over ramps in the lake, and crews were removing grandstands set up for the night before. We walked in Calvin Square and on the Rue de Calvin past the site of his home, showed the children the Hotel de Ville where we had researched in the city archives four years earlier, and found our favorite antique shop and the coffee shop with boxes of marigolds on top its green fence.

In the Protestant Cathedral of Saint Pierre bells pealed a ten-minute prelude to the service, drowning out the sound of a band marching at the riverfront. Then the organ played the *Saint Anne* tune for "O God Our Help in Ages Past." The music lingered among the pillars as it does in all good Gothic churches. During the French service the Rev made efforts to participate while the rest of us inspected the windows, especially the ones of the apostles in the choir. The minister preached from the high pulpit which was a gift to Calvin when he returned the second time to Geneva. Afterward the woman guide on a tour of the church was not very sure of her history or of her English. "Turn over," she said to the group when she wanted them to look in another direction. The boys climbed the north tower and reported on the pigeons, the view, and the *jet d'eau*, the geyser of water which is Geneva's landmark. The girls and I sat in the sun beside the courtyard statue of weeping Jeremiah while Tante and the Rev attended part of a Dutch service in the Auditoire where Calvin lectured.

"It must be a nice place and we must have time to enjoy it," Tante Fenna stipulated when she invited us to be her guests for Sunday dinner. Close to the city there is a quiet outdoor place called Hotel and Restaurant de la Belotte with tables on the lakeshore under big eucalyptus trees. There was even a play area for children, and a tank of fresh fish from which fishlovers might choose for dinner. Service and food were excellent and we spent several hours there, looking out over the lake, talking in our language mixture, and savoring such food as campground cooking does not feature.

Geneva was still celebrating when we left after a stop at the Reformation Wall where Farel, Calvin, Beza, and Knox stand, bearded giants in stone.

We crossed the border into France, riding along the Rhone valley into the hills to Nantua, where we stopped at the Château de Pradon, built at the base of a rocky precipice. Campers are welcome on the grassy approach to the château. The old place is a spot for ghosts — drafty halls, rattling doors, squeaking stairs, and dark empty chambers. New owners converting the château into an inn had not yet made much progress. Tante Fenna was shown an upstairs room with two doors. Neither had lock or bolt, one opened into a cavernous attic, the other onto a spooky back stairs. We offered her a carving knife from the camping gear to defend herself.

When the children were asleep, we ordered Schweppes tonic with fruit pastries in the central room of the château which served as dining and sitting room. It was an old beamed room with fireplace and barred windows, enhanced by an ancient clavichord and candles. The proprietor sat with us and explained that the château dated back to 800, though this structure was a rebuilt one from the 1700's. The château had its own phantom, he said, and brought out framed newspaper articles to prove the point. Something about the daughter of a marquis, a girl named Urzele d'Anglefont. Our French was not good enough to appreciate the details.

In the circle of candlelight Tante Fenna produced a five thousand-*franc* note, remnant of months earlier before the *franc* had been devalued and replaced by more manageable numbers. The flickering light and the phantom helped us imagine the note worth its old value and we plotted how to spend this small fortune. A greater problem was how to protect it through the night behind two rattling unlockable doors. The atmosphere was so conducive to fantasy that we almost believed it.

Breakfast in the château included plates of toast and bread, jam and butter, and steaming pitchers of coffee, tea, and hot chocolate. There were individual bowls to pour the liquid into and huge spoons from which to sip it. Tante Fenna paid for her room and returned to announce that her fortune had evaporated. "Did you see Anglefoot during the night?" the children asked, making their own version of the name.

To Cluny and the Protestant monastery at Taizè we came by accident. We had talked of Taizè but the map did not show it. There was a road sign to Cluny, a quiet faded remnant of the town which was Europe's monastic center in the twelfth and thirteenth centuries, with an abbey church which was the largest in Europe until Saint Peter's. With the help of a sign in Cluny we found Taizè, a very little village standing on a low hill with flat green fields all around it. It is a curious blending of the old and new. The stark lines of the new chapel rise above the old stone walls and medieval streets.

The monks were approaching the chapel for noon worship. Singly or in small groups they came, slipped white cassocks over their work clothes, and entered. Within a three-sided U whose open end faced the altar, they knelt on the floor, motionless in prayer. There were forty-five of them when they all assembled. Almost an equal number of visitors sat behind the U on chairs. We had come in through another entrance, past a large yellow sign in three languages, with the French heading *VOUS QUI ENTREZ ICI RECONCILIEZ-VOUS.* "All you who enter here, be reconciled, the father with his son, the husband with his wife, the believer with the unbeliever, the Christian with his separated brother."

Light streamed in through the opaque glass behind the altar. A simple cross hung on the wall to one side and a wide yellow stripe ran from the floor to the ceiling. At the stroke of twelve the monks rose from prayer and took seats on benches around the sides of the U. One played the *portativ* organ while they sang and spoke. In ten minutes it was over. The men filed out silently, hung their white habits at the exit, and returned to work, some in the fields or in building construction, others at the easel or potter's wheel. Some priests stay forever, some for shorter periods, and the monastery also welcomes men as guests for short periods of retreat. Sometime, the Rev told himself. Here and at Mount Athos.

The art exposition of Frere Eric was displayed in a room with uneven floor boards and a sagging doorsill. There were some remarkable oils and sketches at remarkably high prices. Across the dusty street in a shop beside the stone wall, one could buy records and pottery of Taizè. The monk in charge was happy to take dollars instead of *franc*.

Bourges, Orleans, Chartres, Paris, Senlis, Compiègne, Noyon — we were coasting back. Calvin and Olevianus studied law in Bourges, and Olevianus tried unsuccessfully to rescue a young prince from drowning in the river. The entrance of the cathedral had a row of headless statues and another of statueless niches, though the tympanum above the double door showed rich detail in the afternoon sun.

At Orleans the next day we found Joan of Arc, wielding a sword on a prancing horse in the central square. "Joany on the Pony," the American military there call her. In the smaller branch of the Loire River swans were swimming and quaint storybook houses crowded the banks.

Was it the rain or were we mentally too saturated to absorb any more? Chartres was a disappointment to us. We did not stand awe-struck as we were supposed to do when we saw the unmatched towers of its cathedral rising from the city and the plain around it. The inside was warmed by countless candles and flowers for the Feast of Assumption, and many people were kissing a pillar. There was too much commotion to sit and contemplate the magnificence of the 130 windows, and there was no sun to transform them. We bought Christmas cards at the shop in one corner of the cathedral. Women of Brittany, in white lace caps that stood on their heads like square pillars, were selling laces and felt souvenir caps outside.

A day for Paris is not enough. It is just a taste, a whetting of the children's appetite for more time there and in Versailles and Fontainebleau. We passed the little statue of liberty on one of the Seine bridges and rode the slanting elevators to the top of the Eiffel tower where we almost blew away taking pictures and pointing out landmarks in all directions. They were changing the guard at the unknown soldier's tomb under the Arc de Triomphe. We walked in the Tuileries gardens and pointed out the Louvre.

Napoleon's tomb was peaceful in contrast to the crowds moving to Notre Dame's island, entering the cathedral through the door of Adam and Eve and the serpent. The inside was a mass of lighted tapers for the Assumption. We walked along the bookstalls and watched the river bright with boats. The umbrellas and art displays of Montmartre seemed cleaner than the last time we were there and the round white domes of Sacre Coeur rose with dignity over the people swirling below.

At day's end we drove on for dinner in the restaurant of Le Bourget airport where Lindbergh landed after his Atlantic crossing. Next time we will wait to have dinner in the hotel where we slept in Senlis. Hotel Du Grand Cerf has thirty *chambres* and an abundance of charm — red-flowered chintz at the windows, downy comforters on canopied beds, and in our adjoining rooms with bath a *prie dieu* the Rev longed to take home to his study for morning prayers. We agreed with Tante Fenna who had a room down the hall that we would sleep long in the morning.

Tante tapped on our door before eight, with her hat on. "At seven a maid came to my door with a breakfast for two on a tray."

"Why for two?" said the Rev, groggily. Tante stifled her giggles. Why two or why any at all she did not know. Well, she would shop while we dressed and ate.

Compiègne — here in a wooded park stands a railroad car like the one of the 1918 armistice signing. It is not the same one because Hitler demanded France's surrender in 1940 in the original car and then took it to Germany as a trophy. There, in the bombing of Berlin, it was destroyed.

All the way to Noyon, John Calvin's birthplace, the road winds through wooded area. It passes through Sentingny and Pont l'Eveque where Calvin's grandfather made barrels. Beside the arched stone bridge over the Oise River tents were being set up for a carnival.

Calvin is no hero in his home town, though there is a Calvin house rebuilt on the original site after it was destroyed in 1918. The stone floor of the main room and the front windows made from the bottoms of greenish bottles are original. Nearby, facing the Place de Parvis, is the cathedral, defaced probably in the French Revolution. The heavy wooden doors under the portico are bound in iron. This is the fifth church on the same site. In the second one Charlemagne was crowned in 768. The present church, in which Calvin received the tonsure when he was twelve, was built in the twelfth century. It still displays the bones of a seventh-century bishop, Saint Eloi. All the cathedral windows were destroyed in World War II and it was not opened again until 1952. Noyon had no use for its native son after he became a Protestant and Calvin rarely returned there. Once when he did, he was forced to hide in a town nearby.

Around the corner from the cathedral the Rev bought a beret and Tante

Fenna selected a big natural-straw hat for me. "I'll have to wear it the rest of the trip," I said. "Where would we pack it?"

From Noyon we drove into Guido de Brès territory, through cities in which this Belgian reformer-martyr preached and worked. In Valenciennes, where he was hung in 1567, the old church with its square free-standing tower was being rebuilt. Before reaching Mons, de Brès's birthplace, we had to cross the Belgian border. The official demanded a *carnet,* though the use of one is unheard of in European non-Communist countries. No matter that we needed none in Austria, Switzerland, France. He wanted one, anyway. No, not a photostat. A real *carnet.* For fifteen minutes we sat while he debated. "Just like Hungary," said Clark. Twice the man asked irritably, pointing to Tante's morning purchases in the back of the car, whether we had any liquor or perfume to declare. "None," said the Rev firmly. Finally, grumbling, he tore off the first part of the last photostat sheet.

In Mons the drab buildings were lined up against the street. The gold-topped city hall tower is more imposing than the grey spireless cathedral. Brussels we gave a lingering look. The children were more interested in the *mannelkin,* the little bronze boy statue, than in the medieval gold-trimmed square at the Hotel de Ville where a band was preparing for an evening concert. Through the elegant parts of Antwerp we followed a Dutch-license car past the north harbor to the Dutch border. Here the Belgian official asked for nothing! We did not offer him the second part of the *carnet* sheet, which is intended to assure the country one is leaving that the car has not been disposed of or sold within its borders. Let the man on the first border worry what happened to us, we said.

The children gave a lusty shout as we crossed the border. "We're home," they cried, bouncing on the seats. All things are relative — after the Middle East, the Netherlands was certainly home. At Breda we celebrated with ice cream and cake and called Tante Kundien and Oom Henk. At 11:30 we were in their home in Utrecht.

Sometime after 1 A.M. we were sitting around the table, five adults drinking coffee, discussing the mail and presenting gifts. We had some from Beirut to give and Tante Fenna produced some, too.

Then it was two o'clock, and we were just in bed on the top floor when the knock sounded. Here was Tante Fenna in her nightclothes, hair streaming down her back, holding up a bottle.

"This I bought in Senlis when you were getting up this morning," said the directress of hospitals. "It's a bottle of rum for my colds this winter."

"May you have many of them," answered the Rev, "and after I sleep I will decide what penance you must do for making a liar out of me when we crossed the Belgian border." Whereupon Oom Henk and Tante Kundien came up from their bedroom to see what was going on and we all sat on the bed together and talked and laughed some more.

ONE MORE WEEKEND. Rainy, naturally. I brought four loads of washing to the new launderette and felt like a seasoned traveler translating for some English-speaking boys to the Dutch proprietor. At night we gave a dinner for the uncles and aunts. Father always did this, said the Rev, and who knows how long we will have the older generation with us? So we gathered in the Lage Vuursche with eleven aunts and uncles from all over the Netherlands. The heavy drapes were drawn in the private room, and the oval table gleamed with candles, flowers, and silver.

We wondered whether the circle would be complete next time we came. In the dear Dutch tradition, each of the uncles rose to speak after dinner. They reminisced about father — "the best of the family went to America, we always say" — and thanked us for continuing the strong bond which impelled him to cross the ocean twenty-three times. We tried in vain to explain that we were the debtors, we and our children who had seen for themselves the treasure there is in a family and a faith to share and pass on.

Oom Bee spoke last, as the oldest, the *stamhoofd* of the family. He is gone now, and so is his beloved Tante Yt. They died within six weeks of one another in the spring after our return to Michigan. When the first news came, and again with the second telegram, there was stillness in our busy house. Eyes brimming, we looked at one another and knew why we had to go to Holland when we did.

The boys spent their last weekend with Oom Bee and Tante Yt at the house with the white bench. We all had supper there on Sunday, eating currant buns with cheese, squeezing mayonnaise out of a tube, and avoiding the salt shaker because Oom Bee avowed that overuse of salt contributed to his baldness. Centerpiece this time was a Canadian grenade from the freeing of Ermelo by the Canadians in World War II. It was more appetizing than the snake and proved the launching point for many war stories about Oom Bee's church and life in Ermelo. Oom Bee took pictures with his old box camera, though his eyes were so poor he could not see what he was doing, and somehow all the pictures turned out well and he wrote illegibly on the back of each and sent them to us.

There was a final birthday party in Amsterdam with cousins, and the final Sunday evening at Tante Kundien's hospitable house in Utrecht with special pastries and coffee, during which Dave, of all people, suddenly retreated behind a magazine to hide his emotion at leaving.

Monday morning we lined up luggage on the walk leading from the front door. Since nothing could be left in the car on the ship, we had given away soaps, medicines, and the plastic pail. An extra army foot locker held many of our acquisitions. The Rev wrapped the copper tray in all the foam rubber and then in cardboard. There were two luggage lines, one for the ship's hold to be carried to the pier with the redbus, the other of hand pieces to be carried to London where we would board ship when it reached Southampton. I made a list of twenty-nine pieces plus two coats while Tante Fenna pasted V labels on everything.

Tante Fenna and the Rev left in the redbus for the pier and would take a train from there to Hook of Holland. The other six of us left an hour later with Oom Henk and Tante Kundien, while Agaat in pale pink and exquisite makeup and Annie in unbrushed teeth and wrinkled skirt waved from the middle of the street. By eleven everyone had converged at Hook of Holland, candy bars and candy rolls were pouring into my purse from relatives come to see us on our way. The boys held tightly *half gulden* pieces from Tante Yt. Pictures — Dicker in front with a red shirt hanging out, pulling faces — and kisses and farewells and always our thanks with the comment that makes leaving less difficult, *"Tot ziens,"* till we see you again. And Tante Yt, deep brown eyes clear and unfilled with tears, answered in Dutch, "And if we do not see you again, we know that this is good too, and someday we will all see each other forever."

And so we were waving from the customs desk, from the open hallway to the ferry, and then we were out of sight as we boarded, feeling with the sadness a great relief because the emotional tension of the farewell was over and since it was inevitable, it is better finished.

The ferry plowed out of the channel and on the stretches of beach we could see hundreds of color dots marking swimmers and the larger orange and blue spots of tents. Dicker reached out to the gulls, the buildings receded, the shoreline blurred, and we settled in a confusion of deck chairs to reread the latest mail from home. That is, until chubby Charlotte and her art-teacher mother attached themselves to us. Charlotte was lonesome. Could she play with our children? Her mother showed animal sketches she had made at the Rotterdam zoo, and in the same breath offered to do one of me, which she did, and it was a poor sketch, though perhaps her linking of subject choice was unintentional and conditioned me to dislike the sketch. Charlotte and her mother were from Massachusetts. They had toured the Netherlands on a motor bike.

Predictably the channel weather became cold and cloudy and we went down late in the afternoon for an *uitsmijter* — an open-face sandwich of meat slices with fried eggs on top — and french fries in the dining room. As we approached Harwich at seven, the Rev organized the baggage brigade, assigning to each child the one or two items which would be his for all walking until we boarded ship again in Southampton. To Em was assigned one camera bag which contained the apricot jam for Sandor and the slide camera in its own leather case. Em set the bag down with a thud on the deck.

Customs was a scramble and while we waited in line, the train for London, on which we had reserved seats, filled and departed. Priority slips and reservations meant nothing. Another train left later with those of us who remained. Charlotte's mother was wearing a bicycle tire around her neck, an extra for the motorbike being shipped home. Charlotte produced some card games to play on the tables between our second-class seats. Dicker was hungry and ornery. An old man gave Nan some stamps. In the pink-purple sunset a large ship was silhouetted and I wished we were on it going straight home without a London stopover.

Em shouldered her camera bag as we stepped off the train and said, "This feels squishy." We unzipped it and found that the thud on the ferry deck had broken the glass jar of apricot jam in which the Argus camera case was now swimming. Glass was mixed through the precious preserves. The Rev fished the camera out of the sticky stuff, we dared not reenter the train to get paper towels for fear it would depart and separate us, a conductor came to our rescue by bringing towels, and we all stood around forlornly while the Rev wiped jam off the camera case and then wrapped it in an unread *New York Times* we were saving. Because of the delay we were at the end of the taxi queue, and the old black taxis that came down the ramp were few.

Charlotte's mother had acquired a man from somewhere and we watched her whizz away in an early taxi, the tire still around her neck. For an hour we inched forward, each child moving his pieces with the line, everyone tired and ornery. Finally we squeezed into a cab, four of the children sitting backwards on flip-down seats, windows wide open, riding uncannily on the wrong side of the street. Nan took the occasion to remark, "I read once in my history book that the people from Brittany settled England and that's why it's called Britain. Some of them dyed their faces blue." None of us cared much. Except Dicker, who had revived after a low point.

"Tell you a joke," he said. "Once a boy wanted to go back to school, but he couldn't because if he did his face would turn green. Funny, huh?" The back-to-school part sounded good.

"Tell you another joke. Once a boy ate too many apples and his face turned red like the skin." With this we pulled up in front of the mission house where we had reservations. It was a big old place on a quiet street, and a cluster of little old ladies showed us to four rooms reserved for us. The Rev closeted himself half an hour in the nearest bathroom trying unsuccessfully to flush the apricot jam down the ancient plumbing.

I T WAS A GOOD THING we had only two days in London. We were running out of money and interest and the two meals a day included in the price of our lodging were horrible. They were obviously the reason that the mission house could operate at minimum cost and still make a profit. Food was skimpy, doled out by the bird-like little women who judged appetites by their own fragility. It was unappetizing, like pork and beans — counted — on bread for breakfast and sour bread pudding for supper. Not a drop of coffee the whole two days. After the first evening meal, the Rev in desperation joined six old ladies and one superannuated man for evening prayers in the hope that tea afterward would include some solid food, but there was not so much as a crumb or cracker. We bolstered each other with the glorious thought that in two days we would be hosted by the Holland-America Line and our mouths watered in anticipation.

But we had fun. We rode a double-deck bus downtown, and chose a two-hour, forty-cent bus tour from a fistful of literature in Victoria Station. "Best buy in London," said the bobby on the corner. There was money enough to buy sandwiches and fruit for lunch and we munched while riding. We saw everything, if briefly — Buckingham Palace, Wellington Arch, Hyde Park Corner, Piccadilly, Haymarket, Nelson's Column, Whitehall, Parliament, Westminster Abbey, Lambeth Palace, the War Museum, Tower Bridge, Tower of London, Bank of England, St. Paul's, Fleet Street, the Law Courts, and much more. As we passed Middlesex Hospital a crowd was gathered to cheer Winston Churchill as he left for his home.

We also saw a lot on foot. Buckingham and the changing of the guard, and then through Kensington Park to the Abbey, which we explored thoroughly. Big Ben and parliament we photographed while Dicker poked dirt with a paddlepop stick and the dirt flew into his eyes. Past Downing Street and Whitehall we came to Trafalgar Square with Lord Nelson on his pillar and artists drawing chalk pictures on the sidewalk with their beat-up hats laid out to receive contributions. A negro was having his portrait sketched for two pence by an artist in a brown beret. This inspired Dicker to a version of "Old Black Joe," which continued, punctuated with hunger hiccoughs, all the way to Piccadilly, where we caught a bus to the mission house and the bread-pudding dinner.

Wednesday, gladly, we picked up all our luggage and departed. To save money we walked to the bus and managed to board with all our gear, the four-foot painting roll included. We checked it all in lockers at Waterloo Station, bought tickets for the train to Southampton — unreserved, remembering the Harwich experience — and set out on another trek through the city. Dave found a sixpence in a vending machine and the woman to whom he tried to return it told him pleasantly to keep it. Dicker was possessed of uncommon vitality, considering he had vomited at the pork-and-bean breakfast. Three times around a pole, down a curb, up a curb, pick up a dirty rubber band, and so on. In such fashion we crossed Waterloo Bridge, in the middle of which a woman stopped to ask us what it was like in San Francisco where her daughter lived. With the pigeons we sat on the steps of Saint Paul's a while and Clark spent his last sixpence inside to buy us a bookmark of the painting of Christ knocking on the door which hangs in St.

Paul's. The painting, that is, not the door. Via the 202 feet of fluted Doric column which is the Fire Memorial, we walked to the Tower of London, through which I took the older children while the Rev and Dicker sat on a cannon watching the guards in tall fur hats and the boats passing under Tower Bridge. The boats, that is, not the guards.

Outside the Tower walls a group was watching a trick artist tying a partner in chains while an older man stood ready to deliver a message, with the white letters 'God is Love' emblazoned on the back of his black jacket. We had to leave in the middle of this, while the man was still tied in chains, to find a bus back to Waterloo Station. Not finding one or knowing where to find one, we extravagantly hailed a taxi.

On the train to Southampton reserved seats did mean something so we were shunted about while people claimed their spaces. Nan endeared herself to one couple by returning a package they left in their seat when they got off at the ship. And then we were on board, our rooms were larger than on the *Rotterdam,* dinner was announced and our dining room table was ready for us, assigned to advantage because we had requested it in advance in Rotterdam. Walk, don't run, Dicker. Don't eat all the rolls before we order. Could you bring some coffee while we make our choice?

Grey weather plagued us most of the way and we were seldom on the open deck even though it was the end of August. Dave celebrated his birthday with cake and candles brought by the dining steward, and the waiters helped us sing Dutch and English birthday songs. That was the day a boy said to Clark, "Where've you been?"

"We drove to Israel and back."

"That all?" replied the boy scornfully. "I've seen EVERYTHING in London."

Nearing Newfoundland. The Rev making out customs declarations with the help of the notebooks, Dave and Nan propped on bunks finishing their diaries, Dicker locked contentedly in the playroom, Em and Clark bickering over hats, horns, balloons, and souvenirs from the children's party. I sorted through a mass of papers, menus, matches, and scrapbook materials. Two days till September. People will be wearing dark cottons. Bother the return to styles and seasons! Everyone on board is a little terse. Vacation is over, travel done, and school, work, and unpacking loom. Too many bored children fill the halls and salons because the decks are washed with rain.

At five on the last morning we are on deck while the ship glides past the Statue of Liberty. We should have a lump in our throats. We dock early. After early breakfast the Rev joins the long tourist-class line for customs clearing before disembarking. The official informs him when his turn comes that all passport holders in the family must be in the line. While we debate in our cabin whether to join the line at once or wait a while, a customs official knocks, sent by a good friend who works in the upper echelon of the customs department. This helpful man escorts us to the first-class line, clears us through, and offers to meet us on the pier to effect a final reckoning on the redbus and all other acquisitions.

Twenty family members roar a welcome as we come down the gangplank and the children are borne off with their cousins to Wyckoff, New Jersey, an hour away. Father, brother Jim, the Rev, and I wait for the redbus and the customs reckoning after assembling the thirty-one pieces that belong to us and checking them off on a list:

3 army duffle bags	typewriter
4 square cartons	medicine case
painting carton	2 camera bags
copper tray	hat box
2 blue suitcases	brief case
2 Samsonite suitcases	train case
2 brown-checked suitcases	4 children's duffle bags
1 plaid suitcase	2 coats
2 army foot lockers	

The tray, looking as if it had been dipped in the Hudson, lay bedraggled in a deserted corner of the pier. A prying customs official got his fingers sticky looking for diamonds under the dirty clothes stuffed into the apricot-jam camera bag. The official sent by our friend came along and helped us reckon the duty, and somehow we loaded everything into the redbus and headed for lunch in Wyckoff and a festive family dinner in Monsey, New York. Next morning we took to the highway in cavalcade with father Van and sister Helen whom we lost twice on the Pennsylvania turnpike. The redbus decided to be temperamental after fifteen thousand miles of valiant service abroad, and we needed a push several times when the starter refused to function.

One of the first days home Dicker sat on the screened porch with his friend Tom, reading his favorite picture book of many lands. If the pictures did not look familiar, he came to inquire what country it was and whether we had been there.

"Now, Tom, this is India," he would say. "We haven't been there yet. Not YET."

Tom's mother asked him, "Dick, where are you going next summer?"

"I'm not sure," replied the youngest member of our safari for seven. "Maybe India or Japan. We haven't been there yet."

A

Abner, 171
Abraham, 77, 80, 131, 136, 161, 169, 172, 178, 181
Absalom, 169
Adam, 177, 234
Adana, 138-139, 144
Aesculapius, 93, 98
Agrinion, 53
Ahab, 173, 174
Ahiram, 153
Ahmet I, 79, 202
Akhisar (*Thyatira*), 86-89, 109, 166
Aksehir, 107-109
Albania, 52-53
Alberobello, 51
Alexander the Great, 67, 72, 77, 79, 91, 94, 97, 138-144, 153, 200
Alexandretta (see Iskenderun)
Alexandria, 66, 91, 100, 139, 142, 147
Alexandroúpolis, 70-71
Ali Pasha, 53
Alkmaar, 17, 36
Alt, Albrecht, 174
Altamura, 50
Altdorf, 39, 230
Ambrose, 39
Ameide, 18
Amersfoort, 11
Amfissa, 66
Amman (*Philadelphia*), 3, 162, 163
Amphipolis, 68
Amsterdam, 3, 13-14, 36, 63, 235
Andrew, 183, 184
Ankara, 4, 77, 84, 131-137, 139
Antakya (*Antioch of Syria*), 131, 142-144
Antioch of Pisidia, 102, 107-110, 131, 138
Antioch of Syria (see Antakya)
Antiochus, 103, 108, 188

Antipas, 91
Antoinette, Marie, 225
Antony, Mark, 91, 139, 172, 175
Antwerp, 235
Apollos, 96
Appolonia, 68
Aquila, 96
Arachova, 64, 66
Araunah, 178
Aretas IV, 161
Aristotle, 59
Arius, 77, 85, 86
Arnhem, 24
Arpad, 220
Arta, 53
Aswan, 147, 153
Ataturk, 75, 77, 78, 136, 137
Athanasius, 85-86
Athens, 58-63, 91, 97, 98, 99, 139, 144, 157
Attalia, 103
Attalus III, 59, 92
Augustine, 39
Augustus, Caesar, 108, 136
Aurelius, Marcus, 93, 153, 199, 200
Austria, 98, 215, 223-228

B

Baalbek, (*Heliopolis*), 80, 156-158
Babylon, 141, 142
Baden, 38
Balaam, 92
Balata (*Shechem*), 174
Balikesir, 86
Bamm, Peter, 96
Baniyas, 146
Barak, 173-188
Barbarossa, Frederick, 132
Barcelona, 170
Barnabas, 108, 131, 142, 143, 144
Basel, 38
Baudouin, 12
Beatrix, 18
Becharre, 149
Beersheba, 173

Beethoven, Ludwig van, 224, 225
Beirut, 1, 3, 4, 82, 135, 140, 151, 153-162
Belgium, 3, 55, 235
Ben Gurion, David, 181
Beograd, 206-209, 226
Berchtesgaden, 3, 41, 137, 228, 229
Berea (see Veria)
Bergama (*Pergamum*), 87-93, 96, 103, 105, 198, 200
Berlin (see also East Berlin and West Berlin), 1, 3, 24-31, 35, 75, 92-93, 165
Bernhard, 12, 13
Bethany, 168
Bethesda, 175
Bethlehem, 169-170, 173, 177
Bethphage, 168
Bethsaida, 152, 185
Beza, Theodore, 231
Boaz, 169
Bologna, 41
Bolsward, 17
Bourges, 233
Brahms, Johannes, 225
Braunschweig, 30
Breda, 235
Brindisi, 49-51, 150
Britain (see England)
Browning, Robert, 40
Brugg, 38
Budapest, 3, 211, 212, 215-221
Bulgaria, 3, 68, 70, 75, 166, 196, 202-205
Bursa, 85-86
Byblos (see Jebail)
Byron, George Gordon, 40
Byzantium (see Istanbul)

C

Caesar, Julius, 61
Caesarea, 198
Cairo, 1
Caleb, 168
Calvin, John, 231-234

*Italics denote cities in ruin or earlier names of modern cities.

Cana (see Kafr Kannah)
Canaan, 181
Canterbury, 139
Capernaum (see En Sheva-
   Kefar Nahum)
Caracalla, 93, 156
Carthage, 86
Casemier, 29
Cassander, 67
Castellammare, 49
Chalcedon, 76
Charlemagne, 20, 29, 234
Chartres, 233
China, 78, 100, 142
Chorazin, 152, 185-186
Christ, 77, 83, 85, 87, 88,
   90, 92, 95, 100, 103,
   142, 143, 152, 162, 167,
   168, 175, 178, 179, 183-
   186, 188, 192, 199
Chrysostom, 143
Churchill, Winston, 239
Cicero, 139
Cilicia, 60, 132, 141
Clement, 143
Cleopatra, 91, 139, 172
Cluj (Kolozsvar), 213
Cluny, 232
Clusius, 80
Coen, Jan Pieterzoon, 17
Colosse, 101, 103-106
Compiègne, 233-234
Constantine, 27, 42-44, 46,
   76-77, 80, 83, 85, 86,
   143, 145, 156, 170, 176
Constantinople (see Istan-
   bul)
Corfu, 52
Corinth, 54-58, 66, 96, 99,
   136, 166
Cragg, Kenneth, 155
Crete, 53
Croesus, 94, 95, 97
Cyprus, 3, 144, 149, 197,
   198, 201
Cyril, 100
Cyrus, 94-95

D

Dachau, 16, 181
Dalaas, 230
Damascus, 1, 3, 14, 62,
   146, 152, 156, 158-163
Dan, 173
Daniel, 94, 139
Daphne (see Hariye)
Darius, 138, 140, 141
David, 98, 136, 148, 163,
   165, 168, 169, 178, 181,
   188

Deborah, 173, 188
Debrecen, 221
De Brès, Guido, 235
Delft, 16, 18, 25
Delphi, 64-65, 94
Demetrius, 99
Denizli, 101, 104, 106
Derbe, 110, 131-132
Dimashq (see Damascus)
Dinar, 104
Diocletian, 84
Dionysius, 59, 61
Dothan, 57, 173, 174
Drenthe, 17, 20

E

East Berlin, 30-35, 147
East Germany, 30, 32, 34,
   204
Ecirliköy, 101
Edirne (Hadrianopolis), 75,
   202-205, 211
Egypt, 149, 153, 155, 169,
   170, 191
Elgin (Thomas Bruce), 61
Elijah, 192
Elisha, 172, 174
Elizabeth (Austria), 225
Elizabeth (England), 12
El Jib (Gibeon), 170-171
El Khalil (see Hebron)
Eloi, 234
England, 27, 51, 61, 152,
   155, 182, 187, 237-240
En Sheva-Kefar Nahum
   (Capernaum), 183, 191
Epaphras, 101, 105
Ephesus, 80, 87, 92, 94-105,
   141, 166, 198, 199
Epirus, 53, 55, 62, 63, 81
Erasmus, 16
Erfurt, 30
Ermelo, 236
Ethiopia, 156
Euripides, 59
Eve, 234
Ezekiel, 153

F

Famagusta (Salamis), 197
Farel, Guillaume, 231
Ferrai-Ipsala, 71
Finegan, Jack, 68, 101, 108
Florence, 41, 227
Fontainebleau, 233
France, 3, 230-235
Frankfurt, 67
Frederick III, 26-29

G

Gaeta, 46
Garstang, John, 172
Gaza, 168
Gaziantep, 140
Gebran, Khalil, 149
Geneva, 222, 230, 231
Gerasa (see Jerash)
Germany (see also East
   Germany and West Ger-
   many), 3, 4, 25-35, 228-
   230
Gibeon (see el-Jib)
Gibraltar, 152
Goethe, 29
Gomorrah, 172
Gordon, Charles, 177
Göttingen, 30
Gravina, 50
Graz, 226
Greece, 3, 4, 49, 52-71, 76,
   94
Groningen, 19, 20, 35, 36
Grosseto, 41

H

Haarlem, 9-11, 15, 17, 18,
   22, 24, 36
Hadrian, 61, 93, 98, 139,
   163, 170, 176, 202
Hadrianapolis (see Edirne)
Hague, The, 4, 16, 36, 166
Haifa, 3, 95, 188, 192-194
Hals, Frans, 17
Hannibal, 86
Hanover, 35
Hariye (Daphne), 145
Harlingen, 35
Harwich, 237
Hatunsaray, 110
Hebron (el Khalil), 168-169
Heidelberg, 3, 24-29, 38
Hein, Piet, 16
Helena, 44, 170, 176
Heliopolis (see Baalbek)
Helmstedt, 30
Hennef, 25
Heraclitus, 96
Herborn, 25
Herod Antipas, 182, 191
Herod the Great, 142, 163,
   174, 175, 179
Herzl, Theodor, 190
Hezekiah, 178
Hierapolis (see Pamukkale)
Hilversum, 20
Hiram, 148
Hitler, Adolf, 181, 213, 234

243

244

Holland (see Netherlands, The)
Homer, 96
Honaz, 104, 106
Hoorn, 17
Houphouët-Boigny, Felix, 181, 187
Hungary, 3, 4, 37, 166, 204-223, 225, 226, 235

I

Iconium (see Konya)
Ignatius, 143
Igoumenitsa, 52-53
IJmuiden, 9, 11, 12
India, 69, 141, 155
Innsbruck, 230
Iran, 69
Iraq, 69, 147
Irene (Constantinople), 85
Irsina, 50
Isaac, 169, 178
Iskenderun (Alexandretta), 140-142
Israel, 3, 146, 147, 149, 152, 155, 173, 174, 180, 181, 184, 188, 190, 197, 240
Istanbul (Constantinople and Byzantium), 3, 4, 14, 43, 58, 68, 71-86, 95, 137, 160, 166, 201, 202, 207
Italy, 3, 4, 29-51, 173, 203
Izmir (Smyrna), 3, 87, 88, 95, 99, 108, 197, 198, 200
Izmit (Nicomedia), 84
Iznik (Nicea), 84-85, 99

J

Jacob, 168-169, 174
Jairus, 183
János, Arany, 215
Jebail (Byblos), 152, 153
Jerash (Gerasa), 162, 163
Jericho, 163, 168, 171-173
Jerome, 170
Jerusalem, 3, 4, 27, 57, 58, 59, 63, 99, 163-168, 174-180, 206
Jezreel, 173
Joab, 171
Joanina, 53
John of Antioch, 100
John, the apostle, 87, 93, 96, 97, 99, 175, 189, 199, 200
John the Baptist, 79, 95, 159

John of Nassau, 25
John, Pope, 40, 44, 45
Jonah, 152
Jordan, 162-180, 182, 191
Josef, Franz, 225
Joseph of Arimathea, 175
Joseph (father of Christ), 170, 192
Joseph (patriarch), 173
Josephus, 179
Joshua, 168, 171, 174
Judas (Christ's betrayer), 167
Judas (of Damascus), 160
Judea, 142
Julian, 145, 157
Juliana, 12
Justinian, 79, 80, 83, 96
Justin Martyr, 170
Juvenal, 142

K

Kafr Kannah (Cana probably), 185, 188, 191
Kaiserlautern, 27
Kampen, 22
Karacabey, 86
Karadorde, 206, 207
Karagac, 202
Kavalla, 68-69
Kawania (see Konya)
Kayseri, 137
Keats, John, 45
Keçskemet, 211
Kempis, Thomas à, 17
Kenyon, Kathleen, 172
Kesan, 74
Kilbassan, 110, 132
Kipling, Rudyard, 85
Kirkagac, 91
Kitzingen, 29, 30
Kloosterburen, 19
Knox, John, 231
Köln (Cologne), 25
Kolozsvar (see Cluj, Rumania)
Komotini, 70
Konya (Kawania and Iconium), 102, 107-110, 131-133, 150
Korea, 135, 165
Koster, Laurens, 17

L

Lamb, Harold, 154, 187
Lamia, 66
Laodicea, 87, 88, 101, 103, 105, 133, 198

Larisa, 66
Larnaca, 197
Latakya, 145-146
Lausanne, 230
Lazarus, 168, 197
Leah, 169
Lebanon, 145-158, 221
Le Havre, 7
Leiden, 15, 17, 80
Levadia, 64, 66
Libya, 145-147
Liechtenstein, 230
Lisse, 15
Livorno, 41
Locorotondo, 51
London, 3, 221, 237-239
Loosdrecht, 17
Lot, 161, 163
Lot's wife, 172
Loyola, Ignatius, 170
Lucerne, 38-39
Lugano, 39
Luke, 43, 68, 96
Lusignan, Guy de, 187
Luther, Martin, 25, 143
Lydia, 69, 90
Lysimachus, 85, 91, 200
Lystra, 110, 131, 132

M

Macedonia, 67-68
Mac Innes, Campbell, 167
Maes, Nicholaes, 14
Magdala (Taricheae), 183
Magdeburg, 32
Manisa, 93
Mark, 162
Marmara, 65, 75, 79
Mary, 79, 99-100, 169-170, 191, 192, 207
Mary Magdalene, 177, 178, 183
Matera, 50
Matthew, 183
Maximilian, 25
Mecca, 76, 80, 165
Megiddo, 173
Memnon, 100
Mendelssohn, Felix, 199
Meppel, 20, 22
Mesalongi, 54
Meta, 49
Michelangelo, 41, 43, 44
Milan, 39
Miletus, 198
Mindszenty, Josef, 216
Mohammed, 72, 76, 79, 178
Mondragone, 46
Mons, 235

Moses, 153, 157, 174
Mozart, Wolfgang, 224-225
Muller, Herbert, 76, 93, 132, 176
Mumpf, 38
Mussolini, Benito, 213

N

Nablus, 174
Nagykörös, 211-215, 225
Nantua, 231
Naples, 43, 46-47
Napoleon, 31, 153, 154, 234
Nazareth, 173, 185-188, 190-192
Neapolis (see Kavalla)
Nea Appollonia, 68
Nebuchadnezzar, 153
Nemanja, Stevan, 207
Nero, 43, 58
Nestorius, 100
Netherlands, The, 2-5, 7-24, 35-37, 80, 166, 209, 235-237
Neuss, 38
Neustadt, 27, 28, 110
Nicator, 108
Nicea (see Iznik)
Nicodemus, 177, 190
Nicomedia (see Izmit)
Nicopolis, 53
Nicosia (*Paphos*), 197
Nijeveen, 20, 21, 22
Nineveh, 152
Nis, 205-206
Noah, 197
Noci, 51
Novi Sad, 206, 209, 226
Noyon, 233-235

O

Old Stamboul (see Istanbul)
Olevianus, 25, 27, 29, 233
Onesimus, 96, 105
Oplenac, 206-207
Orhangazi, 85
Orleans, 233
Ostuni, 50
Otto Henry, 29
Overveen, 13, 18

P

Palestine, 191
Pamukkale (*Hierapolis*), 101, 103, 105, 166
Paphos (see Nicosia)

Paris, 78, 95, 233
Patmos, 95, 96, 97
Patras, 52, 54
Paul, 43, 45, 46, 56, 57, 60, 61, 63, 66, 67, 68, 69, 77, 96, 98, 99, 100, 101, 105, 108, 109, 131, 138, 142, 143, 144, 160, 161, 175, 198
Pella, 67
Pergamum (see Bergama)
Pericles, 58, 59, 63
Persia, 59, 79, 94-95, 105, 140, 173
Pest (see Budapest)
Petar I, 207
Peter, 43, 101, 143, 183, 184, 185, 186
Petra, 161
Pharaoh(s), 149
Phidias, 60
Philadelphia (in Jordan — see Amman)
Philadelphia (in Turkey), 87
Philaeterus, 91
Philemon, 96
Philip, 101
Philip of Macedon, 72
Philippi, 68, 69, 90
Phoenicia, 151-153
Phrygia, 105
Piaam, 17
Picerno, 49
Pilate, 175
Pindar, 60
Piraeus, 57, 59, 62, 144
Pisa, 2, 41, 45
Plato, 58, 59
Plovdiv, 204
Podersdorf, 223
Polycarp, 200
Polycrates, 101
Pompeii, 48, 184
Pompey, 162
Pont l'Eveque, 234
Positano, 49
Potenza, 49
Potsdam, 213
Priscilla, 96
Pritchard, James B., 171
Puteoli, 43

R

Rachel, 168
Ramsay, William M., 87, 108
Ramses II, 153
Rebecca, 169

Rembrandt van Rijn, 14
Revere, 41
Rheinfelden, 38
Rhodes, 105
Robinson, David M., 108
Rome, 1, 4, 20, 27, 40-46, 53, 67, 68, 69, 75, 76, 77, 83, 92, 101, 142, 156, 157
Rotterdam, 3, 7, 16, 18, 19, 240
Rumania, 226
Ruppert I, 29
Russia, 29, 30, 34-35, 41, 75, 139, 211, 219
Ruth, 169

S

Saarbrucken, 27
Saladin, 187
Salamis (see Famagusta)
Salerno, 49
Salt, 163
Salzburg, 197, 228-229
Samandag, 144
Samaria, 173
Samson, 168
Santpoort, 18
Sarah, 169
Sarajevo, 207
Sardinia, 41
Sardis (see Sart)
Sárospatok, 220, 222
Sart (*Sardis*), 1, 87, 88, 93-97, 105, 198
Sassenheim, 15
Sattel, 39
Saul, 173
Schubert, Franz, 224, 225, 226
Schwanden, 230
Schwyz, 39
Sebaste, 174
Selçùk, 96
Seleucia, 131, 132, 142, 144
Seleucus I, 142, 145
Semiramis, 138
Senlis, 233-235
Sentingy, 234
Sepphoris, 191
Serbia, 206, 207
Severus, Septimius, 42
Shechem (see Balata)
Shelley, Percy B., 44
Sicily, 41
Sidon, 152, 153, 186
Silas, 69
Silenen, 39
Silivri, 75
Simmern, 26

246

Sindirgı, 86
Sisera, 173, 188
Smyrna (see Izmir)
Socrates, 59-60
Sodom, 172, 184
Sofia, 202, 204
Solomon, 148, 149, 157, 163, 178, 179, 182
Soma, 91
Sorrento, 48
Southampton, 6, 237, 239, 240
Spaarnwoude, 11
Spain, 27
Speyer, 28
Spiegelberg, 39
Stalin, Joseph, 213
Staphorst, 17
Stephan (Hungary), 221
Strabo, 105, 139
Strauss, Eduard, 225
Strauss, Johann, 225
Strauss, Josef, 225
Stuttgart, 26
Subotica, 206, 209, 226
Switzerland, 3, 38, 39, 149, 208, 230, 231, 235
Syria, 139, 140-142, 145-148, 151, 158-162, 183, 186
Szeged, 211

T

Tabgha, 185
Tabor, 188
Taizè, 232-233
Taranto, 50
Taricheae (see *Magdala*)
Tarrasa, 132, 170

Tarsus, 138, 139, 143, 145
Tekirdag, 71, 74-75
Tel Aviv, 181, 192
Terracina, 46
Thecla, 131
Themistocles, 59, 61
Theodosius, 157, 159
Theophilus, 143
Thessalonika, 67-68
Thyatira (see Akhisar)
Tiberias, 181-182, 191
Timothy, 96, 131
Titus, 42-43
Topola, 206-207
Trier (*Treves*), 27
Trieste, 1
Tripoli (Lebanon), 145-151
Troas, 69
Tromp, Cornelis, 16
Troy, 96
Turgutlu, 93
Turkey, 3, 53, 60, 66, 71-145, 148, 155, 166, 198-205, 220
Tychicus, 105
Tyre, 149, 152, 153, 186

U

Ursinus, 27, 28, 29
Utrecht, 16, 29, 36, 222, 235

V

Vaduz, 230
Valenciennes, 235
Venice, 2, 40, 61
Veria (*Beria*), 66
Verona, 4, 40, 45, 186, 228

Versailles, 233
Vespasian, 188
Vester, Bertha Spafford, 179
Vesuvio, 47-48, 56
Vienna, 3, 224-227

W

Wagner, Richard, 40
West Berlin, 35, 147
Westerstede, 35
West Germany, 32, 34, 35
Wilhelm (Germany), 31
Wilhelmina, 16
William the Silent, 16, 25
Wirdum, 20
Wittenberg, 143

X

Xanthi, 69
Xenophon, 77
Xerxes, 105

Y

Yalta, 213
Yalvac, 107, 108, 109
Yugoslavia, 3, 4, 166, 202, 204-211, 226

Z

Zahle, 156
Zandvoort, 5, 8, 9, 10, 14, 27, 35, 36, 166
Zoutkamp, 17
Zürich, 38-39
Zwolle, 17

GRONINGEN

BERLIN

AMSTERDAM

LONDON

BRUSSELS

HEIDELBERG

VIENNA

PARIS

TRIER

BUDAF

SALZBURG

ATLANTIC OCEAN

LUZERN

VENICE

GENEVA

BELGRA

MILAN

ADRIATIC SEA

ROME

NAPLES

Safari

MEDIT

for Seven